ALLERTON PARK INSTITUTE

Number 20

Proceedings of a Conference
Sponsored by the
Illinois State Library
and the
University of Illinois
Graduate School of Library Science
and
University of Illinois
Office of Continuing Education and Public Service

Collective Bargaining in Libraries

edited by
FREDERICK A. SCHLIPF

University of Illinois
Graduate School of Library Science
Urbana-Champaign, Illinois

© Copyright 1975 by the
Board of Trustees of the University of Illinois
LC Card Number: 75-25240
ISBN: 0-87845-042-4

CONTENTS

INTRODUCTION ix
FREDERICK A. SCHLIPF

EMPLOYEE RELATIONS IN LIBRARIES: THE CURRENT SCENE .. 1
ARCHIE KLEINGARTNER and JEAN R. KENNELLY

UNIONIZATION OF LIBRARY PERSONNEL:
WHERE WE STAND TODAY 23
DON WASSERMAN

THE LEGAL ENVIRONMENT 30
ANDREW M. KRAMER

RECOGNITION AND BARGAINING UNITS 43
MARTIN H. SCHNEID

THE DUTY TO BARGAIN 54
R. THEODORE CLARK, JR.

GRIEVANCES 76
MARTIN WAGNER

IMPASSE RESOLUTION IN THE PUBLIC SECTOR 84
JAMES L. STERN

NEGOTIATION SIMULATION 107
ROBERT E. BROWN

IMPLICATIONS FOR PUBLIC LIBRARIES 117
MILTON S. BYAM

IMPLICATIONS FOR ACADEMIC LIBRARIES 122
MARGARET BECKMAN

COLLECTIVE BARGAINING IN LIBRARIES: A BIBLIOGRAPHY ... 146
MARGARET A. CHAPLAN

GLOSSARY OF COLLECTIVE BARGAINING TERMS 165
LABOR RELATIONS TRAINING CENTER

INDEX 177

INTRODUCTION

In the past decade, collective bargaining between library employees and library management has emerged as a major pattern in library personnel administration. Although library unions have existed since early in the twentieth century, it is primarily in the last eight or ten years that they have become collective bargaining agents rather than employee associations. The current expectation is that within the next few years a great many public and academic libraries will have encountered unionization of professional, clerical and support staff, and will have experienced collective bargaining, often for the first time.

Historically, there appear to have been two major periods of interest in the unionization of library employees. In his paper in this volume, Kleingartner suggests that the first period of high interest occurred in the late 1930s, in reaction to the general union movement of that era and to the National Labor Relations Act of 1935. By 1939, however, the total membership in library unions was probably less than 1000 individuals. The second major era in library unionization began in the 1960s with the unionization of the staffs of the Brooklyn Public Library and the Berkeley library.

As a group, librarians have had extremely mixed reactions to the prospect of unionization. Most of the library literature on the subject ranges from apprehensive to censorious, and the American Library Association (unlike such other professional organizations as the National Education Association and the American Federation of Teachers) has shown no signs of becoming directly involved in union activities. The ambivalence which librarians have displayed toward unions can probably be traced to several factors, one of which is the domination of the professional associations and journals by administrators rather than by rank-and-file library employees. Another factor is the traditional fear among librarians that professionalism and collective bargaining are incompatible concepts, and that the unionization of professional staffs will almost surely result in a decline in the quality of public service. A third factor has been the fear of librarians that unionization will establish a permanent adversary relationship between librarians and library administrators, thus splitting into hostile camps groups that have common professional goals and should function as colleagues. Associated with this factor is the concern on the part of many administrators that library clerks and lower-level professionals will band together for collective bargaining purposes, thus linking two groups which theoretically have vastly different training, ability, and dedication. A final factor is that the library profession is traditionally a feminine one; a profession dominated by educated, middle-class women is not the most likely candidate for the labor organizer. The reactions of librarians to the prospect of unionization are similar in many ways to those of school teachers, as one might expect given the somewhat comparable labor situations.

A few topics are of particular interest in the area of collective bargaining in libraries. One is the entire area of management rights. Bargaining in the public sector in general has been characterized by union invasion of areas traditionally regarded as under the jurisdiction of management; the insistence of school teachers on bargaining over class size and other organizational matters of this type is an example. It will be interesting to see what role issues of this nature will eventually play in negotiations with library unions.

A second area of particular interest is the strength of library unions themselves. Will library unions be able to function as separate units, or will they be forced to amalgamate with larger unions, sacrificing autonomy for necessary leverage? In most areas, librarians are a highly dispersed minority group fulfilling what is probably viewed as a nonessential function; amalgamation with larger groups may therefore be required if any kind of leverage is to be developed, even though such groups may regard librarians' needs as of minor importance.

The twentieth annual Allerton Park Institute, at which the papers in this book were originally presented, was designed to examine in an unemotional way the field of library unionization. Rather than to examine once again the good or evil inherent in collective bargaining, or to provide helpful pointers for fending off this development, the Institute was designed to present a thorough overview of the way in which collective bargaining actually functions in libraries. This was accomplished by reviewing the background and current problems of library unionization, providing participants with a basic knowledge of collective bargaining methods and techniques, and examining the impact of collective bargaining on various types of libraries. The papers presented at the Institute can be divided into three groups on this general basis.

The first group consists of two papers on the general problems and

INTRODUCTION

current extent of library unionization. The first of these is by Archie Kleingartner, Professor and Associate Executive Director of the Institute of Industrial Relations at the University of California, Los Angeles, and Jean Kennelly, Assistant Professor in the School of Librarianship, University of Washington, Seattle. They review the current nature and extent of library union activity and consider such issues as the problem of professionalism, alternative forms of organization (professional associations and single library staff associations), the problems of introducing professional goals into the negotiation process, and the general future of library unionization. In the second paper, Don Wasserman, Assistant to the President for Collective Bargaining Services, American Federation of State, County, and Municipal Employees (AFSCME), deals with the general problems of collective bargaining in the public sector, with particular emphasis on the experience of AFSCME in this area.

The second group of papers deals with specific technical issues in the area of collective bargaining: the legal environment, recognition, bargaining units, scope of negotiations, grievances and disputes. The first of these papers is by Andrew Kramer, Executive Director of the Office of Collective Bargaining, Springfield, Illinois, who reviews the confusing legal status of library unionization. Kramer places emphasis on the public sector, to which the National Labor Relations Act does not apply, and he reviews the great variety of patterns which exist in various states. In the following paper, Martin Schneid, Assistant to the Regional Director at the National Labor Relations Board (NLRB), Chicago, discusses the area of recognition and bargaining units, particularly as they apply to libraries in the private sector. Schneid's background is of particular interest because of his involvement with the University of Chicago library case, which was concerned in part with the definition of supervisory personnel, an issue of particular importance in library unionization. Schneid also discusses the problem of including professional and nonprofessional personnel in the same bargaining unit and devotes considerable space to the nature of unfair labor practices and the activities of the NLRB in this area. R. Theodore Clark, partner at Seyfarth, Shaw, Fairweather & Geraldson, Chicago, discusses two general areas: the obligation to negotiate in good faith, and the determination of the proper scope of negotiations. In the first area he explains what union and management representatives may and may not do under current labor law. In his explanation of the scope of negotiations, he pays particular attention to the public sector, where the determination of this scope is particularly difficult. Here he examines the impact of state management rights laws and civil service laws, as well as the impact of other state statutes and municipal charters and ordinances. Martin Wagner, Professor at the Institute of Labor and Industrial Relations, University of Illinois at Urbana-Champaign, discusses the general area of grievances, emphasizing how the problem of grievances relates to the entire area of unionization and the various ways grievances are handled in actual situations. In the final paper of this section, James L. Stern, Professor at the Department of Economics, University of Wisconsin at Madison, discusses and evaluates the various methods of impasse resolution in the public sector. Impasse resolution in this area is complicated by the fact that the use of certain tactics (such as the strike) has traditionally been legally denied to public employees. Stern describes each of the possible techniques—including mediation, factfinding, arbitration, nonstoppage striking, continuous bargaining, referenda and strikes—describing how they have been used and evaluating their relative effectiveness in the resolution of disputes.

At the Institute the presentation of these five papers on the particular issues and techniques of collective bargaining was followed by a seven-hour training session on negotiating a union contract. This session was organized with the help of Morris Sackman of the Division of Public Employee Labor Relations, Labor Management Services Administration, U.S. Department of Labor. Participants at the conference were divided into ten small negotiating groups, each consisting of five-person union and management negotiating teams, which had to resolve an elaborate hypothetical labor-management situation to avoid resorting to strike. This simulation session is discussed in a paper by Robert Brown, Assistant Director of the Graduate School of Library Science, University of Illinois at Urbana-Champaign.

The final section of the volume consists of three papers concerned with the impact of unionization on the library world. The first of these papers is by Milton Byam, Director of the Queens Borough Public Library, New York City. Byam discusses the evolution and variety of public library unions, and he describes the special problems encountered in negotiating and resolving grievances and impasses, in coping with special legislation, and in operating in the public sector. The second paper in this section is by Margaret Beckman, Library Director at the University of Guelph, Ontario. Beckman discusses the implications of unionization for academic libraries and covers a wide variety of areas, ranging from the appropriate general approach to management and the various possible formalized personnel procedures to the problems of protecting library services and permitting future technological changes. She examines the impact of strikes on academic libraries and suggests methods for developing workable personnel relations before an impasse occurs.

Two additional items are included as appendices to the volume. The first is a glossary of collective bargaining terms prepared by the Labor Relations Training Center, Bureau of Training, United States Civil Service Commission. This glossary defines more than 100 common terms encountered in collective bargaining and will be helpful to the reader in dealing with the papers in this book. The second item is a selective, annotated bibliography of publications

INTRODUCTION *xiii*

on collective bargaining in libraries, prepared for this book by Margaret Chaplan, Librarian at the Institute of Labor and Industrial Relations, University of Illinois at Urbana-Champaign. This bibliography is in part a bibliographic essay and is structured on a subject basis.

No published conference volume can reproduce the actual experience of attending an institute. The papers in this volume were all followed by extensive discussion when presented at the Institute, and this discussion has not been reproduced here. The Institute was concluded by an informal panel discussion on the future of unionization in libraries, led by Milton Derber, Professor at the Institute of Labor and Industrial Relations, University of Illinois at Urbana-Champaign, and including Katherine Armitage, Coordinator of Library Instructional Services at Sangamon State University Library in Springfield, Illinois; Margaret Bikonis, member of the Park Forest, Illinois, Library Board; and Morton Coburn, Assistant Chief Librarian, Chicago Public Library. This discussion also has not been included in this volume. Two of the papers—those by Wasserman and Wagner—are actually edited transcriptions of tape recordings, and Byam's paper, which was quite brief, has been augmented by the inclusion of several additional observations he made while presenting it. Only a brief summary can be made of the collective bargaining simulation session, and no volume can reproduce the experience of being isolated for three days on a semi-rural estate with 100 librarians concerned with collective bargaining.

Any institute of this type involves the work of many individuals. In addition to the speakers and other authors mentioned above, the many people who helped to plan and organize the Institute deserve special thanks. My colleagues on the planning committee included Robert Brown, Assistant Director, Graduate School of Library Science, University of Illinois; Milton Derber, Professor, Institute of Labor and Industrial Relations, University of Illinois; and Mary Quint, Manpower Consultant, Library Development Group, Illinois State Library, Springfield. Herbert Goldhor, Director, Graduate School of Library Science, University of Illinois, served on the committee in an ex-officio capacity. Brandt Pryor of the University of Illinois's Office of Continuing Education and Public Service, Conferences and Institutes, served as institute supervisor and handled the many problems associated with the day-to-day management of the Institute. A large group devoted several days of their time to the preparation and management of the simulation session; in addition to Morris Sackman and the members of the planning committee, these included: Ray Gilbert, Labor Management Services Administration; Mary Jo Detweiler and Kathleen Kelly Rummel, Illinois State Library; Gerald Podesva and Jack Prilliman, Lewis and Clark Library System; Margaret Chaplan, Gary Frank and Daniel Gallagher, Institute of Labor and Industrial Relations, University of Illinois; Jean Baron, Trustee of the Evanston Public

Library, Evanston, Illinois; and Jerry Parsons, University of Illinois Library. Arlynn Robertson and her staff at the Publications Office at the Graduate School of Library Science transcribed and typed papers, corrected errors and verified citations, and beat me into line when I showed signs of falling by the wayside. Without the efforts of all of these people, the twentieth annual Allerton Park Institute could never have taken place and this book would have been impossible.

FREDERICK A. SCHLIPF

Editor

ARCHIE KLEINGARTNER
Professor of Industrial Relations
Graduate School of Management
University of California, Los Angeles
Los Angeles, California
and
JEAN R. KENNELLY
Assistant Professor
School of Librarianship
University of Washington
Seattle, Washington

Employee Relations in Libraries: The Current Scene

> Although only a small proportion of the librarians in the country have actually become union members, the issue of library unionization has attracted attention throughout the profession, and much of the most active library discussion of recent years has been concerned with it.[1]

Those words were written thirty-five years ago by Bernard Berelson in an influential article about unionization and employee relations in American libraries. What Berelson described was basically the reaction to passage of the National Labor Relations Act (NLRA) in 1935, and to the economic and social conditions of the 1930s which precipitated a wave of union organization in the mass production industries of America. Not only librarians and the American Library Association took note of these developments; some salaried professions went much farther than the librarians in responding to the circumstances of the 1930s.

During that decade and in the 1940s, a number of professional engineering societies (e.g., the American Society of Civil Engineers) sponsored collective bargaining programs.[2] The major motivation of these societies was, however, to prevent the unionization of engineers. Because the NLRA gave no special consideration to the problems and interests of professional employees, many persons during that period were concerned that professional employees in industry would be absorbed by bargaining units in which the majority were

1

nonprofessionals.[3] The rationale of the engineering societies to justify this departure from their traditional opposition to all forms of collective bargaining is described as reflecting the view that: "while unionism is unprofessional, collective bargaining, if conducted on a conservative and dignified plane is not, in itself, objectionable. It was therefore argued that the collective bargaining device be taken over ... and the societies were urged to take on collective bargaining functions or to organize an all-inclusive association for this purpose."[4]

The engineering societies quickly lost interest in collective bargaining after passage of the Taft-Hartley amendments to the NLRA in 1947, which provide in Sections 2(12) and 9(b) that professionals are not to be included in a unit with nonprofessionals unless a majority of the professional employees vote for such inclusion. Since they were never really committed to the principle of collective bargaining, the professional provisions of Taft-Hartley and the subsequent decline in union activity among engineers served the societies' purposes well. One might question whether they served the interests of working engineers equally well.

Unlike some of the engineering organizations, the various library associations tended during that period to emphasize their professional orientation and remained aloof from collective bargaining. Berelson estimated in 1939 that the total number of librarians who were union members was somewhat over 700.[5] In a modest way, the 1930s represented an upsurge of interest by librarians (as distinguished from library associations) in collective bargaining.

We have called attention to the actions of the engineering societies in order to emphasize the long history of efforts by professionals to devise a system of decision-making in the employment relationship that would protect personal, professional, and economic goals. A realistic appraisal of the current scene of employee-management relations in libraries must be viewed against the backdrop of this evolution.

In 1939, Berelson correctly observed a growing interest in unionization and collective bargaining among librarians. The fact that the total volume of union activity in the post-1939 period remained extremely modest does not diminish the importance of that development.

In the 1970s we are observing another period of intense interest in collective bargaining. The fact that the 20th Annual Allerton Park Institute is devoted entirely to the question of collective bargaining in libraries is strong, but by no means the only evidence of the resurgence of interest in this topic by the library profession.

The skeptic will ask, "Is the current scene any different from what occurred thirty-five years ago?" That is, have we simply reached another one of those points in time when librarians get excited about unionism and overreact to developments—all with little prospect for lasting impact on libraries, the library profession or individual librarians? In retrospect, it is not hard to understand why large-scale unionization of librarians did not occur in the 1930s. At the time, most union activity was concentrated in the private sector of the economy—the NLRA applies only to employees in the private sector—but most librarians are employed in public institutions. From the 1930s until roughly 1960, relatively little union activity occurred anywhere in the public sector.

We believe that the current interest among librarians in collective bargaining is justified by emerging developments. Unlike the 1930s, union growth and activity is now concentrated where librarians are—in the public sector and among salaried professional occupations. The NLRA is the Magna Carta for manual workers providing the right to organize and bargain collectively in the private sector. We are witnessing in the 1970s a rapid extension of legislative protection for union activity in the public and nonprofit sectors. Neither librarians nor most other salaried professionals can escape the challenges posed by these developments even if they wish to do so. Thus, the question in 1974 is not really: Are librarians interested in collective bargaining? The question is: In what form will the library profession be swept up by the general growth of union activity in the public sector?

However, it is not only the rapid expansion of collective bargaining legislation for public employees that has changed: there is also a vastly different atmosphere in the 1970s from that in the 1930s which affects librarians as much as it does other professionals. Several elements have contributed to this new climate. Union growth and collective bargaining among professionals have had a slow but continuous expansion since the 1930s. Today few professionals would argue that collective bargaining per se is incompatible with professionalism. There is a new appreciation of what it means to be a salaried professional and a concurrent change in professionals' expectations of what they want to derive from the employment relationship. Both established unions and traditional professional associations have become more sophisticated in effectively representing salaried professionals. Library administrators as well as leaders of professional organizations everywhere are being forced into a reappraisal of their style of leadership, their relationship to individual professionals, and their role in the collective bargaining process. The concept of participation in decision-making has for many professions become a slogan in promoting various methods to bring about a greater degree of involvement in the management of the employing organization, one of these methods being collective bargaining. The many concrete and visible achievements of collective bargaining by the organized work force since the 1930s have not gone unnoticed by unorganized professionals. We intend in this paper to touch on the implications of these elements in the course of analyzing the current labor relations scene in libraries.

Type of Library	Number of Librarians[b]	Percentage of U.S. Librarians[b]	Number Involved in Bargaining	Percentage Involved in Bargaining
School (elementary-secondary)	52,000	46	17,160[c]	33[c]
Academic (community college through university)	19,500	17	3,900[d]	20[d]
Public	26,500	23	2,650[e]	10[e]
Special	16,000	14	160[f]	1[f]
Total	114,000	100	23,870	20

Table 1. Estimated Extent of Collective Bargaining[a] among Librarians by Type of Library

[a]The term "collective bargaining" as used here should be interpreted broadly in that it refers to that negotiations process entered into by librarians and employers or their representatives with the intention of bringing about bilateral determination of employment matters of mutual concern. Only the figures given for school librarians represent bargaining completed through the contract stage.

[b]Estimates of the numbers of U.S. librarians by type of library are those from the Bureau of Labor Statistics given in *The Bowker Annual of Library and Book Trade Information*, 19th ed.[6]

[c]*Negotiation Research Digest*[7] states that at the close of the 1972-73 school year, 934,000 NEA members (two-thirds of the organization's 1,500,000 members) were covered by bargaining contracts. Assuming also a two-thirds representation by the AFT (membership 229,000, *World Almanac*, 1974, p. 107), a total of 1,010,333, or approximately one-third of the teaching work force in the United States, are represented through collective bargaining. Presumably one-third of the school librarians are also represented, the school librarian's identity resting as it does with the teaching work force. The figure given here includes only those school librarians under bargaining contracts and does not reflect the many school librarians who are members of NEA or AFT but are not yet represented by bargaining contracts.

[d]A rough estimate which rests on the figures reported in the 1971 survey of bargaining in institutions of higher education reported by Kennelly.[8] Thirty percent of the national random sample surveyed reported bargaining in progress. Sixty percent of those institutions which reported bargaining also reported that librarians were included in the faculty bargaining unit. These precentages have been applied to the number of academic librarians given in *The Bowker Annual*.[6]

[e]An estimate of unionized public librarians reported by Guyton.[9]

[f]An arbitrary estimate only; no systematic data regarding bargaining by special librarians have come to the authors' attention.

EXTENT OF UNION ACTIVITY

There are no precise figures on the number of librarians who are covered by collective bargaining agreements, who are union members, or who are engaged in bargaining under other than union auspices. Although such figures are not available (there is an obvious need for research in this area) the estimated involvement by librarians in collective bargaining is approximately 10 percent of the public librarians, 20 percent of the academic librarians, 33 percent of the school librarians, and a scattering of special librarians. Table 1 provides a comparison of the extent of bargaining among librarians within each of the four types of libraries together with the number of librarians employed in each type of library, as reported by the Bureau of Labor Statistics.

The aggregate of these estimated percentages of unionized librarians appears to be about 20 percent or approximately 23,870 of the 114,000 American librarians. Librarians, however, represent only a little over 1 percent of the professional labor force. In contrast, for example, elementary level teachers alone represent 13 percent of the total American professional work force.[10]

One measure of increase in union activity which holds special import for academic librarians has resulted from the rapid growth of bargaining by college and university faculties. In its annual summary of such activity in two-year colleges, four-year colleges, and universities, the *Chronicle of Higher Education* in 1971 reported 81 campuses with recognized bargaining agents.[11] By the spring of 1974, the figure had risen to 338 American campuses with recognized bargaining agents for faculty.[12] A 1971 survey inquiring into the inclusion of librarians in faculty bargaining units found that approximately 60 percent of those campuses engaged in faculty bargaining did include librarians in such units.[8] More recently, John Weatherford's survey for the Council on Library Resources identified several schools which had specifically excluded librarians from faculty bargaining units, among them the sizable University of Delaware.[13]

Elementary and secondary school librarians are even more closely identified with teaching faculties than are academic librarians with faculties in higher education. The National Education Association (NEA) and the American Federation of Teachers (AFT) together represent in bargaining over one-third of the country's teachers. It is reasonable to assume, and we have done so in Table 1, that this figure includes approximately one-third of the country's 52,000 school librarians.

Although the number of librarians represented by unions in a bargaining relationship is only about one-fifth of the potential, this figure substantially understates the number of librarians who are affected by bargaining activity, and omits entirely the number of librarians who receive some form of representation from quasi-union professional associations and from single library staff organizations.

Another measure of the fact that unionism for librarians is attracting wide and active discussion is the number of articles on the subject published and indexed in *Library Literature*. In the ten-year period between 1960 and 1970, approximately eighty citations have appeared,[14] and in the first three and one-half years of the present decade, from 1970 through April 1974, more than 100 citations have been counted under the heading "library unions" alone. Numerous additional articles can also be found under headings such as "strikes" and "labor and the library."

PROFESSIONALISM AND COLLECTIVE BARGAINING

William Goode, in analyzing professionalism from the viewpoint of a sociologist, made himself unpopular with librarians by concluding that librarianship, along with nursery school teaching and podiatry, will never become a profession in the full sense.[15] Louis Vagianos, a librarian, argues that librarians should stop seeking the unnecessary and elusive label of *professional* in favor of skilled service worker status which would improve—among other things—their potential for unionization.[16] Discounting the complaints of the many librarians who assert that "librarians are just as professional as lawyers and professors and should be paid a comparable salary and be given the same respect," the truth probably lies somewhere between the view that librarianship will never become a profession and the view that librarians should accept their skilled worker status and do away with the wishful talk about professionalism. Wherever the truth may lie, however, the concept of professionalism is central to the many questions which surround and touch upon employee relations and collective bargaining in libraries.

Clark Kerr has described the American university as a mass of uneasy confusion.[17] So we might describe the library in America today, especially with regard to the status of its professional staff: the library is seen in varied roles such as book depository, information storehouse, educational agency, and community or social center; the librarian assumes varied roles such as bookperson, custodian, information scientist, educator, and social activist or community helper. There is widespread disagreement about the function, purpose and appropriate organizational scheme of the library, as well as about the chief function of a library. That is, how different are the functions and purposes of public, academic, school and special libraries? Who is in charge of the library? Who should be? Should the library director or chief librarian carry principal authority? Or should the staff of librarians themselves as autonomous professionals serve as the library's chief decision-makers? These questions touch upon crucial aspects of the librarians' concerns with their professional status.

In a collective bargaining environment the decision as to whether an occupation is designated as professional may have an important influence on the composition of the bargaining unit, the scope of negotiations, status as managerial employees, eligibility for certain perquisites, and related matters.

Professionalism impinges on unionism and collective bargaining, but the opposite also occurs. For example, has collective bargaining enhanced the status and autonomy of the librarian as a professional, or has it had the opposite effect? How does collective bargaining affect the ability of both administrators and professional staff to achieve their personal goals and meet their professional and organizational responsibilities? Be it public, school, special or academic library, the American library today is not likely to escape struggling with such pressing questions associated with the concept of professionalism. Research into the literature on professionalism and the rise of various occupations to professional status reveals no general agreement on the meaning of the terms "profession" and "professionalism." Nor is this the place to attempt such a definition. Yet it is apparent that recognition of professionalism has important social and economic consequences for the members of the occupation who wish to be accorded professional standing in our society; it carries for its members an important assignment of differential prestige. For some occupations the label rather than the substance of professionalism may be the end being sought.

An important element of the ideology of professionalism has been that there exists an essential harmony of interests between the employer and the professional staff. As an expression of ideology, few of us would quarrel with this formulation. Undoubtedly most librarians and library administrators would agree that fundamentally they share in the same responsibilities and have a joint interest in developing the field of librarianship. However, many employers and professional administrators have used the concept of harmony of interest as the basis for a broadside attack on efforts of salaried professionals to organize for purposes of collective bargaining. In effect, these administrators argue that professionals should eschew unionism and collective bargaining on the grounds that it constitutes unprofessional conduct; because there exists a fundamental harmony of interests, mutual confidence is endangered and effectiveness blunted when a union enters the picture; the union is perceived as driving a wedge between staff professionals and administrators. These same persons would argue that any problems arising in the employment relationship can be solved through improved communication and consultation. What this kind of argument does is equate professionalism with loyalty to management. An interest in unionism is automatically viewed as an expression of disloyalty, and by extension as unprofessional conduct. In our mind there is no doubt that this argument reflects purely managerial interests rather than a concern with maintaining high professional standards.

A more realistic conceptualization of the essential nature of the relationship between staff professionals and administrators can be found in a series of six propositions set out by Jack Barbash:[18] (1) management-employee relations inevitably generate problems; (2) the character of the work makes little difference; (3) it makes no difference who the employer happens to be; (4) although the essential differences of interest between those who are employed and those who employ may be made more bearable, they cannot be eliminated; (5) if there is a difference of interest between the two parties, neither side can be trusted adequately to protect the interests of the other—no matter how high-minded the management, it cannot adequately protect the interests of the employees, and even if it could the employees would not trust management to do so unilaterally; and (6) the only practical way to resolve this inherent conflict between employer and employees rests with a mechanism in which either side can say "no" to the other.

Barbash's principles seem applicable to the situation of librarians. Librarians as salaried personnel are in a direct relationship with the employer. Because the employer has many of his own goals to achieve, there will develop conflict at various points between his legitimate goals and the equally legitimate goals of the employees who have their own definition of the imperatives for success and survival. Librarians, like other groups of salaried professionals, form protective organizations to speak for and defend their interests in dealings with the employer.

PROTECTIVE ORGANIZATIONS AMONG LIBRARIANS

There are basically three kinds of protective organizations that claim the ability to represent the job and professional interests of librarians—the professional association, the labor union, and the single library staff association. Considerable variations exist among the organizations within each of the three types. Of the three, the library staff association is perhaps the least important insofar as labor relations are concerned; thus, it will be treated last and very briefly.

The Professional Association

Among librarians, the dominant form of organization has been the professional association. Librarians have shown a tendency toward proliferation of associations to the point where there are now, in addition to the ALA, more than thirty organizations which are national in scope although oriented toward various specializations and service areas.[19]

The predominant association, the ALA, is broadly based with a fairly open membership policy. This is not to say that the ALA is fully representative of American librarians. In 1973, ALA's membership stood at 30,172 (28,267 personal members) or about 25 percent of the 114,000 American librarians. But this membership figure includes many who are not librarians—trustees, friends of libraries, etc. Interestingly, too, the 30,172 figure represents a decline in membership by some 7,000 from the peak membership year, 1969.[20]

The ALA, as the most visible professional association—and the oldest, now approaching its one-hundredth anniversary—may be taken as the librarians' counterpart to the National Education Association (NEA), the American Nurses Association (ANA), and the American Association of University Professors (AAUP). Unlike these other organizations, however, the ALA has paid relatively little attention to immediate job matters and has concentrated instead on broad professional objectives such as establishing standards for professional practice, accrediting library schools (although there are still more nonaccredited than accredited schools), holding annual conferences, and publishing journals.

The ALA's leadership posts are often filled by persons high in the management hierarchy. Like many other professional organizations, the ALA has fostered an attitude of full cooperation between employer and employee under the assumption that there exists a fundamental identity, not a conflict of interest, among members regardless of their status as employee, employer, or even trustee. In its view, improved communication, consultation and education of members, with the organization acting as catalyst, would work to solidify and strengthen the bonds of common concern and interest to all members. By contrast, the ANA, the NEA, and the AAUP all have developed collective bargaining programs and compete with established unions to obtain representation rights. The ANA adopted such a policy as early as 1946, and today collective bargaining on behalf of registered nurses is undoubtedly its most important function. The NEA reluctantly turned to collective bargaining in the early 1960s, largely as the result of the pressure created by the success of the AFL-CIO-affiliated American Federation of Teachers (AFT). Today the NEA and AFT pursue very similar collective bargaining policies, and there is talk about a merger of the two national organizations. The AAUP formally adopted a collective bargaining program in 1968, in part as a result of the success of both the NEA and the AFT among college and university faculties.

The ALA has never officially or actively opposed library unionism.[21] As early as 1919, speakers were invited to discuss the advantages and disadvantages of union membership at a trustees section meeting. (However, ALA trustees did not present their views at this meeting.) In 1938, the ALA Library Unions Round Table (LURT) was formed by library union members to coordinate the work of existing unions and to act as a clearinghouse and advisory agent for employees forming new unions. By the late 1940s the LURT had become inactive, its recommended resolutions never having been acted upon by the ALA council. The ALA's first semiofficial comment on unionism was made in 1939, when the Third Activities Committee included in its final report on reorganization and evaluation of association purposes a strong statement in favor of unions.[22] The report was sent to the 1939 council but was not discussed. Thirty years later, in 1968, the subject again surfaced officially. ALA's President Roger McDonough, in his inaugural address, stated, "I am not against unions per se; I don't feel that unions can or will exhibit the same concern for the profession that we do."[23] Stimulated by this statement, a 1969 preconvention conference explored the problem of professional associations versus unions, and in 1970 the Library Administration Division Board of Directors adopted a position statement on collective bargaining. Although approved by the executive board of the ALA in April 1970, the position statement has not appeared in the association's official publication, *American Libraries*, nor has it been approved by the membership. The position paper states that the ALA will promote bargaining legislation, inform its constituents about bargaining trends, assist library personnel in data gathering, and encourage training programs relating to bargaining. However, the document also states: "The collective bargaining concept and collective bargaining laws generally preclude the membership of both managers and other personnel in the same union or bargaining group...constitutional provision precludes ALA's becoming a bargaining organization within its current membership and dues structure."[24] Such a stand reasserts ALA's position as an old-line professional association virtually unmoved by the current trend toward bargaining. Its position is in striking contrast to the posture taken by those professional organizations mentioned previously that have not only officially endorsed bargaining, but also have actively engaged in collective bargaining on behalf of their members.

We may contrast the ALA's position with that of the AAUP, for example. The AAUP's statement on collective bargaining, although retaining professional association ideology, makes a firm commitment to collective bargaining as an appropriate mechanism for achieving faculty goals. The 1972 council position on collective bargaining reads in part: "The AAUP will pursue collective bargaining, as a major additional way of realizing the Association's goals in higher education and will allocate such resources and staff as are necessary for a vigorous selective development of this activity beyond present levels... there is pressing need to develop a specialized model of collective bargaining for higher education rather than simply to follow the patterns set by unions in industry."[25]

In summary, it would appear that professional library associations have not actively opposed collective bargaining efforts, nor have they significantly encouraged movement in this direction. The fact is that over the years, these associations have been relatively passive regarding the employment problems of professional librarians. A study completed in the mid-1960s concluded "that the professional associations among nurses, teachers, engineers, and, in all probability, other salaried professions as well, appear to have the capacity—by adapting to the changing needs and conditions of the professions—for discouraging large-scale unionization in the forseeable future. Even while eschewing any identification with labor unions, these associations appear quite willing to act like unions to protect their dominant positions in the professions."[26]

The major associations among teachers and nurses have effectively made the adjustments in structure and function to encompass the need for effective bargaining on behalf of their members. The AAUP seeks to remain the dominant professional organization among faculty by adopting a collective bargaining stance; the outcome is still uncertain. In the case of librarians, the actions taken by the ALA in 1970 probably preclude the association from becoming a collective bargaining representative for librarians. However, were the ALA inclined even now to develop a collective bargaining program and to seek representation rights for librarians, we suspect that effort would not have much prospect for success. Such a decision might have succeeded during the 1960s; now it appears too late. Therefore, the basic pattern of labor relations in libraries is being developed within the framework of employee organizations already deeply committed to collective bargaining.

The Labor Union

What distinguishes the unions from the various associations in light of the present discussion is their early acceptance of the concept of collective bargaining with the employer. The unions, being characterized by varying degrees of militancy and success, were vigorously opposed by many librarians and by library management.

In the case of salaried professionals it is generally an oversimplification to draw a sharp distinction between the professional association and the union model. This matter requires some elaboration here because for many professionals the word "union" invokes an image of industrial unions in the mass production industries. The stereotype in many people's minds is that of a strike-happy organization, led by power-hungry leaders who care about nothing but getting more money, tying management's hands, and stifling any opportunity for individual growth and achievement. That this stereotype does not describe the unions with which the writers are familiar needs to be stated, but not belabored. We wish to emphasize, however, that many of the unions seeking to represent professional employees differ in significant ways from those usually portrayed as being the mainstream American labor movement. The more successful of them tend to comprise an amalgam of characteristics drawn from both traditional professional associations and traditional trade unions. Perhaps a more accurate description would be to call them quasi-unions or quasi-professional organizations.[27]

The 1960s saw a marked movement in the direction of convergence of goals, tactics and strategies of the two kinds of protective organizations—the associations and the unions. That convergence has advanced farther among some salaried professionals (e.g., teachers and nurses) than it has among others (e.g., engineers and scientists).

We have seen actual mergers of associations and unions, notably those of the NEA and the AFT affiliates in the city of Los Angeles and on a statewide basis in New York. We have also seen significant functional changes on the part of professional associations; a notable example is the American Association of University Professors. We have even seen shifts in identity from professional association to union, as exemplified by the NEA. In short, we are witnessing the demise of the primacy of pure professional associations and the pure union in the world of professional employee relations. Among professional associations of librarians, however, we have witnessed neither mergers nor functional or identity changes.

Because librarianship lacks a professional association as trend setter in bargaining—the ALA having gone on record as refusing to function in this role—librarians have tended toward diversity in the kinds of bargaining undertaken. Those employed in academic libraries, as already noted, have more often than not been included in a faculty bargaining unit, represented variously by the NEA, the AFT, the AAUP, or independent bargaining agents.

Librarians in public libraries have bargained chiefly through established unions, notably the American Federation of State, County, and Municipal Employees (AFSCME). AFSCME locals of library personnel tend to vary as to the composition of the bargaining unit. In New York, for instance, extremely successful AFSCME locals at three major libraries—the Brooklyn Public Library, the Queens Borough Public Library, and the New York Public Library—have been composed of approximately the same number of clerical and blue-collar employees as of librarians. Librarians in the city of Los Angeles, which along with the Brooklyn and New York Public libraries is considered one of the three largest library systems in the country, organized through an AFSCME local which represents librarians only. Librarians employed by the Los Angeles County Library are represented by the Service Employees International Union in a unit consisting entirely of librarians.

Another pattern of bargaining unit composition consists of multiple occupational categories at several levels of government in the same bargaining unit. Librarians in Philadelphia, Milwaukee, and Rochester, New York are represented in such mixed bargaining units.[28]

While the AFSCME's share of organized librarians has grown considerably with the nationwide increase in public sector collective bargaining since the 1960s, numerous independent mixed units of public employees also represent librarians.[29] The Civil Service Employees association of White Plains, New York is an example of the independent municipal employees' union. Opinion is divided as to the appropriateness of a mixed unit for librarians. In response to an attitudinal survey conducted in 1968 as a project of the ALA's Library Administration Division, both administrator and union views differed sharply. Asked if library employees should be part of the same bargaining unit as other city employees, one administrator replied "No," while another suggested that fifty library employees within the city's employee group of 2,000 would have less leverage in a separate unit than in one which included nonlibrarians. Similarly, one union spokesman supported the strength-in-numbers argument while another noted that mixed units were especially inappropriate for professional librarians who have no counterparts in other city departments.[30]

There is mounting evidence of concern over strength through size of bargaining units. Dennis Stone emphasized this in his assessment of the prospect of unionism as of summer 1974. He noted that the consensus of union and association offices in Washington, D.C., was that librarians were simply too small a group to be effective in bargaining units representing only librarians.[31] Stone believes that two public employee bargaining bills supported by organized labor, if enacted at the federal level, would bring considerable impetus to bargaining among librarians and other public employees. One of the bills (HR 8677) would set up a National Public Employment Relations Commission (NPERC) for public employees. The other bill (HR 9730) would bring public employees under the jurisdiction of the present National Labor Relations Act. Should either bill pass—and many persons predict that such legislation will be passed—bargaining unit composition would undoubtedly become more uniform along the guidelines or provisions of the NPERC or the NLRB.

Benjamin Aaron, in his analysis of both pieces of proposed legislation, questions the underlying premise of these bills, that is, the desirability of the federal government's preemption of the entire field of labor-management in the public sector. He suggests that neither bill will be needed if the present trend continues among the states toward passage of bargaining legislation at the state level for public employees. Aaron argues for a simpler approach than the full-scale federal control over public employee bargaining as proposed in both these bills. He suggests instead a federal statute which would establish basic bargaining rights for public employees, those rights having been already established in most large states. The statue would apply only in those states in which legislation has not already been passed affirming, for example, the absolute right of public employees to organize and to engage in collective bargaining (as opposed to so-called meet and confer procedures) as well as five related basic bargaining rights.[32]

The bargaining units established under the National Labor Relations Act, Executive Orders 10988 and 11491 for federal employees, and most of the legislation adopted for state and local employees, rest on the fundamental criterion of "identifiable community of interest" rather than the "broad common goals" criterion which is favored by many library administrators. Management often considers as the most appropriate bargaining unit the broadest grouping of employees, because this permits dealing with one large all-inclusive unit rather than a multiplicity of competing organizations.

An appropriate unit with an identifiable community of interest is usually defined in terms of distinctiveness of function, similarity of job skills, and mutual interests in job-related problems and grievances. In the case of a library, the broad goals which all employees presumably hold in common—for example, high quality service to the public—might be the basis for the most appropriate unit. With identifiable community of interest currently being the single most important consideration in unit determination, the criteria distinguishing professionals from other categories of employees become significant. In professional work the emphasis presumably is on the intellectual as opposed to the manual activity, on using independent judgment as opposed to routine decision-making, on qualitative rather than quantitative output, and on specialized and advanced knowledge in contrast to general academic education or vocational training. In the private sector and in federal employment, professional personnel may not be included in a unit with nonprofessional employees unless a majority of the professional personnel vote for such inclusion. The same options are available to professionals in much of the state and local legislation that has been enacted for public employees.[33] Many questions still remain about how to deal with supervisory personnel. Executive Order 11491 for federal employees provides that unless required by practice, prior agreement, or special circumstances, no unit may include both supervisors and the employees they supervise. Yet, because of unevenness in legislation, there are many exceptions. The Washington State Professional Negotiations Act of 1965, for example, provides that all professional employees in a given school or community college district, except the chief administrative officer, are automatically included in the same bargaining unit.

The Staff Association

A discussion of library employee relations would not be complete without mention of the staff association and its potential as a mechanism for structuring professional employee relations. However, because staff associations do not and could not engage in collective bargaining without transforming themselves into at least a quasi-union type of organization, they will not be treated here in great detail. Historically, the staff association has served principally to organize and to promote social activities, and only informally to improve the economic welfare and working conditions of the staff. Bryan's 1949 study included in the Public Library Inquiry, documented the predominance of social activities over all others on the part of staff associations.[34] Ninety-five percent of the librarians in her survey, however, expressed a desire that their staff associations work toward improved economic welfare. Another 93 percent see aiding the professional development of librarians as a focus for many staff associations. This aim was indicated as a desired activity by some 93 percent of the 2,000 public librarians who responded to Bryan's survey.

In academic libraries on campuses where librarians are not represented in the faculty senate or by formal collective bargaining, the staff association may serve as a representative body for the librarians or as a mechanism to improve personnel policy or to bring out greater participation in policy development or implementation. Overall, however, if measured on a continuum or scale of effectiveness in structuring employee relations, the staff association would lie at the laissez-faire extreme.

PROFESSIONAL GOALS IN BARGAINING

We have suggested the hypothesis that the wages, hours, and other terms and conditions of employment for librarians will increasingly be established through negotiations between the employer and a certified bargaining agent. Bargaining creates a number of difficult problems for librarians, not shared by many other salaried professionals. Most crucial in this regard is the makeup of the bargaining unit. School librarians typically find themselves in the same unit with teachers, where of course they constitute a small minority, or in a unit composed of an assortment of supportive professional and semiprofessional staff such as school nurses, playground directors, and counselors. In colleges and universities we typically find librarians together with the teaching faculty, where they again constitute a small percentage of the unit or with other nonteacher professionals such as professional researchers, extension specialists, and accountants. It is unlikely that there will be many bargaining units for school and academic librarians containing exclusively librarians or even units where librarians constitute a majority. Public librarians are somewhat more likely to have their own units, but their problem may be whether the unit is large enough or strong enough to be taken seriously by anyone. There is little evidence to suggest that the interests of librarians are being given special attention in collective bargaining legislation or by agencies such as employee relations commissions. Part of the responsibility for this must rest with the library profession itself because of its failure over the years to articulate a consistent philosophy about the vital job and professional goals of librarians and the extent to which collective bargaining might serve to achieve these goals.

There is now enough experience with professional worker collective bargaining in the public sector to suggest, at least in broad outline, the basic bargaining strategy of professionals who are in a position to establish their own goals and devise their own bargaining policies.

In many respects, what professionals seek to achieve in their jobs and careers is no different from what all other employees—professional, as well as white- and blue-collar—strive to obtain. But there are also important differences. Of course, differences also exist among those occupations typically placed within the category "professional." Professionals everywhere seem to hold in common the idea that work is more than "just a job." They expect to give a good deal of effort to their work and careers, and they hope to obtain a high level of reward for their efforts. To illustrate this commonality, it is helpful to separate into two categories the goals sought by professionals. We can call then Level I and Level II goals.

Level I goals may be defined as those relating to fairly short-run job and work rewards. These goals are common to all categories of workers, irrespective of education, function, status, and related qualities; they have a "now" focus. Typical Level I goals include the fundamental concerns of satisfactory wages or salaries, suitable working conditions, fair treatment, reasonable fringe benefits, and a measure of job security. While conflicts do develop over the employers' obligation to meet employees' specific demands with respect to these goals, wherever collective bargaining exists in the public sector there is general recognition that they are appropriate subjects for the bargaining table.

Level II goals may be defined as the longer-run professional goals—those not generally held by manual workers as realizable objectives. Although they may be viewed as highly desirable by all workers, these goals are seldom translated into concrete objectives except by professionals. They are centrally related to the mission and content of the functions performed by members of the profession. Much of the substance of Level II goals is encompassed in the concepts of autonomy, occupational integrity and identification, individual career satisfaction, and economic security and enhancement.[35] Taken together these four concepts define much of the substance of professionalism.

While Level I goals may lack the glamor associated with Level II goals, their importance must not be underestimated. Like the first levels of Maslow's hierarchy of needs, they serve as the necessary foundation for higher level needs— for Level II goals.[36] Historically, librarians as a group have experienced greater frustration than many other salaried professionals in achieving Level I goals, particularly satisfactory salaries.

Each of the Level II goals is important to the current reappraisal of employee relations in libraries. Salaried professionals no longer derive much satisfaction from the rhetoric of professionalism. They are demanding its substance, and more and more they are resorting to collective bargaining to achieve it. They are no longer satisfied with being told that they are sharing in management decision-making, that they are expected to live up to a high professional calling, and that unionism is incompatible with professionalism.

Autonomy, whether for self-employed or for salaried professionals, suggests the professionals' right—indeed, obligation—to practice in their work that which they know. They expect to be trusted—not judged—by those to whom they make available their specialized knowledge. Once admitted to full membership in the profession, they expect to adhere to a code of conduct formulated by the profession and binding on all its members. They desire an authority structure which recognizes the characteristics of their professional role. Reference librarians in a large university library, for example, who must operate under a single-copy purchase policy imposed over their objection by the library director and the board, have suffered an erosion of professional autonomy.

Occupational integrity and identification refers to delimitation of professional boundaries in dealings with clients and employees and to attainment of public recognition. With respect to internal organization, a profession will adopt a policy on entry, will take protective action against threats to its prerogatives and status, and will resist transfer of primary loyalty away from the profession to the goals of the employing organization. The recent employment of a nonlibrarian as head of the San Francisco Public Library has received considerable negative response from librarians on the West Coast. The upcoming selection of the Librarian of Congress highlights the same issue.

The matter of individual career satisfaction concerns the professionals' desire to retain a good deal of direct control over decisions affecting their work and careers. The hierarchical authority structure of most libraries interposes a screen between the professional employees and the library administration, with administrators making most of the critical decisions regarding the deployment of professional staff and rewards for performance. "To be recognized as experts in their field, especially by their employers," "to be protected from unqualified outsiders," "to do satisfying and socially useful work," and "to have a predictable line of career development without leaving the profession," are phrases commonly used in the literature to describe this area of interest. Individual career satisfaction has been thwarted, for example, for the children's librarian who wishes to practice in his or her area of specialization rather than to assume administrative functions, but who finds no career ladder available.

Finally, the concept of economic security and enhancement in the Level II goal context goes beyond simple monetary gain. What makes this category important is the notion that the level of reward should be pegged not so much to the contribution made to the employing organization directly, nor to the need for adequate income to sustain a certain standard of living, but rather to the direct relationship of rewards and the quality of service rendered. Thus, the quality of the library service performed at a branch, rather than the number of books circulated or the senoirity of the branch librarian, would be the base from which to measure professional worth.

Several observations may be made in comparing Level I and Level II goals. Whereas Level I goals were defined as being more "now" oriented than Level II goals, at some point the Level II goals may become just as instantly compelling for professionals as Level I goals.[37] In collective bargaining, Level I items may involve greater immediate dollar cost to the employer than Level II items. On the other hand, Level I items are less frequently disputed as appropriate subjects for bargaining. The Level II issues, while clearly having economic consequences, are from the employer's viewpoint of greatest concern because they may provide a fundamental challenge to managerial authority. For that reason, Level II goals are frequently more intractable in terms of conflict over whether they are appropriate subjects for collective bargaining.

The evidence from bargaining by professionals with considerable experience in the process indicates that, early in the relationship, the primary stress of the bargaining organization seems to be on securing Level I goals, or "bread and butter items" as they are frequently called. However, it is also true that no sooner are acceptable Level I benefits established than the professional bargaining organization turns its attention to Level II issues. In actual negotiations, this often takes the form of initially negotiating a concept into the contract (such as peer review) and working out in subsequent negotiations the details of its implementation. The final outcome often is deep penetration into areas of decision-making formerly reserved exclusively for management.

In general (with some notable exceptions), unions composed of and oriented toward the problems of manual workers tend to concentrate in their bargaining activities on achieving more benefits in the Level I area; if tradeoffs are to be made in bargaining, they are typically willing to give up the Level II goals for increased Level I benefits. In the case of professional worker bargaining, the process becomes considerably more complex. Any bargaining organization that wishes to retain the support of its professional constituents in a collective bargaining environment must demonstrate, on a continuing basis, its ability to secure Level I goals at an acceptable level. It also seems clear, however, that this same organization, if it is responsive to the central concerns of professionals, will strive continually to secure Level II goals. Stated another way, the organization will work continually to expand participation in decision-making in all the areas of concern to professional employees. Indeed, it can be argued that if an employee organization does otherwise, it would forfeit its claim to being able to represent the full range of job and professional interests of its members. The hypothesis may be suggested that the greater the degree of professionalism of the occupation involved, the greater the pressure on the bargaining agent to work effectively in the Level II area.

This analysis, if correct, raises a number of very important issues for librarians in view of the wide assortment of organizations which represent them. Do such organizations give the kind of attention to the job and professional interests that librarians feel they are entitled to? From our perspective, the problem is not that of having to decide whether an AFL-CIO-affiliated union or a professional association-turned-bargaining agent can do a better job. Each type of organization has demonstrated its basic ability to work effectively on behalf of professionals in the employment relationship. The dilemma confronting librarians is a more parochial one. In those cases in which they have their own bargaining unit, the unit will almost invariably be extremely small, in a relative sense, raising questions about its potential effectiveness. In those cases in which librarians are combined with nonlibrarians, the former almost invariably constitute a minority in the unit, raising the question of whether the distinctive needs and interests of the librarians will be given adequate attention. There are so far no easy solutions to these problems; nor is it clear to us that librarians will be given much choice in the matter.

The question of unionism and collective bargaining among librarians has been a topic of active interest since the 1930s. Although there has been a union presence among librarians for many years, its total impact has not been great. This situation is likely to undergo drastic change. The 1960s saw the beginning of large-scale unionism and collective bargaining among public employees, and especially among professionals, a pattern which has continued into the 1970s. A substantial majority of the nation's 114,000 librarians are employed in public institutions.

There is nothing that even approaches a consistent pattern in the type of organization representing librarians in bargaining or in the composition of the bargaining units in which librarians find themselves. One can only conclude that the quality of representation librarians receive varies considerably from case to case.

The central conclusion which emerges from our view of the library labor relations scene is that librarians, as professionals, appear to have little opportunity to exert real influence on the critical decisions involving composition of bargaining unit and choice of bargaining agent. In this sense librarians are in a dependent position—an uncomfortable one for a proud profession to find itself in.

Librarianship constitutes a small profession; its members are dispersed geographically and work in many different institutional settings. These and related factors undoubtedly contribute to the dependency of librarians on the good will of others for their job and professional enhancement. As a profession, librarianship has been less vigilant in advancing its professional interests and in developing structures for collective action in the employment relationship than is true of most salaried professions.

It seems that the future of employee relations in libraries will depend upon the appropriateness and success of existing and changing governance structures in libraries. It will depend on the passage of new—and changes in existing—bargaining legislation. It will depend heavily upon the extent of professionalization and the projection of this development outside the profession. It will depend upon congruence in perceptions of the nature of the profession among librarians themselves, as well as among the public at large.

REFERENCES

1. Berelson, Bernard. "Library Unionization," *Library Quarterly*, 9:477, Oct. 1939.
2. McIver, M.E., *et al. Technologists' Stake in the Wagner Act.* Chicago, American Association of Engineers, 1944; and Northrup, Herbert R. "Collective Bargaining by Professional Societies." *In* Richard A. Lester and Joseph Shister, eds. *Insights into Labor Issues.* New York, Macmillan, 1948, pp. 134-62.
3. *Matter of Globe Machine and Stamping Company*, 3 NLRB 294 (1937). This fear among many engineers was to a large extent unfounded. In fact, professional engineers were given special consideration by the NLRB in the establishment of bargaining units under the Wagner Act. As early as 1937 the NLRB was applying the "Globe Doctrine," which provides that within a plant "where the considerations are evenly balanced, the determining factor is the desire of the men themselves."
4. Shlakman, Vera. "Unionism and Professional Organizations Among Engineers," *Science and Society*, 14:330, Fall 1950.
5. Berelson, *op. cit.*, p. 497.

6. Green, Joseph. "A Three-Year Comparison of Urban-Suburban Library Statistics." *In* Madeline Miele, ed. *The Bowker Annual of Library and Book Trade Information.* 19th ed. New York, Bowker, 1974, p. 236.
7. "Negotiation Notes," *Negotiation Research Digest*, 7:15, Jan. 1974.
8. Kennelly, Jean R. "Collective Bargaining in Higher Education in the United States: Conceptual Models and a Survey of Incidence among Faculty and Supportive Professional Personnel." Unpublished Ph.D. dissertation prepared for the University of Washington, 1972.
9. Guyton, Theodore L. "Unionization of Public Librarians: A Theoretical Interpretation." Unpublished Ph.D. dissertation prepared for the University of California, Los Angeles, 1972.
10. Blitz, Rudolph C. "Women in the Professions, 1870-1970," *Monthly Labor Review*, 97:36, May 1974.
11. *Chronicle of Higher Education*, 5:1, May 10, 1971.
12. *Chronicle of Higher Education*, 6:24, June 10, 1974.
13. Weatherford, John. "Librarians in Faculty Unions," *Library Journal*, 99:2443, Oct. 1974.
14. Boaz, Martha. "Labor Unions and Libraries," *California Librarian*, 32:104, April/July, 1971.
15. Goode, William J. "The Librarian from Occupation to Profession," *ALA Bulletin*, 61:544-55, May 1967. See also_____. "The Theoretical Limits of Professionalization." *In* Amitai Etzioni, ed. *The Semi-Professions and their Organizations.* New York, The Free Press, 1969.
16. Vagianos, Louis. "The Librarian and the Garbageman: Professionalism Reconsidered," *Library Journal*, 98:391-93, Feb. 1, 1973.
17. Kerr, Clark. *The Uses of the University.* Cambridge, Mass., Harvard University Press, 1963, p. 18.
18. Barbash, Jack. "The Elements of Industrial Relations," *British Journal of Industrial Relations*, 2:66-78, March 1964.
19. *The Bowker Annual . . ., op. cit.*, pp. 461-513.
20. *ALA Membership Directory 1973.* Chicago, ALA, 1973, p. 215.
21. Guyton, *op. cit.*, pp. 111-14, Chapter 4.
22. Dudgeon, Matthew S., et al. "Final Report of the Third Activities Committee," *ALA Bulletin*, 33:796, Dec. 1939.
23. McDonough, Roger H. "An Inaugural Address," *ALA Bulletin*, 62:874, July-Aug. 1968.
24. "The American Library Association and Library Collective Bargaining" (Position Paper adopted by the Library Administration Division Board of Directors, Jan. 21, 1970). *In* American Library Association. *Executive Board Minutes. 1970 Spring Meeting, Chicago, Illinois, April 29-May 1, 1970.* Exhibit 6, unpaged.
25. Davis, Bertram H. "Council Position on Collective Bargaining," *AAUP Bulletin*, 57:511-12, Winter 1971.
26. Kleingartner, Archie. "Professional Associations: An Alternative to Unions?" *In* Walter Fogel and Archie Kleingartner, eds. *Contemporary Labor Issues.* Belmont, Calif., Wadsworth, 1966, p. 255.
27. Schlachter, Gail. "Quasi-Unions and Organizational Hegemony within the Library Field," *Library Quarterly*, 43:185-98, July 1973.
28. Gardiner, George L. "Collective Bargaining: Some Questions Asked," *ALA Bulletin*, 62:973-76, Sept. 1968.

29. Ibid., p. 975; see also *National Trade and Professional Associations of the United States and Labor Unions*. Washington, D.C., Columbia Books, 1974, p. 39.

30. American Library Association. "Collective Bargaining: Questions and Answers," *ALA Bulletin*, 62:1388, Dec. 1968.

31. Stone, Dennis. "The Prospect of Unionism," *American Libraries*, 5:365, July/Aug. 1974.

32. Aaron, Benjamin. "Federal Bills Analyzed and Appraised by Expert," *LMRS Newsletter*, f:2-4, Nov. 1974.

33. Prasow, Paul. *Unit Determination in Public Employment–Concept and Problems* (Reprint No. 198). Los Angeles, Institute of Industrial Relations, University of California, 1969.

34. Bryan, Alice I. *The Public Librarian: A Report of the Public Library Inquiry*. New York, Columbia University Press, 1952, pp. 264-71.

35. Kleingartner, Archie. *Professionalism and Salaried Worker Organization*. Madison, Industrial Relations Research, University of Wisconsin, 1967, Chapter 3.

36. Maslow, A.H. "A Theory of Human Motivation," *Psychological Review*, 50:370-96, July 1943.

37. Vollmer, Howard M., and Mills, Donald L. eds. *Professionalization*. Englewood Cliffs, N.J., Prentice Hall, 1966, Chapter 8.

DON WASSERMAN
Assistant to the President for Collective Bargaining Services
American Federation of State, County, and Municipal Employees
Washington, D.C.

Unionization of Library Personnel: Where We Stand Today

During the past decade a rapid change has been taking place in public employment: public sector employees of all types are joining employee organizations. Unlike the employee organizations of the past, these are being formed for the major purpose of engaging in collective bargaining with employers, including state governments, county governments, school boards, local governments, universities, colleges, and nonprofit institutions.

The growth of our own organization, AFSCME (American Federation of State, County, and Municipal Employees), may indicate what has happened among public employees over the last fifteen years. In 1964, for example, the dues-paying membership of our union was about 235,000; today the membership stands at 700,000, and is made up exclusively of people who work for state and local governments and for nonprofit institutions. There has been continual pressure on the part of public employees throughout the nation to join unions such as AFSCME and other employee organizations. The major issue involved seems to be the desire of public employees to introduce the concept of bilateralism into the employee relationship. Public sector employees number fewer than their private sector counterparts, and in terms of employee relations, most institutions and local governments have been run on a unilateral basis. Public employees are unhappy with this, and as a result the organization of public employees has taken place across the board, including not only blue-collar workers, nonprofessional white-collar workers, technicians and hospital workers, but also professional employees, especially where they are hired in large numbers. For example, AFSCME has substantial numbers of social service employees, engineering personnel, and librarians. Many of the teachers' groups—the National Education Association, the

This article is an edited transcription of Mr. Wasserman's presentation at the Institute.

23

American Federation of Teachers, and the American Association of University Professors—have also witnessed considerable growth during this period.

Until recently, most public employers in most states really did not care whether employees joined associations or unions. It was relatively immaterial to them, because even when employees joined unions, that was about the end of the story. Although the unions may have become involved in some handling of personal grievances and matters of that nature, there was really no genuine collective bargaining.

Our union was founded in the midst of the depression, during the same period when some of the more militant industrial unions, such as those of the auto workers, the steel workers, and the rubber workers, were founded. AFSCME had a different birth, however, for it was founded by a group of management employees in Wisconsin who were fearful that a newly elected state administration would attempt to destroy the recently established civil service system in that state. To protect that civil service system, the organization which later became the American Federation of State, County, and Municipal Employees was founded in 1932 and became active in 1935. From the beginning, therefore, AFSCME was linked very closely to the problems of administration of public service affairs and the encouragement of civil service.

These goals remained very much the same until after World War II. Then the nature of the organization slowly began to change. In the 1950s we had the first movement anywhere on the part of public employees to sit down at a bargaining table and actually negotiate conditions of employment with the public employer. The earliest instances of what might be called the birth of collective bargaining in the public sector took place in a few large cities—first Philadelphia, then Cincinnati and New York. As a matter of fact, the framework of the New York bargaining situation later provided the background for the Federal Employees' Executive Order 1098, which was promulgated by President Kennedy in 1962 and established the framework for the limited form of bargaining which federal employees have.

Actually, most of the movement in the public sector toward collective bargaining took place on a *de facto* basis—i.e., without benefit of law. When Congress passed the Wagner Act in 1935, it specifically excluded from coverage all public employees, as well as most employees of nonprofit institutions such as hospitals. The Wagner Act was amended in 1947 by Taft-Hartley, and by Landren and Griffin in 1959, but all amendments to the original law continued to bar public employees from engaging in collective bargaining and from the protections of the national labor relations policy of the country. Because of this, when collective bargaining appeared in the public sector it grew up on a piecemeal basis, state by state, county by county, school board by school board, municipality by municipality. It was about 1960 in the state of Wisconsin when the first public sector bargaining law was passed, giving public employees for the first time the legal right to sit down with employers and mutually determine the conditions under which they would work.

In the last several years there has been a rash of bargaining legislation, but thus far only about one-half the states have enacted any general legislation covering most public employees. I am not considering here laws which deal specifically with a single group such as teachers, police, firefighters, or university personnel, but am concerned with laws applying to the broad range of public employees working for state and local governments. Although about one-half of the states have enacted some kind of general legislation, coverage varies widely. In some states, coverage extends to both state and local governmental employees; in others only state employees are covered. Ironically, a number of state legislatures have enacted legislation covering local government employees only, excluding state employees.

One of the interesting things about state legislation on collective bargaining is the great variety that exists throughout the country. No two public sector bargaining laws are alike, and for a single state there may be as many as four or five laws, one dealing with teachers, one with state employees, one with municipal employees, and another with police and firefighters. Within a state, different municipalities and counties have different codes concerning the right of public employees to bargain collectively. In one municipality, therefore, it is quite possible that employees have more or fewer rights than they have in a neighboring jurisdiction.

For a number of years AFSCME has been seeking federal legislation in this area, either through amendment of the present statutes or, preferably, through a special piece of legislation which would take into account the specific needs and concerns of public employees. We have sponsored a public employees' relations act in Congress for a number of years, and in 1974 we succeeded in having a bill introduced in both the House and the Senate. This bill would provide a collective bargaining framework for all state and local government employees throughout the nation. At the same time, however, it would permit a state which had enacted legislation that was substantially equivalent to that enacted by Congress to continue to administer its own law.

The important problem in this area is that when we bargain in the absence of law, on a *de facto* basis, the mechanism and procedures are generally controlled by the employer. This leaves the employees at a very distinct disadvantage.

It is certainly true that the initial thrust for collective bargaining rights for public employees has come from blue-collar workers, just as the thrust in the private sector toward collective bargaining and unionization came from blue-collar workers in the mid-1930s. But unlike the private sector, the public sector has witnessed an expanded concept of unionism that has far transcended the blue-collar field. For example, AFSCME represents substantial numbers of professional employees in most of the major local governments throughout the United States and in many of the large state governments.

State governments have typically lagged behind local governments in affording any rights to employees. In the absence of legislation we are very frequently able to sit down and negotiate on a *de facto* basis with a local governmental employer, but it becomes much more difficult to do this with the state employer. The state of Ohio may serve as an example here, for it has no collective bargaining legislation. The state service there mirrors the fact that there is no legislation, for there is very little bargaining at the state level, and what bargaining takes place is concerned with an individual institution or facility. By contrast, we have developed agreements with virtually every large municipal employer in Ohio.

The spread of collective bargaining from its historical beginnings in the blue-collar field through white-collar workers and into professional employees is not based on any great organizing campaign on the part of AFSCME. It is based very simply on the fact that professional employees, especially those hired in large numbers, quickly come to realize that they are not treated as professional employees, particularly in such very basic areas as decision-making. One needs only to look, for example, at the detailed regulations and restrictions which surround the job of an experienced social service employee in many jurisdictions to realize that he is treated as a clerk, not as a professional employee. Although AFSCME does not represent teachers, we may note that one of the main reasons that they began to bargain about a decade ago was the fact that they were not treated as professionals. This clerical status, coupled with low salaries, was a prime reason for the tremendous thrust by teachers to engage in collective bargaining during the 1960s. We are now witnessing this same development on the part of other professional employees. For example, a group of professional employees in Philadelphia organized themselves into an association a few years ago and then asked to be affiliated with AFSCME. We have witnessed this in other cities as well.

A distinctly new development of the past three or four years is the move toward collective bargaining by state employees who are professionals. In a sense these represent the last bastion. State employees, state professional employees, and university and college faculty seem to be organizing concurrently, and there seems to be no doubt that this will continue on an accelerated basis. One thing that is going to accelerate this movement is that general economic conditions in the United States are going to get worse before they get better. We have witnessed a contraction of public budgets, especially on the municipal level, in the past five or six years, and this condition will probably worsen in the next year or two. This budget cutting has already affected colleges and universities, and has begun to affect state governments too. Despite what might be told to those seeking wage increases, most states have been operating at a surplus; in fact, the state surpluses overall were greater in fiscal 1973 than in 1972. As a result of general revenue sharing help from the federal government, many states have been able to increase their surpluses without increasing state taxes. Some states have at the same time decreased their services to local governments within the state and have generally started to tighten their belts. I expect some of these rather large state surpluses will soon start to wither away as the economic conditions in the nation generally worsen and state revenues decline.

It seems that when governors, mayors, and university trustees start to look for a place to engage in a little belt tightening, they will look for what they consider to be fringe areas of state, city or university operations. They will look for things that may easily be cut back, and every area that can be considered nonessential will be hit. For example, in large local governments we have seen tremendous cutbacks in recreational facilities—cutbacks in personnel and in number of hours—and this kind of operation is spreading. Another area that administrations will examine for budget cutting will certainly be libraries. Libraries and librarians are going to be in for a rough time for the next few years.

This problem relates to the idea of collective bargaining for public employees in several ways. Typically, public employees, like their counterparts in the private sector, wish to sit down in some mutually satisfactory way to determine the wages, hours, and conditions of employment under which they will work. Many professional issues fall under the heading of conditions of employment. The decision of how facilities are to be staffed is an example. These issues become more crucial for discussion and negotiation among professional employees than they do among nonprofessional employees. We have seen this in the arguments over classroom size in the teacher negotiations and over case loads for social service employees. There are similar problems throughout the area of public employment, including library services. In the case of budget cuts, the questions are: How is the situation to be handled? If there is going to be a cutback in services, how is this cutback to be performed? What will be the impact on employment and employment opportunity? These are all areas that we have made subject to the collective bargaining procedure.

My experience has been that negotiations by professional employees have dealt with many professional issues and have tried to deal with a much wider range of issues than negotiations in the private sector. As a result, when professional employees want to talk about services, the first response by the employer has been that these areas are concerned with the mission of the agency and are therefore a management prerogative and not subject to negotiation. But in AFSCME we look at it from another perspective: we believe that anything which has an impact on the employee and how he functions is in essence a condition of employment. Even some of the more restrictive laws under which we bargain in the public sector—those laws which have spelled out management rights—still generally permit the public employee to engage in dialogue where there is a management prerogative that affects employment conditions. Most of our collective bargaining procedures, even in situations where the law has a management-rights clause, provide that we have the right to bargain over subject matters which affect the employees, the way in which they perform their jobs, and the general conditions under which they work. The negotiations of most professionals have therefore much more readily entered those areas which are called the "mission of the agency" or "management prerogatives" than have negotiations among, for example, blue-collar workers in the private sector.

I expect this trend to continue, but I do not accept the argument that has been made by observers of and participants in professional negotiations that monetary items take a back seat in such negotiations. It isn't even necessary to consider today's economy to realize that "bread and butter" issues—wage and pension matters and health insurance matters—are of primary significance. To suggest that these issues have little meaning to the professional employee, who is concerned only with performing a service to the employer and to the public at large, is nonsense. I don't know who started this story, but I suspect that it came in part from the employer; by claiming this he almost puts his employees on a pedestal, and I suspect that they are somewhat receptive to the idea. It puts a halo around their heads, and it sounds nice. It also makes a nice public appeal if the professional workers say they are more concerned about quality of service or how children learn than they are about the fact that they are still working for $4500 a year. If this was ever true, it is not so today. Professional employees are interested in wages, in providing their families with a decent standard of living, in having a measure of security and a decent retirement system, in being covered by reasonable health and life insurance plans. This is nothing shameful, for you really cannot take pride in your job unless you can have a certain amount of self pride as well. It is important that service employees be interested in these "bread and butter" issues.

Of course it is true by the very nature of the job that professionals—librarians, social service employees, teachers, engineers, chemists or physicists—should be interested in the way in which the service they perform is going to be delivered to the people who want, request and need that service. Their entire training has told them this is proper, and to expect otherwise of them is to ask them to demean themselves. I contend that the only way professionals can have a voice in how services are to be established and delivered is by having a collective voice. This is particularly important in the case of large facilities and large institutions where there are many professionals and many employees under supervision. The only way that public employees may have a voice in setting the conditions of employment under which they will work—wages, fringe benefits, hours, etc.—is again by having a collective voice. Whether the vehicle is an out-and-out labor union like the American Federation of State, County, and Municipal Employees, or whether it is an employee association given some more euphemistic or appealing name, is a decision that public employees will make on a city-by-city, state-by-state, service-by-service basis.

I think, however, that the problems that librarians have faced up until now will increase considerably over the next year or two. They are going to increase as a result of the real budget crunch that employers will face. Libraries will in many cases be looked at first when sacrifices need to be made, and public employees in general will be scrutinized regardless of the kinds of services they perform. This is only one further reason why self-organization becomes absolutely essential. Librarians will need to have a voice in determining how crises will be met, how decisions are going to be made. Only through a collective voice does any individual professional, public employee have any voice at all.

ANDREW M. KRAMER
Executive Director
Office of Collective Bargaining
Springfield, Illinois

The Legal Environment

The legal environment surrounding the unionization of library personnel must be discussed from several different standpoints. At the outset, one must differentiate among library personnel on the basis of whom they work for. Library personnel working for private universities come under the National Labor Relations Act (NLRA). Library personnel working for public employers in some states come under the jurisdiction of a state public employee labor relations act, while such personnel in other states have no statutory protection and must rely on judge-made law which varies from state to state.

For many years library personnel were in the no-man's land of labor relations, outside the reach of any statutory framework to guide them in their dealings with their employer. The National Labor Relations Board (NLRB) had refused to assert jurisdiction over private, nonprofit colleges and universities until 1970, when in its *Cornell University* (183 NLRB 41) decision it decided to assert jurisdiction over such institutions.

Library personnel working for public employers are not under the jurisdiction of the NLRA. As public employees, they have been slow to achieve many of the rights which have long been enjoyed by employees in the private sector. Since a large number of library personnel work in the public sector, it is important to provide some background with respect to public sector bargaining.

When we consider public employee bargaining from a historical perspective, we are not talking of bargaining but rather of the restraints imposed in preventing union organization and bargaining from ever taking place. Nearly two decades ago, the report of the American Bar Association Committee on Labor Relations of Governmental Employees suggested that: "a government which imposes upon other employers certain obligations in dealing with their employees may not in good faith refuse to deal with its own public servants on a reasonably similar basis, modified, of course, to meet the exigencies of the public service."[1]

At the time of that report it was generally accepted that public employees did not have any right to bargain. Indeed, in 1945 the Supreme Court had occasion to note that "under customary practices government employees do not bargain collectively with their employer."[2]

A central rationale leading to the denial of bargaining rights in the public sector was the concept of sovereignty. Since collective bargaining is premised on a bilateral determination of conditions of employment, it was viewed as an interference in the sovereign's affairs. Typical of the attitude which prevailed is the opinion of the Florida Attorney General in 1944 in which he stated:"no organization, regardless of who it is affiliated with, union or non-union, can tell a political subdivision possessing the attributes of sovereignty, who it can employ, how much it shall pay them, or any other matter relating to its employees. To countenance such a proposition would be to surrender a portion of sovereignty that is possessed by every municipal corporation."[3]

During the same time that bargaining rights were being denied, certain groups of public employees were thwarted even in their efforts to organize. Various courts sustained discharges of public employees for becoming members of labor unions on the grounds that such membership either violated a state statute or the court's perception of state public policy.

It is of some interest to note that public employees were on several occasions granted the right to organize on the basis of a state right-to-work law. In a reversal of the popular concept of their role, some courts construed state right-to-work laws as allowing public employees the right to organize and join labor unions.[4]

Until recently, and even now with rare exception, public employees have been denied the right to strike. In enjoining strikes, courts noted the need for government services to be unobstructed and held that such strikes contravene public welfare.[5]

Historically, courts have generally been either disinclined or compelled to analyze at length the basis for enjoining public employee strikes. A finding that such strikes result in a denial of government authority seems to reflect the conclusion that strikes compel governmental decisions that would otherwise not be made.

Many of the decisions prohibiting public employee strikes have arisen in states which have "Little Norris-LaGuardia Acts" prohibiting the issuance of injunctions in labor disputes. Even in the absence of express exclusion, however, these anti-injunction statues have not been held applicable to public employees.[6]

While the role of the law in the past has been a negative factor with respect to public employee bargaining, significant changes have occurred over the past fifteen years. Federal courts have recognized the constitutional rights of public employees to join and form labor unions and have struck down statues prohibiting public employees from joining unions.[7] Federal and state courts have also become increasingly sensitive to the due process rights of public employees.

In more than thirty-six states and in the federal government the debate over the legitimacy of public employee organizational and bargaining rights is academic as a result of legislation or executive order. The public sector bargaining legislation which has been enacted raises numerous issues which have no analogy to the private sector. While space does not permit discussion of all of these issues, some of the present approaches to public employee bargaining deserve mention.

It is often suggested that one of the distinguishing features between the private and public sectors is that in the private sector management and unions negotiate under the constraints of the market place. Management in the private sector considers the effects of increased labor costs on the price of items being manufactured as well as competitive forces and consumer preference. In the public sector, however, services are not generally dependent on the revenues they produce and most often are exclusive in nature. This does not mean, however, that the constraints found are no less effective than those in the private sector.

It is the political process which imposes some of the major constraints in the public sector. The type of service provided, the location where such services are to be provided, and the allocation of revenue to provide such services is often dependent upon political opinion and political pressures. Thus, it has been argued, opening the door to full-scale bargaining, as has evolved in the private sector, will "institutionalize the power of public employee unions in a way that would leave competing groups in the political process at a permanent and substantial disadvantage."[8]

In applying these views, some states and the federal government have chosen to limit the scope of bargaining by executive order. Thus, in some states public employers are not required to bargain over matters of "inherent managerial policy," including "the functions and programs of the public employer, standards of services [and] standards of work." Other states such as Michigan have not chosen to limit the duty to bargain, however, and have imposed a duty similar to that imposed under the NLRA.

In addition to the impact of the political process on defining the scope of bargaining, another factor which has played a significant role is the presence of civil service systems. In many states and municipalities, civil service systems have come to encompass all aspects of employee relations and not just those aspects related to the merit principle. In Illinois, for example, the personnel code and its implementing rules cover most of the matters found in private sector collective bargaining agreements.

Unfortunately, many states have ignored the pervasive impact of civil service statutes and rules in drafting public sector bargaining legislation. The failure to deal adequately with this issue leads ultimately to judicial accommodation—a solution ill suited to treat fully the complexities presented.[9]

Another issue which has not been fully considered in drafting public sector legislation is the definition of who the public employer really is. Is it the executive branch, or does that title belong to the legislature or a county board which ultimately approves the monetary terms of any ageement through the appropriation process?

Very little attention has been given to this issue which bears directly on the implementation of a statutory duty to bargain in good faith. One state which has at least addressed itself to this problem is Wisconsin. Under the Wisconsin Public Employee Relations Act, the term *employer* is defined to reflect the differences between the legislative and executive branches. While the state is considered as a single employer, the act sets out the role of the legislature with respect to the implementation and approval of collective bargaining agreements.

One of the critical issues faced in the public sector is the determination of appropriate bargaining units. While Martin Schneid discusses this issue in depth elsewhere in this volume, it is necessary for me to touch upon some of the problems posed.

Bargaining unit determinations in the public sector have far-reaching consequences since the establishment of a given unit affects the structure of bargaining and has a measurable impact on the traditional governmental policy of maintaining, where possible, uniformity of terms and conditions of employment.

Unit determinations in states which do not have legislation are made either by the parties or by the employer. For example, in *Chicago High School Assistant Principals Association* v. *Board of Education of the City of Chicago* the court was faced with the issue of whether the Board of Education had to recognize high school assistant principals as a separate unit for purposes of collective bargaining. Assistant principals were covered under the Board of Education's collective bargaining agreement with the Chicago Teachers Union. The agreement contained no provision for the severance of assistant principals and the board refused to recognize this group as a separate unit. In supporting the board's action, the court noted that it was "clear [that] the Board wanted to deal with just one bargaining unit" and that if each of the groups covered under the contract "were allowed to carve out its own bargaining unit, the extended negotiation would work an undue hardship on the Board in carrying out its necessary public purpose."[10]

The absence of criteria to govern unit determinations generally brought about a proliferation of units since public employers and state legislatures gave little consideration to this issue. For example, in New York City more than 380 separate units were established—some containing as few as two employees. Similar patterns were found under Executive Order 10988, in Wisconsin, Massachusetts and Oregon.

Among the factors most frequently mentioned in determining bargaining units are: (1) clear and identifiable community of interest among employees; (2) establishment of units which will promote effective collective bargaining; and (3) establishment of units in light of the operational efficiency of the agency or agencies involved. In addition to these general considerations, numerous states have now imposed explicit criteria to deal with the problem of fragmented bargaining units.

When dealing with state employees, legislatures have been even more explicit in terms of unit determinations. The Pennsylvania act requires the board to consider "that when the Commonwealth is the employer, it will be bargaining on a statewide basis unless issues involve work conditions peculiar to a given governmental locale."[11] The Illinois Executive Order covering state employees requires the office of collective bargaining to "promote the interest of the State in bargaining on a statewide basis by considering statewide units presumptively appropriate."[12] Similarly, the Minnesota act draws a distinction between municipal employees and state employees by requiring the director of mediation services to "define appropriate units of state employees as all the employees under the same appointing authority except where professional, geographical or other considerations affecting employment relations clearly require appropriate units of some other composition."[13]

The trend toward statewide units is not uniform. Several states have found separate units appropriate in cases involving educational institutions. For example, in *Ft. Hays Kansas State College*, the Kansas Public Employee Relations Board stated that it "would allow public employees at each unit of higher education to organize an individual institutional unit."[14] In discussing the rational of its decision the board noted:

> Each institution, we feel, is a separate distinct operating entity with a complex relationship already existing between the public employees and the administration therein. The principles of efficient administration will be maintained inasmuch as the evidence before this board indicates that most problems concerning conditions of employment with university employees have been handled on a local basis; i.e., between the local university administration and the employee. . . . Some previous history of employee organization, specifically KU Medical Center, was noted but not considered as having great weight. However, geographical location posed a possible serious problem, especially when considered with the concept of the separate identity of each institution as mentioned above. The difficulties of employees organizing over a great distance (i.e., the distance between Wichita and Fort Hays) when considered in light of

the fact that each institution has operated as a separate identity made the unit determinations on an individual basis seem most logical. The board did not view the problems of overfragmentation and splintering of a work force as automatically requiring a statewide unit in every case, but that each case must be reviewed on its own merit, thus our decision of the individual institutional units.[15]

The above approach can be contrasted with the approach taken in New York and New Jersey. The New York board held that a university-wide faculty bargaining unit was appropriate since "the concomitant differences among the campuses do not establish such conflicts of interest between their respective professions as to warrant geographic fragmentation."[16] A similar result was reached by the New Jersey commission when it reversed its earlier determination that separate units were appropriate.[17]

Recently the director of public employment practices and representation of the New York Public Employment Relations Board was faced with a decertification petition on behalf of nonacademic professionals who were in a statewide unit combined with academic professionals.[18] The nonacademic professionals sought separate representation and a reversal of the board's earlier decision including academic and nonacademic professionals in a statewide unit. The director of public employment practices and representation held that there was no evidence to justify fragmenting the existing bargaining unit and found that the history of collective bargaining which existed after the establishment of the initial unit demonstrated that nonacademic professionals "did enjoy effective and meaningful negotiations on salaries as well as other matters."[19]

Even where a single campus is held to constitute an appropriate unit, questions arise with respect to the composition of that unit. In 1972 the Pennsylvania Public Employee Relations Board held that the faculty members in the university's law, dental and medical schools should be excluded from an overall unit and directed an election in the law school unit.[20] The Michigan Employment Relations Commission, however, rejected the establishment of separate units within a given institution and rejected the establishment of a separate medical school unit on the grounds that "it would unduly fragmentize a *teaching faculty unit* if individual schools or colleges are permitted to have separate representation."[21]

It is evident from the decisions rendered by state public employee relations boards that the trend is toward large units, particularly when dealing with state employees. It is obvious that the early problems faced in New York and Wisconsin have greatly influenced subsequent action with respect to unit determinations. The trend toward large units does not preclude the establishment of separate institutional units as evidenced by the Minnesota and Kansas decisions affecting state colleges and universities.

The trend toward large units is also evident from the National Labor Relations Board decisions concerning university employees. For example, at New York University in 1973 the board noted that while librarians were distinguished from faculty members with respect to tenure requirements, retirement age and lack of proportional representation on the university senate, they should be included in a university-wide unit with faculty members.[22] While in several cases the board has rejected units composed solely of library personnel, it did find a separate unit appropriate at Claremont University in 1972.[23]

In contrasting some of the rights granted employees under the National Labor Relations Act and the rights of public sector employees, we can first look at the whole concept of collective bargaining. In the private sector, a fundamental premise of national labor relations policy is the concept of free collective bargaining. Collective bargaining has long been viewed as a process by which parties settle disputes without the intervention of a third party. The strike or threat of a strike plays a fundamental role in the private sector since it is the threat of something worse which is viewed as a means to secure agreement between an employer and a union. Thus, federal courts have prohibited state interference with the collective bargaining process.

In the public sector the concept of free collective bargaining has really never surfaced since, with rare exception, public employees are denied the right to strike. Impasse resolution devices in the public sector are viewed as the means to bringing about the settlement of a dispute between two unyielding parties.

The reasons given for denying public employees the right to strike are varied. According to some, the acceptance of the right of public employees to strike would take away the authority of public officials to administer government for people. President Roosevelt had occasion to observe that "a strike of public employees manifests nothing less than an intent on their part to obstruct the operations of government until their demands are satisfied."[24] The Taylor Committee in New York stated that the right to strike in the public sector is not compatible with orderly functioning of a democratic form of representative government.

The future, in my opinion, will bring about a re-evaluation of the traditional notion that all public employees should be barred from striking. It is obvious that certain governmental services are essential and must be provided. This does not mean, however, that free collective bargaining with the concomitant presence of economic force cannot exist in certain areas. Indeed, one should consider whether the public is paying a higher cost by denying all public employees the right to strike and substituting for that right impasse resolution devices which might reflect higher settlements than would have been achieved had the test been one of economic warfare rather than third-party decision-making.

Moreover, declaring public employee strikes illegal has not meant the end of strikes. States which have enacted punitive antistrike legislation have often had to forego enforcement of the law since the penalties were too extreme. This was particularly true in New York under the Condon-Wadlin Act.

The failure to enforce stringent laws regarding public employee strikes is further evidence of the deep political involvement in public sector collective bargaining. A governor or mayor is both an employer and politician. These roles are not consistent since a chief executive's actions as an employer carry political overtones. Thus, in New York it was shown that the Condon-Wadlin Act was not enforced in cases where the striking union was politically strong.[25]

In considering whether public employees should be granted the right to strike, one should also focus on the question of what issues are appropriate for strike action. There has been little consideration of this question since most states prohibit public employee strikes and even in the states providing a limited right to strike no distinction is made over the issues on which strike action can be taken.

An example of this problem is a decision of an agency to go from a program of providing institutional care to the utilization of private facilities. Some of the groups affected by such a decision are the employees at the state institution, the patients being treated, the municipality where the institution is located and special interest groups involved in the health care field. While a union representing the employees should be able to bargain with the public employer over the impact of such a decision, one can persuasively argue that decisions such as this should not be subjects over which unions can strike.

To remove an issue which might affect a broad range of social and community interests from the arena of economic warfare is not to say that public employees and their bargaining representatives should not have input with respect to that issue. Bargaining and political pressure, a tool used by public employee unions and other interest groups, offer ways in which the public employee can participate in the decision-making process.

Another troublesome issue in the public sector concerns union security agreements. As an exclusive representative, a union must represent, without discrimination, all employees in the unit regardless of union affiliation. In the private sector union security agreements are legal, except in states where right-to-work laws are in effect. Section 7 of the NLRA grants employees the right to organize and bargain collectively and the right to refrain from such activities "except to the extent that such right may be affected by an agreement requiring membership in a labor organization as a condition of employment as authorized in Section 8(a)(3)."[26]

In *NLRB* v. *General Motors*, the Supreme Court discussed the differences between an agency shop and a union shop in the following terms: "Under the second proviso to §8(a)(3), the burdens of membership upon which employment may be conditioned are expressly limited to the payment of initiation fees and monthly dues. It is permissible to condition employment upon membership, but membership insofar as it has significance to employment rights, may in turn be conditioned only on payment of fees and dues. 'Membership' as a condition of employment is whittled down to its financial core."[27] Thus, the distinction between union shop and agency shop is the choice of membership. Under an agency shop the employee is given the "option of membership" while under a union shop, that option is removed. Recently the NLRB held that the term "membership" in Section 8(a)(3) means "a financial obligation limited to payment of fees and dues."[28]

The primary challenge to negotiating agency shop or union shop clauses in the public sector centered around the provisions in various state laws giving employees the right to refrain from union activity. In the private sector, this question has arisen within the context of right-to-work laws.

In 1963 the Florida Supreme Court held that a clause requiring the payment of service fees as a condition of employment was violative of the right-to-work section of the Florida Constitution.[29] The court based its decision on the fact that an individual's "right to work" without regard to union membership was "abridged" when the individual was required to pay a fee to continue working.

A contrary view of a right-to-work provision is found in *Meade Electric Co. v. Hagberg*. There, the court held that the Indiana right-to-work law did not bar negotiation of agency shop since the statute "merely prohibits agreements and conduct which conditions employment on membership in a labor organization."[30] Membership, however, under the NLRB's rationale is the payment of fees and dues. Thus, one should question the rationale employed by the court in *Hagberg*.

Various decisions have been rendered in the public sector concerning the legality of agency shop clauses. In *New Jersey Turnpike Employees, Local 194 v. New Jersey Turnpike Authority*, a New Jersey court was faced with the task of determining whether such a clause was permissible in light of the following statutory provision: "Public employees shall have, and shall be protected in the exercise of, the right to freely and without fear of penalty or reprisal, to form, join and assist any employee organization or to refrain from such activity."[31]

In interpreting the above language, the court held that the execution of an agency shop agreement violated an employee's right to refrain from assisting an employee organization. Relying on the right of employees to refrain from "assisting" an employee organization, the court concluded that the enforcement of an agency shop clause would have the effect of "inducing, if not compelling, union membership, participation, and assistance on the part of non-member employees."[32]

Similarly, in *Monroe-Woodbury Teachers Assn.* the New York Public Employment Relations Board (PERB) held that an agency shop clause was illegal. In reaching its decision the New York board relied on several factors. First, it found that an "agency shop ... is inconsistent with the statutory grant of right that employees may refrain from 'participating in' an employee organization."[33] In addition, the Public Employment Relations Board found that the negotiation of an agency shop clause was in conflict with the New York Teachers Tenure Act and the New York dues deduction law.

On appeal the PERB's holding was affirmed. The Appellate Division of the New York Supreme Court found that to require the payment of dues "would be in violation of the law as constituting, at the very least, participation in an employee organization."[34] The court also held that the negotiation of an agency shop was inconsistent with the provisions of the New York Public Employee Relations Act, which makes it unlawful to "discriminate against any employee for the purpose of encouraging or discouraging membership in, or participation in the activities of any employee organization."[35]

In Illinois, the Attorney General has issued a recent opinion which has held that employees of a county highway department cannot be required to join a union should the county board recognize and bargain with the union as the exclusive representative of the highway department employees. In addition, the Attorney General held that union dues can be deducted only if the employee requests to have this done. In light of these opinions and the current state law, the union security issue in Illinois can only be resolved through legislative action.

Some of the issues present in both the public and private sector with respect to the unionization of librarians concern the status of librarians as professional employees and their role as supervisors. The National Labor Relations Board has considered librarians to be professionals and have therefore included them in units with other faculty members. The board has also rejected the argument that the supervision of nonprofessional personnel by librarians automatically makes them supervisors so as to deny them bargaining rights. The board considers the amount of time that librarians spend supervising and the group which is supervised.

In discussing the legal environment, it is important to point out that various changes are currently being proposed which would affect library personnel. Several bills are now pending in Congress to either extend NLRA coverage to public employees or to create a national public employee relations act. The wisdom of having federal legislation cover public employees is in doubt since there are great differences among states which must be considered in drafting and enacting any public employee relations bill. It seems better to deal with this issue on a state rather than a federal level, even though it might be necessary to set some minimum federal standards which states are required to meet.

Until there is legislation in states like Illinois, the great majority of library personnel have to depend on judge-made law which is an inadequate means to solve the major problems posed in this area. In the absence of a statutory framework, courts are ill equipped to deal with the myriad of issues raised in this area.

The current labor relations scene in Illinois represents a patchwork of thoughts and ideas, most of which are confusing and not very meaningful. Other than Executive Order 6, which Illinois Governor Daniel Walker issued in September 1973, there is no framework to guide labor relations for public employees in that state.

The legal environment surrounding the unionization of library personnel illustrates the difference between the public and private sectors. While librarians in the private sector can negotiate virtually all matters, their public sector counterparts are generally not given such a generous menu to negotiate. While librarians in the private sector can strike, their public sector counterparts are generally denied recourse to this tool of economic warfare. But while librarians in the private sector must rely on the economic force they can generate to bring about a settlement, their public sector counterparts can often rely on impasse resolution devices to solve differences.

To this already confusing environment we add the fact that the rights of librarians in the public sector may often vary from employer to employer. The situation will not become any clearer until legislation is passed which establishes a basic framework to protect employers, employees and the public.

REFERENCES

1. Kaplan, H. Eliot, et al. "Report of the Committee on Labor Relations of Governmental Employees." In *Section of Labor Relations Law. American Bar Association. 1955 Proceedings.* Chicago, American Bar Center, 1956, p. 90.

2. *Railway Mail Association* v. *Corsi*, 326 U.S. 88, 95, 65 S. Ct. 1483, 1488, 89 L. Ed. 2d 2072 (1945).

3. Florida Attorney General's opinion, March 21, 1944, reprinted *in* Rhyne, Charles S. *Labor Unions and Municipal Employe Law* (National Institute of Municipal Law Officers, Report No. 116). Washington, D.C. National Institute of Municipal Law Officers, 1946, pp. 252-54.

5. *Anderson Federation of Teachers* v. *School City of Anderson*, 252 Ind. 558, 251 N.E. 2d 15, 37 A.L.R. 2d 1131, cert. denied, 399 U.S. 928 (1969).

6. *City of Pana* v. *Crowe*, 57 Ill. 2d 547, 316 N.E. 2d 513 (1974).
7. See, for example, *McLaughlin* v. *Tilendis*, 398 F. 2d 287 (C.A. 7th cir., 1968); *American Federation of State, County and Municipal Employees* v. *Woodward*, 406 F. 2d (C.A. 8th Cir., 1969); *Atkins* v. *City of Charlotte*, 296 F. Supp. 1068 (W.O.N.C., 1969).
8. Wellington, Harry, and Winter, Ralph. *The Unions and the Cities.* Washington, D.C., Brookings Institution, 1971, p. 30.
9. See, for example, *Civil Service Commission* v. *Wayne County Board of Supervisors*, 384 Mich. 363 (1971); and *Laborer's International Union, Local 1029* v. *Delaware*, 72 L.C. 53, 238 Del. (1974).
10. *Chicago High School Assistant Principals Association* v. *Board of Education of the City of Chicago*, 5 Ill. App. 3d 672, 675, 284 N.E. 2d 19 (1972).
11. Pennsylvania Public Employee Relations Act, Ch. 19 §604(4).
12. Government Employee Relations Report (GERR) Ref. File, 51:2211, 1975.
13. Minnesota Stat. Anno. Supp., Ch. 179 §197.74(4).
14. In *Ft. Hays Kansas State College*, GERR No. 487, B-3 (1973).
15. *Ibid.*, No. 487, B-4.
16. In *State of New York (State University of New York)* 2 PERB 3492 (1969); aff'd. sub. nom., *Wakshull* v. *Helsby*, 35 A.D. 2d 183, 315 N.Y.S. 2d 371 (1970).
17. In *State of New Jersey*, GERR No. 484, B-6, F-1 (1973).
18. *State of New York (State University of New York)*, 7 PERB 4007, par. 7-4010 (1974).
19. *Ibid.*, 7 PERB 4007.
20. In *Temple University*, GERR No. 472, B-1 (1972).
21. *Michigan State University*, Michigan Employment Relations Commission (MERC) Lab. Op. No. 82 (1971); and *Wayne State University*, MERC Lab. Op. No. 140 (1972).
22. *New York University and New York University Chapter, American Association of University Professors, et al.*, 205 NLRB 16, 1973 CCH, NLRB par. 25, 587 (1973).
23. *Claremont University Center et al., and Office and Professional Employees International Union, Local No. 30, AFL-CIO*, 198 NLRB 121, 1972 CCH NLRB par. 24, 508 (1972).
24. Quoted *in* Rhyne, *op.cit.*, p. 437.
25. Hildebrand, Geroge H. "The Public Sector." *In* John T. Dunlop and Neil W. Chamberlain, eds. *Frontiers of Collective Bargaining.* New York, Harper & Row, 1967, p. 38.
26. *NLRA*, 29 U.S.C.A. § 157.
27. *NLRB* v. *General Motors*, 373 U.S. 734, 742, 83 S. Ct. 1453, 1459, 10 L. Ed. 2d 670 (1963).
28. *Hershey Foods Corporation et al., and Lloyd Brewer*, 207 NLRB 141, 1974 CCH NLRB, par. 26, 506 (1973).
29. *Retail Clerks Local 1625* v. *Schermerhorn*, 141 So. 2d 269 (1962), aff'd. 375 U.S. 96, 84 S. Ct. 219, 11 L. Ed. 2d 179 (1963).
30. *Meade Electric Co.* v. *Hagberg*, 129 Ind. App. 631, 159 N.E. 2d 408, 413 (1959).
31. *New Jersey Turnpike Employees Local 194* v. *New Jersey Turnpike Authority*, 123 N.J. Super 461, 467, 303 A. 2d 557 (1973).

32. *Ibid.*, 470.
33. In *Monroe-Woodbury Teachers Association* v. *Monroe-Woodbury Board of Education*, 3 PERB 4545, par. 3-3104, 3-4510 (1970), aff'd. 4 PERB 7097, par. 4-7014 (1971).
34. *Farrigan* v. *Helsby*, 68 Misc. 2d 952 (1971), aff'd. 346 N.Y.S. 2d 39, 41 (1973).
35. *McKinney's Consol. L. of New York, Anno., Civil Service Law*, Ch. 392, Art. 14 (1967). *See also Ritto* v. *Fink*, 58 Misc. 2d 1032 (City Ct. of Rochester, 1968); and *Foltz* v. *Dayton*, 27 Ohio App. 35, 272 N.E. 2d 169, 56 Ohio Op. 2d 213 (1970).

MARTIN H. SCHNEID
Assistant to the Regional Director
National Labor Relations Board
Chicago, Illinois

Recognition and Bargaining Units

Any meaningful discussion of recognition and bargaining units must include general aspects of the National Labor Relations Act (NLRA) and reference to specific provisions, policies and procedures which have a significant, if indirect, impact on the subject.

The first consideration is: When does the act apply? The phrase "assert jurisdiction" is of primary importance here. The statute itself, in its definitions, excludes as employers the United States or any wholly-owned government corporaton, or any Federal Reserve Bank, or any state or political subdivision thereof, or persons subject to the Railway Labor Act. By decision of the National Labor Relations Board, with court approval, jurisdiction was at one time not asserted over certain industries or enterprises such as hotels, noncharitable hospitals, nonstate-owned educational institutions or professional sport organizations, although the statute did not exclude them. But in time, again under court approval, the board extended its jurisdiction over these enterprises, among others. By amendment of the statute, the board was given jurisdiction over the U.S. Postal Service and over charitable, nonstate hospitals. The board, however, still does not assert jurisdiction over race tracks, sheltered workshops, and some other enterprises.

In addition, and probably more relative to libraries, on September 23, 1974, the board announced that it was considering declining jurisdiction over private secondary and elementary schools and preschools. Interested parties were invited to submit comments, views or arguments within thirty days.

Before jurisdiction is asserted, after having been extended to a class of enterprises by statute or discretion, it must appear that the particular employer unit involved (and this may entail a number of employers banded together in an acknowledged bargaining unit), meets stated annual dollar standards. These standards may be either gross, as in the case of retail operations, or in terms of interstate inflow or outflow, in the case of various nonretail operations.

The work of the board lies primarily in two areas: (1) handling charges of unfair labor practices against employers or unions, or both, and (2) handling representation or bargaining agent election cases. In any type of case, before the board may act, it must appear that the employer involved is subject to the jurisdiction of the board. This is true if the charge is against a union or an employer, or in a representation case.

If these qualifications are not met, regardless of the other elements of the case, no action will be taken on the charge or petition. Thus, the phrase "assert jurisdiction" truly applies to the situations at hand. Employees working for noncovered employers, e.g., a state university, do not have the rights set out in Section 7 of the act, nor can the board processes protect them. The board cannot conduct representation elections if the employer is one over whom jurisdiction is not asserted, nor can it act against a labor organization, if the employer, being only indirectly involved, is likewise one over whom jurisdiction is not asserted.

However, knowledge of the NLRA, its procedures, and its policies can be of significant value to employers, trade union officials and employees, whether or not the enterprise involved is one over which jurisdiction would be asserted. If a covered employer is involved, such knowledge will point to the legal limitations, rights and available avenues of procedure. If the enterprise is not subject to the act, following the policies enunciated under the act can lead to better employer-employee relationships. If a union is a bargaining agent, it can lead to more productive, meaningful handling of industrial relations problems. Further, many states have, or may soon have, labor relations laws or executive orders which would apply to noncovered employers, and these are generally modeled after the NLRA.

Assuming that the employer is covered under the act, how are librarians affected? First, not all librarians are employees. Section 2(3) of the act, in defining *employee* excludes supervisors. Section 2(11) defines *supervisor*, and if an individual falls within that definition, he does not enjoy the rights guaranteed in Section 7, nor, except in rare cases, can a remedy be afforded him for discrimination by an employer or restraint or coercion by a union. Further, on April 23, 1974, the Supreme Court, in *NLRB* v. *Textron Inc.*, found that employees properly classified as managerial are excluded from protection of the act. While the court did not define managerial, it cited with approval the board's definition which recognized as managerial executives who formulate and effectuate management policies by expressing and making the operative decisions of their employers. Further, the board has deemed to be managerial buyers those who regularly and to a substantial degree make substantial purchases for the employer.

Relevant to the supervisory status of professionals is the problem of whom they supervise. In the *University of Chicago* case (205 NLRB 220), decided on August 3, 1973 (and, by chance, concerning librarians), the board decided that professional librarians who supervise other professional librarians are supervisors within the meaning of the act, but that professional librarians who supervise only clerical (nonprofessional) employees are not supervisors within the act's meaning. This decision was affirmed on October 22, 1974, by the U.S. Court of Appeals for the Seventh Circuit.

The third, and perhaps most cogent, consideration is whether librarians are professional within the meaning of Section 2(12) of the act. If they are professional (and not supervisory or managerial), they possess all the rights of nonprofessional employees. They are, however, accorded special treatment in representation cases to the following extent: under Section 9(b) it is provided that the board shall not decide that any unit is appropriate for the purposes of collective bargaining if such unit includes both professional employees and employees who are not professional employees unless a majority of such professional employees vote for inclusion in the unit.

The National Labor Relations Act includes the following definition of "professional employee":

(a) any employee engaged in work (i) predominately intellectual, varied in character as opposed to routine mental, manual, mechanical, or physical work; (ii) involving the consistent exercise of discretion and judgment in its performance; (iii) of such a character that the output produced or the result accomplished cannot be standardized in relation to a given period of time; (iv) requiring knowledge of an advanced type in a field of science or learning customarily acquired by a prolonged course of specialized intellectual instruction and study in an institution of higher learning or a hospital, as distinguished from a general academic education or from an apprenticeship or from training in the performance of routine mental, manual, or physical processes; or
(b) any employee, who (i) has completed the courses of specialized intellectual instruction and study described in clause (iv) of paragraph (a), and (ii) is performing related work under the supervision of a professional person to qualify himself to become a professional employee as defined in paragraph (a).[1]

The board has had many occasions to apply the definition to a particular case. Recognizing that the definition speaks in terms of the work performed, the board did not pass on the individual qualifications of each employee involved, but rather upon the character of the work required of them as a group.[2] But the background is examined to decide whether the work of the group satisfies the "knowledge of an advanced type" requirement of the statute.[3] The requirement that professionals possess "knowledge of an advanced type," does not mean that such knowledge must be acquired through academic training alone; it is the character of the work required that determines professional status.[4]

The board makes its findings independent of other governmental decisions. For example, a Wage and Hour Act finding that employees are nonprofessional does not affect a board finding of professional status,[5] nor does the fact that the persons acting need not be licensed to practice their profession in the state.[6]

With the foregoing distinctions noted, the act applies equally to librarians as to other employees. Section 7 of the act provides: "employees shall have the right to self-organization, to form, join, or assist labor organizations, to bargain collectively through representatives of their own choosing, and to engage in other concerted activities for the purpose of collective bargaining or other mutual aid or protection, and shall also have the right to refrain from any or all of such activities."[7]

To protect these rights, Congress declared certain activities by employers and by unions to be unfair labor practices. Free speech without threat of reprisal or force is not a violation of the act: "the expressing of views, arguments or opinion, or the dissemination thereof ... shall not constitute or be evidence of an unfair labor practice ... if such expression contains no threat of reprisal or force or promise of benefit."[8] When speech contains a threat of reprisal, force, or promise of benefit, dependent upon the employees' union sympathy or concerted protected activity, it becomes violative of Section 8(a)(1), by an employer, or 8(b)(1)(A), by a labor organization. Employers may not question employees about their union activities or membership in such circumstances as will tend to restrain or coerce them, may not spy on union gatherings, may not grant or withhold wage increases deliberately timed to defeat self-organization among employees, and may not make or promulgate rules restricting employees in solicitation for or against unions on nonworking time or distribution of union or anti-union literature in nonworking areas on nonworking time.

Under Section 8(a)(2), an employer violates the law if he dominates or interferes with the formation or administration of any labor organization, or contributes financial or other support to it, such as taking an active part in organizing a labor organization or a committee to represent employees, bringing pressure upon employees to join a union, or showing favoritism to one of two or more unions which are competing to represent employees.

Section 8(a)(3) forbids an employer to discriminate against an employee "in regard to hire or tenure of employment ... [or] *to encourage or discourage membership in any labor organization"*[9] (emphasis added). Under this section, preferential or closed shops are prohibited, while union shops are permissible but not mandatory.

Section 8(a)(5) and Section (d) bar an employer from refusing to bargain in good faith concerning wages, hours and other conditions of employment with the representative chosen by a majority of employees in a group appropriate for collective bargaining.

How does the duty to bargin arise? An employer, faced by a demand for recognition as bargaining agent by a labor organization which he has in no way assisted, and in the absence of any evinced interest in such representation by another labor organization, may accord such recognition if the claiming labor organization represents an uncoerced majority of the employees in the proposed bargaining unit. This voluntary recognition is permissible, but not mandatory. Or, the employer must recognize a union if it obtains a majority in an election conducted by the board, a state agency or a neutral third party, with substantial adherence to the board's election procedure. Finally, if a union, in the absence of any other union claiming to represent any of the employees involved, makes a claim to represent the employees, and the employer refuses to recognize that union, he may be ordered to bargain with that union, without an election, or in the face of a lost election which has been set aside upon objections properly filed, provided that (1) the union in fact represents an uncoerced majority of the employees, and (2) the employer has committed such unfair labor practices as to make the holding of a fair election impossible.

However the duty to bargain arises, it entails various obligations upon the employer and the union. The employer (and the bargaining agent union) must (1) be willing to meet at reasonable times and places; (2) have present a representative with sufficient authority to engage in bargaining; (3) not refuse to meet because of whom the other party has designated as its bargaining representative; (4) upon request, bargain about (but not necessarily agree upon) subjects within the scope of wages, hours and conditions of employment; and (5) upon request, furnish information reasonably necessary to the bargaining process.

Unions, in addition to what has gone before, are also subject to limitations. Section 8(b)(2) prohibits a union from causing, or attempting to cause, an employer to discriminate against an employee in violation of Section 8(a)(3). For example, a union may not ask the employer to discharge an employee because he is running for union office or has failed to pay a fine or assessment, nor may it ask that he make a contract which provides that seniority (or other benefits) shall be dependent on union membership.

Under Section 8(b)(3), in addition to the obligations of the employer under 8(a)(5), the union does not fulfill its obligation to bargain if, for instance, it insists upon the inclusion of an illegal provision, such as a closed shop, or strikes to compel changes in an existing contract either without giving proper notice or during the term of such contract. Under Section 8(b)(4), unions may not engage in secondary boycotts or jurisdictional strikes, or other prohibited strikes.

One other aspect of the proscriptions against strikes deserves note—the ban on strikes for recognition under certain conditions, e.g., when another union has been lawfully recognized, when the employees have voted (and rejected a union) within the preceding twelve months, or where the union pickets for recognition for more than thirty days without a formal petition being filed for an employee representation election. By statute, there are variations on some of the foregoing for health care facilities.

The National Labor Relations Board cannot act upon its own motion. Only when a charge of unfair labor practices is filed may investigation be made. If no merit is found, the case is dismissed, absent withdrawal. Appeal from a regional dismissal may be taken to the General Counsel, who has final authority in denying the appeal or reversing the regional dismissal. If the case has merit, either upon original investigation or upon General Counsel's reversal of a regional dismissal, settlement is sought. If no settlement is effected, a complaint issues and a public hearing is held before an administrative law judge. When he issues his decision, the board may review the case and issue a decision and order. The board's decision is subject to review or enforcement by the U.S. Court of Appeals, and by the Supreme Court. In meritorious cases, injunctive relief may be sought.

The other major aspect of the board's work is in the determination of collective bargaining representatives. This arises only when a petition has been filed by a union seeking certification as bargaining agent, by an employer upon whom a union has made a claim to represent (or continue to represent) his employees, or by employees seeking to decertify an incumbent union bargaining agent.

When such petition is filed, investigation is made of the following questions: Is the employer subject to the NLRA? Is the union named a labor organization within the meaning of the NLRA? Is the petition properly supported? (In the case of a union or employee petition, 30 percent of the employees must support the petition; in the case of an employer petition without an incumbent union, proof of claim made by the union is required; and in the case of an employer petition with an incumbent union, the employer must show he has objective reasons to believe that the union no longer represents a majority of the employees involved.) Is the unit involved appropriate for collective bargaining? (In employee petitions the unit must be coextensive with the unit represented.) Is the petition timely? (Petitions may not be filed during the year following certification of a union as bargaining agent, during ten months after an election in which no bargaining agent was selected, or in the face of a valid collective bargaining agreement except during the period sixty to ninety days prior to the expiration of such contract—not to exceed three years in length.) The remaining issue is that of majority, which, in a representation case, can only be determined by an election.

In 80 percent of the cases, the parties agree to the election. If the questions are all answered in the affirmative, but parties who are entitled to do so refuse to consent to the election, a public hearing is held, and the regional director either directs an election, dismisses the petition, remands the case for further hearing, or refers it to the board in Washington for decision. Any party dissatisfied with the regional director's decision may request the board to review it, and the board's decision is final.

Once the election is held, if the number of challenged votes cannot affect the results, and if the parties file no objections within five working days, a certification of representative or a certification of results will issue. However, if the number of challenges could determine the results, or if timely objections are properly filed and served, an investigation will be made of the eligibility status of the challenged voters, the facts surrounding the alleged objectionable conduct, or, in some cases, both.

If there are no objections, the challenges will be disposed of. If the election is so close that the challenged votes could affect its outcome, a sufficient number of these are ruled on to render the results definitive. If merit is found to the objections, the election will be set aside and a new election directed. If the objections are found to have no merit, the results of the election will be certified.

Under Section 9(b) of the act, the board is empowered to: "decide in each case whether, in order to assure the employees the fullest freedom in exercising the rights guaranteed by this subchapter, the unit appropriate for the purposes of collective bargaining shall be the employer unit, craft unit, plant unit, or subdivision thereof."[10] When the parties agree to the unit, provided the unit *could* be appropriate, although it is not the only, ultimate, or most appropriate unit, the board will accept such agreement.[11] However, where there is disagreement as to the unit, the board must resolve the differences, which can be of various kinds.

As to the width of the unit, presumably the plant unit is appropriate, but a narrower unit, e.g., a craft unit, or a wider unit, e.g., two or more plants of the same employer, or in some cases, several employers, may be appropriate. Of prime consideration is the community of interest[12] and duties of the employees involved. Functional integration, common supervision, various employee skills, interchangeability and contact among employees, the work situs, general working conditions and fringe benefits are determinative of the community of interest.[13] In other words, one might ask: Does the proposed unit include all employees sharing this community of interest and does it exclude those employees who do not share such community of interest?

When there is a disagreement as to the unit, the board will give weight to a successful valid history of bargaining, but will not consider establishing a contested unit solely on the basis of extent of organization of the union involved.

Once the width of the unit has been decided, so long as more than one employee is in that unit, the number of employees is not a factor,[14] nor are such items as the mode of payment,[15] age,[16] sex,[17] race,[18] union membership,[19] or the union's territorial or work jurisdiction.[20] The desires of the employees, while not controlling,[21] may be a factor in craft severance cases, and certainly are in the case of professional employees.

In all cases, the board must observe the statutory exclusions. The act does not apply to agricultural laborers or individuals employed by their parent or spouse, nor to independent contractors. Briefly, when faced with a contention that certain individuals are independent contractors and therefore not employees, the board applies a "right-of-control" test. If the employer retains the right to control the manner and means by which the result is to be accomplished, the relationship is one of employment, but if the right of control is only as to the result sought, the relationship is that of independent contractor.[22]

Disagreements tend to occur most frequently in the designation of supervisors. Guided by the language in Section 2(11) of the act, the board considers these criteria: "the term 'supervisor' means any individual having authority, in the interest of the employer, to hire, transfer, suspend, lay off, recall, promote, discharge, assign, reward, or discipline other employees, or responsibly to direct them or to adjust their grievances, or effectively to recommend such action, if in connection with the foregoing the exercise of such authority is not of a merely routine or clerical nature, but requires the use of independent judgment."[23] The board, however, also takes into account such factors as substitution for supervisors,[24] training for supervisory positions,[25] ratio of supervisors to supervised employees,[26] varying terms and conditions of employment,[27] and ostensible authority.[28]

As to professional employees and their supervisory status, I have alluded to the pending *University of Chicago* case, concerning professionals as supervisors, and have discussed the board's approach to professionals in general. As to specific cases concerning librarians or libraries, in the recent case of *Queens Borough Public Library* the board, reviewing the history of the establishment and the statutory authority under which it operated, decided that because "the nexus between the library and city of New York, is such that without city support, the library would cease to exist," it would not effectuate the policies of the act to assert jurisdiction over the library.[29]

Some of the later cases concerning librarians deserve mention. In *CW Postcenter, L.I.U.* (189 NLRB 904) the petitioning union sought a unit of all professionals, including librarians. The employer would exclude the librarians, among others, but the board, finding that the twenty-seven librarians who served all the libraries (except that of the graduate center) were professionals and had sufficient community of interest with the other professionals, included them.

The board excluded the library director, who hired and supervised all nonprofessional employees for the libraries. The decision is silent on whether he supervised professional librarians, a question which has thus far been answered by the board in the *University of Chicago* case and the *Catholic University* case to which I will refer later.

In *Fordham University* (193 NLRB 134) one union sought an overall professional unit including professional librarians but excluding the law school faculty. Another union sought a unit of the law school faculty. The employer contended that all faculty members were supervisors, a contention the board denied, and found two separate units, as requested. Finding some librarians not to be professional, the board excluded them. As to the professional librarians, the board noted that the record was insufficient to decide their supervisory status and permitted them to vote under challenge.

Tuscolum College (199 NLRB 28) involved a disagreement as to the unit placement of, among others, the library staff, consisting of a librarian, an assistant librarian, and an assistant to the librarian. The board, citing the Fordham case, found the librarian and the assistant librarian to be professionals and included them with other professionals,[30] but excluded the assistant to the librarian as being a clerical employee.

Catholic University (201 NLRB 929) concerned itself with a law school faculty unit. Disagreement arose as to the status of the head librarian, whom the board found to be a professional. As to his supervisory status, since his duties in this regard were minor supervision over one full-time assistant librarian and four part-time student assistants, the board found him not to be a supervisor, and included him in the unit.

What has been set out thus far is, at best, a fundamental framework on which 214 volumes of board decisions and 18 volumes of court decisions must be consulted to elaborate and explicate the nuances and variations of such basic principles.

I would propound a caveat: When one has occasion to consider a board case, he should not rely upon the august pronouncements of self-styled oracles who rarely are properly informed, more infrequently objective, and even less frequently direct their comments at the proper target. If one who is in the daily arena of industrial or labor relations reads the law and the actual board decision, is aware of whether the law as Congress passed it or the board's interpretation is at issue, and regards the decision as to its effect on the total industrial community, he can provide a meaningful evaluation of the decision. The board, as shown in the proposed rule change regarding jurisdiction over private secondary and primary schools, welcomes and is guided by such significant viewpoints.

Finally, the board's regional offices and Washington offices are available for general or specific inquiries. While no official or interlocutory judgment can be made in the absence of a pending case, board personnel can acquaint people with board policies or status of cases. They will not, of course, suggest what course to follow. They also may, under appropriate circumstances, refer people to other agencies. The board also has various informational pamphlets which could be of help, and hopes that people feel free to use these services.

REFERENCES

1. *National Labor Relations Act*, 29 USCA152 (12).
2. *Northwestern Bell Telephone Co.*, 79 NLRB 549 (1948).
3. *Western Electric Co.*, 126 NLRB 1346 (1960).
4. *Ryan Aeronautical Co.*, 132 NLRB 1160 (1961); *Chrysler Corporation Space Division*, 154 NLRB 352 (1965); and *Robbins and Myers*, 144 NLRB 295 (1963).
5. *Standard Oil Co.*, 107 NLRB 1524 (1954).
6. *Westinghouse Electric Corporation*, 89 NLRB 8 (1950); and *C.T.L. Testing Laboratories, Inc.*, 150 NLRB 982 (1965).
7. *National Labor Relations Act*, 29 USCA 157(64).
8. *Ibid.*, 158(c)
9. *Ibid.*, 158(a)(3).
10. *Ibid.*, 159(b).
11. Donald H. Parsons and James C. Homes, d/b/a the *Parsons Investment Co.*, 152 NLRB 192 (1965).
12. *Berea Publishing Co.*, 140 NLRB 516 (1963).
13. *Sylvania Electric Products, Inc.*, 135 NLRB 768 (1962); and *Curcie Brothers, Inc.*, 146 NLRB 380 (1964).
14. *Koppers Company, Inc.*, 117 NLRB 422 (1957).
15. *Palmer Manufacturing Co.*, 105 NLRB 812 (1953).
16. *Metal Textile Corporation*, 88 NLRB 1326 (1950).
17. *Cuneo Eastern Press, Inc. of Pennsylvania*, 106 NLRB 343 (1953).
18. *New Deal Cab Co., Inc.*, 159 NLRB 1838 (1966).
19. *Delta Manufacturing Division Rockwell Manufacturing Co.*, 89 NLRB 1434 (1950).
20. *Pennsylvania Garment Manufacturers' Association, Inc.*, 125 NLRB 185 (1959).
21. *Ideal Laundry and Dry Cleaning Co.*, 152 NLRB 1130 (1965).
22. *Western Nebraska Transport Service Division of Consolidated Freightways*, 144 NLRB 301 (1963); and *Pure Seal Dairy Co.*, 135 NLRB 76 (1962).
23. *National Labor Relations Act*, 29 USCA 152(11).
24. *Birmingham Fabricating Co.*, 140 NLRB 640 (1963).
25. *Augusta Chemical Co.*, 124 NLRB 1021 (1959).
26. *Sanborn Telephone Co., Inc.*, 140 NLRB 512 (1963); and *Formco, Inc.*, 156 NLRB 1471 (1966).
27. *Heck's, Inc.*, 156 NLRB 760 (1966).
28. *The Bama Co.*, 145 NLRB 1141 (1964).

29. *Queens Borough Public Library*, 195 NLRB 974 (1972). *See also Nassau Library System*, 196 NLRB 864 (1972).
30. *See also University of Miami*, 213 NLRB No. 54 (1974).

R. THEODORE CLARK, JR.
Partner
Seyfarth, Shaw, Fairweather & Geraldson
Chicago, Illinois

The Duty to Bargain

The legal regulation of the obligation to bargain collectively in both the private and public sectors has two primary thrusts. The first is concerned with the mechanics of negotiations and the requirement that the parties negotiate in good faith. The second concerns the scope of negotiations, i.e., the determination of what subjects the parties must, upon request, negotiate.

THE OBLIGATION TO NEGOTIATE IN GOOD FAITH

Under the National Labor Relations Act (NLRA) as originally enacted in 1935, it was an unfair labor practice for an employer to refuse to bargain. There was no similar obligation placed on employee organizations and there was no statutory definition of what the duty to bargain entailed. The primary purpose of the NLRA was to get employers to the bargaining table. As the Senate report stated: "The bill ... leads them [employee representatives] to the office door of their employer with the legal authority to negotiate for their fellow employees. The bill does not go beyond the office door. It leaves the discussions between the employer and the employee, and the agreements which they may or may not make, voluntary."[1] The National Labor Relations Board and the courts, however, soon added certain requirements, such as the duty to meet at reasonable times and to execute in writing any agreement reached. Many of these requirements were subsequently incorporated in Section 8(d) of the NLRA with the passage of the Taft-Hartley Act in 1947. Section 8(d) states that:

> to bargain collectively is the performance of the mutual obligation of the employer and the representative of the employees to meet at reasonable times, and confer in good faith with respect to wages, hours,

and other terms and conditions of employment, or the negotiation of an agreement, or any question arising thereunder, and the execution of a written contract incorporating any agreement reached if requested by either party, but such obligation does not compel either party to agree to a proposal or require the making of a concession.[2]

A substantial number of the public sector collective bargaining statutes contain identical or similar provisions.[3]

Parties' Representatives

Virtually all the public sector statutes grant employees the right to negotiate through representatives *of their own choosing*. This has been uniformly interpreted to mean that the union has the right to select the individuals who will negotiate with representatives of the employer and that interference with this right by an employer is an unfair labor practice. Thus, the fact that an employer finds one or more of the union's representatives personally objectionable does not ordinarily justify an employer's refusal to negotiate. The Wisconsin Employment Relations Commission made the following comment:

> Personal differences arising between the representatives of the parties engaged in negotiations with respect to wages, hours and working conditions of municipal employes do not constitute a valid reason for refusing to bargain in good faith. Both municipal employers and representatives of their employes have the right to designate whomever they choose to represent them at the bargaining table. To allow either or both parties to refuse to bargain with each other because of alleged or actual conflicts between their representatives would be contrary to the intent and purpose of [the act]."[4]

Similarly, the Assistant Secretary of Labor, in a decision under Executive Order 11491, ruled that: "the right to choose its representatives at such discussions must be left to the discretion of the exclusive bargaining representative and not to the whim of management."[5] A good illustration of the scope of this right lies in a recent decision of the Michigan Employment Relations Commission which held that a county board of commissioners was not free to refuse to negotiate merely because the employees' bargaining representative designated *another* union as its bargaining agent, since the bargaining representative was not giving up its right to represent the employees in question.[6] It should be noted, however, that the size of a union's bargaining team, especially where negotiations take place on the clock, is negotiable and that a public employer is within its rights in requesting that the union negotiate over the size of its bargaining team.

While employee organizations thus have broad rights to designate their representatives for the purposes of collective bargaining, this does not generally include the right to include on their bargaining team individuals who are excluded from the bargaining unit on the basis of their supervisory and/or managerial authority. In fact, in many instances public employers would be committing an unfair labor practice if they negotiated with a union bargaining committee that included such supervisory or managerial personnel. In this regard, the Wisconsin Employment Relations Commission in *City of Milwaukee* stated:

> The active participation by supervisory employes in the affairs of an employe organization could result in impeding and defeating the primary purpose of the employe organization—that of representing municipal employes in conferences and negotiations concerning their wages, hours and conditions of employment. Since supervisors are the agents of the municipal employer, a municipal employer, by permitting supervisory employes to participate actively, in any manner similar to that described above, in the affairs of an organization representing employes for the purposes set forth in Section 111.70, could, in the proper proceedings, be found to have committed prohibitive practices by interfering, restraining and coercing its employes in the exercise of their rights granted to them under the law.[7]

While both parties have broad rights in terms of selecting their bargaining representatives, the selected representatives must be clothed with sufficient authority to engage in meaningful negotiations. The use of representatives who do not have any power to agree and who must continually check back with their principals constitutes bad faith bargaining. This does not mean, however, that a party's representatives must have authority to reach binding agreements without any need for ratification. To the contrary, both parties in the public sector typically take any tentative agreements back to their principals for ratification. The Michigan Employment Relations Commission stated: "Obviously, the negotiating team must receive instructions from the governing body and submit oral or written reports to it, if its concessions and tentative commitments are to be meaningful. ... [I]t need not, and probably cannot, be vested with final authority to bind the public employer, since that would seem to involve an illegal delegation of the lawmaking power of the City Council."[8]

Duty to Supply Relevant Information

An employer has a clear duty to furnish relevant data and information to a union which represents its employees.[9] The courts and the various labor boards have uniformly held that employers are required upon request to furnish unions with sufficient data with respect to wage rates, job classifications and other related matters in order to permit the union to bargain intelligently, administer the contract, and prepare for negotiations. In this regard it should be noted that the "union is not required to show the purpose of their requested data unless the data appears to be clearly irrelevant."[10] Rather, the burden is on the employer to show that the requested data is not relevant. An employer is not required to necessarily supply the information in the same form requested as long as it is submitted in a manner which is not unreasonably burdensome to interpret.[11]

Related to the duty to supply information is the obligation of an employer to supply financial data upon request if an employer pleads inability to pay higher wages or fringe benefits. As the U.S. Supreme Court has stated in a case arising under the NLRA:

> Good-faith bargaining necessarily requires that claims made by either bargainer should be honest claims. This is true about an asserted inability to pay an increase in wages. If such an argument is important enough to present in the give and take of bargaining, it is important enough to require some sort of proof of its accuracy. And it would certainly not be far-fetched for a trier of fact to reach the conclusion that bargaining lacks good faith when an employer mechanically repeats a claim of inability to pay without making the slightest effort to substantiate the claim.[12]

Unilateral Action

Another constituent part of the duty to bargain in good faith is the requirement that an employer not make unilateral changes in wages, hours or working conditions which are subject to negotiation without first negotiating with the union. Thus, the Connecticut State Board of Labor Relations observed that: "it is well recognized that unilateral employer action upon a matter which is the subject of current collective bargaining between the parties constitutes a failure and refusal to bargain in good faith upon the issue in question."[13] In one case, for example, the Connecticut board held that an employer acted improperly when it unilaterally adopted a new classification plan while negotiations were in progress.[14]

However, once an employer has given the union an opportunity to negotiate over a given proposal and it appears that the parties are at an impasse, the employer is permitted to unilaterally implement the proposal. In upholding the right of a board of education to take such unilateral action, the Connecticut Supreme Court stated that: "it was not the intention of the legislature to permit progress in education to be halted until agreement is reached with the union."[15]

Overall Obligation to Bargain in Good Faith

Although the courts and the various labor boards are not supposed to sit in judgment concerning the results of negotiations, they do review negotiations to determine whether the parties have in fact negotiated in good faith. What constitutes good faith bargaining has been variously defined. The Connecticut Supreme Court stated in *West Hartford Education Ass'n* v. *Decourcy*: "The duty to negotiate in good faith generally has been defined as an obligation to participate actively in deliberations so as to indicate a present intention to find a basis for agreement. . . . Not only must the employer have an open mind and a sincere desire to reach an agreement, but a sincere effort must be made to reach a common ground."[16] In determining whether there has been good faith bargaining, the courts and labor boards consider the totality of the parties' conduct throughout the negotiations. Thus, while an employer has a clear right to insist upon a management rights clause,[17] it has been held that an employer's good faith is suspect if it insists on retaining such absolute unilateral control over wages, hours and working conditions that it in effect would require the union to waive practically all of its statutory rights.[18]

A classic example of a case in which the NLRB looked at the totality of conduct is the case of General Electric (GE).[19] GE's approach to bargaining—called Boulwarism—involved several different elements, including the submission of a firm offer on a take-it-or-leave-it basis, a massive communications campaign, and what in effect amounted to an end run to the employees. In finding that this approach to bargaining did not comport with an employer's obligation to negotiate in good faith, the NLRB stated:

> a party who enters bargaining negotiations with a take it or leave it attitude violates its duty to bargain although it goes through the forms of bargaining, does not insist on any illegal or nonmandatory bargaining proposals and wants to sign an agreement. For good faith bargaining means more than 'going through the motions of bargaining'. . . . '[T]he essential thing is rather the serious intent to adjust differences and to reach an acceptable common ground'. . . . On the part of the employer, it requires at a minimum recognition that the statutory representative is the one with whom it must deal in conducting bargaining negotiations, and that it can no longer bargain directly or indirectly with the employees. It is inconsistent with this obligation for an employer to mount a campaign, as Respondent did, both before and during negotiations, for the purpose of disparaging and discrediting the statutory representative in the eyes of its employee constituents, to seek to persuade the employees to exert pressure on the representative to submit to the will of the employer, and to create the impression that the employer rather than the union is the true protector of the employees' interests. . . . '[T]he employer's statutory obligation is to deal with the employees thru the union, and not with the union thru the employees.'[20]

It should be specifically noted, however, that it is not ordinarily illegal for an employer to advise its employees of what is occurring at the bargaining table. As one court noted in construing its public sector act: "The act does not prohibit an employer from communicating in noncoercive terms with his employees while collective negotiations are in progress. ... The element of negotiation is critical. Another crucial factor in these cases is whether or not the communication is designed to undermine and denigrate the union."[21]

General Bargaining Guidelines

While it is impossible to set forth ironclad rules on how to fulfill the obligation to bargain in good faith, the following general guidelines may be helpful:

1. Select negotiators with meaningful authority to engage in the give and take of negotiations.
2. Provide, upon request, relevant information in a timely fashion.
3. Do not take unilateral action on matters that are subject to negotiations unless and until such matters have been presented to the union's bargaining team and the parties are at impasse on those matters. It should be noted that this prohibition does not apply during the term of an existing collective bargaining agreement under which the employer has specifically or implicitly retained the right to take the action in question.[22]
4. Do not make proposals on a take-it-or-leave-it basis. This does not mean, however, that after a reasonable period of negotiations an employer cannot legitimately state its final position. For example, in *Philip Carey Mfg.*,[23] the NLRB held that an employer did not commit an unfair labor practice when it made a final offer at the eleventh meeting after having participated in the traditional give-and-take of negotiation.
5. Do not communicate proposals to employees until after they have been presented to the union's bargaining team across the bargaining table.
6. Avoid categorical statements such as: "We will never sign a contract."
7. Take good notes at bargaining sessions. Good notes serve a two-fold purpose: (1) they are helpful in reconstructing what actually occurred in negotiations if it is ever necessary to defend against a charge of refusing to bargain in good faith; (2) negotiating notes are often useful in terms of ascertaining the intent of the parties in agreeing to given provisions in the contract. As such, they can be extremely useful in terms of administering the contract and in presenting evidence of the parties' intent in arbitration proceedings. Parenthetically, it should be noted that it is

generally indicative of bad faith bargaining for one party to insist that there be a verbatim transcript of negotiations or that negotiations be tape recorded.[24] As the NLRB stated: "many authorities and practitioners in the field are of the opinion that the presence of a stenographer at [bargaining] meetings has an inhibiting effect. The use of a stenographer or mechanical recorder to create a verbatim transcript does tend to encourage negotiators to concentrate upon and speak for the purpose of making a record rather than to direct their efforts toward a solution of the issues before them."[25] However, nothing prohibits *both* parties from agreeing to have a verbatim transcript of negotiations.

THE SCOPE OF NEGOTIATIONS

The determination of the scope of negotiations in the public sector is considerably more complex and difficult than in the private sector.[26] As one commentator has observed: "In the private sector the employer's right to design and control the kind and quality of a product he wishes has been relatively unchallenged. In education, many of the demands frequently made in negotiations challenge these same professional prerogatives."[27] Thus, the NEA, in its *Guidelines for Professional Negotiations*, states:

> A professional group has responsibilities beyond self-interest, including a responsibility for the general welfare of the school system. Teachers and other members of the professional staff have an interest in the conditions which attract and retain a superior teaching force, in the in-service training programs, in class size, in the selection of textbooks, and in other matters which go far beyond those which would be included in a narrow definition of working conditions. Negotiations should include all matters which affect the quality of the educational system."[28]

Many others, however, feel that such policy matters must be excluded from bilateral collective negotiations. Wellington and Winter, for example, have observed: "The issue is not a threshold one of whether professional public employees should participate in decisions about the nature of the services they provide. Any properly run governmental agency should be interested in, and heavily reliant upon, the judgment of its professional staff. The issue rather is the method of that participation."[29] Wellington and Winter concluded that if the scope of bargaining was not effectively limited, it "would, in many cases, institutionalize the power of public employee unions in a way that would leave competing groups in the political process at a permanent and substantial disadvantage."[30] The resolution of this fundamental conflict has occupied the attention of not only state legislatures, but also the various labor boards and courts which are charged with the responsibility of deciding what the parties must negotiate.

Any discussion of the scope of negotiations usually begins with a review of what the applicable statute provides. Rather than spelling out in elaborate detail what subjects are negotiable, virtually all of the public sector statutes define the obligation in generic terms. In fact, most statutes use the same wording found in the NLRA, i.e., the parties are required to negotiate in good faith "with respect to wages, hours and other terms and conditions of employment." In one case where a teacher bargaining statute referred to only wages and other terms and conditions of employment and made no reference to hours, the court held that the omission "evidences a legislative judgment that teachers' 'hours of employment' determine students' hours of educaton and that this is an important educational policy which should be reserved to the board of education."[31] As a result, the court held that "the length of the school day and school calendar are not mandatory subjects of negotiation."[31]

In determining the scope of negotiations, then, the initial inquiry is with respect to what falls within the phrase "wages, hours and other terms and conditions of employment." Under the NLRA, if a subject is deemed to fall within this area, it is considered to be a mandatory subject of bargaining.[32] A mandatory subject of bargaining is defined as a subject over which the parties must negotiate and over which the parties may insist upon to the point of impasse. Among the subjects that have been held to be mandatory subjects of bargaining are pensions, paid vacations, holidays, merit increases, incentives, bonuses, health and accident insurance programs, meal allowances, no-strike clause, management rights clause, severance pay, reporting pay, subcontracting, overtime, premium pay, shift work, and grievance procedures. It is an unfair labor practice for a party to refuse to negotiate over a mandatory subject of negotiation. Moreover, an employer's sincere belief that a proposal is not a mandatory subject of bargaining is not a valid defense.[33]

Mandatory subjects of bargaining are to be distinguished from permissive and illegal subjects of bargaining. A permissive subject of bargaining is one which a party can legally propose, but which cannot be insisted upon to the point of impasse. Examples include a demand that the other party withdraw an unfair labor practice charge, a proposal that the employer's last offer be voted upon by the employees prior to any strike occurring, and a proposal that the bargaining unit be expanded to include additional employees not previously covered. An illegal subject of bargaining is one which would be illegal for the parties to include in an agreement, e.g., a union security clause which is contrary to law.

Despite the expansive interpretation of the number of mandatory subjects that fall within the phrase "wages, hours and other terms and conditions of employment," the courts have repeatedly held that the scope of negotiations is not unqualified. Thus, in a recent case the Supreme Court stated that the NLRA "does establish a limitation against which proposed topics must be measured."[34] The most significant limitation is with respect to matters that are deemed to go to the core of entrepreneurial control. In *Fibreboard Paper Products* v. *NLRB*,[35] Justice Stewart in his concurring opinion noted:

> While employment security has thus properly been recognized in various circumstances as a condition of employment, it surely does not follow that every decision which may affect job security is a subject of compulsory collective bargaining. Many decisions made by management affect the job security of employees. Decisions concerning the volume and kind of advertising expenditures, product design, the manner of financing, and sales, all may bear upon the security of the workers' jobs. Yet it is hardly conceivable that such decisions so involve "conditions of employment" that they must be negotiated with the employees' bargaining representative.
>
> In many of these areas the impact of a particular management decision upon job security may be extremely indirect and uncertain, and this alone may be sufficient reason to conclude that such decisions are not "with respect to ... conditions of employment." Yet there are other areas where decisions by management may quite clearly imperil job security, or indeed terminate employment entirely. An enterprise may decide to invest in labor-saving machinery. Another may resolve to liquidate its assets and go out ot business. Nothing the Court holds today should be understood as imposing a duty to bargain collectively regarding such managerial decisions, which lie at the core of entrepreneurial control. Decisions concerning the commitment of investment capital and the basic scope of the enterprise are not in themselves primarily about conditions of employment, though the effect of the decision may be necessarily to terminate employment. ... [T]hose management decisions which are fundamental to the basic direction of a corporate enterprise or which impinge only indirectly upon employment security should be excluded from that area.[36]

Significantly, other courts and public employee relations boards have accepted the concept that "management decisions which are fundamental to the basic direction of a corporate enterprise" are not mandatory subjects of negotiation. For example, the Michigan Employment Relations Commission has held that it "will not order bargaining in those cases where the subjects are demonstrably within the core of entrepreneurial control."[37] While the

Michigan commission acknowledged that "such subjects may affect interests of employees," it stated that "it did not believe that such interests outweigh the right to manage."[37] As the Connecticut Supreme Court recently stated, "the notion that decisions concerning the 'core of entrepreneurial control' are solely the business of the employer appears to have a special kind of vitality in the public sector."[38]

The New York Public Employee Relations Board (PERB) has adopted a similar approach. In its *New Rochelle School District* decision it held that decisions concerning the number of employees and whether a given service should be curtailed were not mandatory subjects of negotiation: "The determination as to the manner and means by which education service is rendered and the extent of such service is the duty and obligation of the public employer. A public employer should not be required to delegate this responsibility. The decisions of a public employer as to the carrying out of its mission—a decision to eliminate or curtail a service—are not decisions that a public employer should be compelled to negotiate with its employees."[39] The New York PERB further noted that the underlying rationale "was the concept that basic decisions as to public policy should not be made in the isolation of a negotiation table, but should be made by those having the direct and sole responsibility therefor and whose actions in this regard are subject to review in the electoral process."[39]

In *Board of Higher Education of New York City*, the New York PERB held that student membership on a faculty evaluation committee is not a mandatory subject of bargaining. The New York PERB stated that: "the composition of committees that evaluate employees is not a term or condition of the employees being evaluated."[40] In hesitating to allow college teachers to shut out nonfaculty members, the board noted that policy questions about a university's responsibilities "often involved issues of social concern to many groups within the community other than the public employer's administrative apparatus and its employees. It would be a perversion of collective negotiations to impose it as a technique for resolving such dispute and thus disenfranchising other interested groups."[40] Member Joseph Crowley dissented, rejecting what he regarded as the majority's overreliance on transposing an industrial model of collective bargaining into an academic setting. He noted that appointment and promotion matters have traditionally been matters for mandatory negotiation.

In a recent case the Kansas Supreme Court was faced with the task of defining what was negotiable under the Kansas teacher statute which requires the parties to negotiate in good faith "with respect to terms and conditions of professional service."[41] In addition to wages and other economic matters, the court held that negotiations were required over "such things as probationary period, transfers, teacher appraisal procedure, disciplinary procedure, and resignation and termination of contracts."[41] On the other hand, the court held that negotiations were not required over "curriculum and materials, payroll mechanics, certification, class size and the use of para-professionals, the use and duties of substitute teachers, and teachers' ethics and academic freedom."[41] The court stated that "the key ... is how direct the impact of an issue is on the well-being of the individual teacher, as opposed to its effect on the operation of the school system as a whole."[41]

In a case under the New Jersey act, the New Jersey Supreme Court held that a college board of trustees is not required to negotiate over the length of the college year or the placement of vacations since these matters involve major educational policy determinations which traditionally have been the exclusive responsibility of the board of trustees.[42] After noting that the lines concerning what is negotiable "may often be indistinct," the court stated:

> [The lines] drawn by the Burlington Board of Trustees seem to us to have fairly effectuated the legislative goals. It negotiated on the matters directly and intimately affecting the faculty's working terms and conditions, such as compensation, hours, work loads, sick leaves, personal and sabbatical leaves, physical accommodations, grievance procedures, etc. It declined to negotiate the major educational policy of the calendar though it did make provision in its governance structure for a calendar committee with student, faculty and administration representatives. While, in the interests of sound labor relations, it might well have also discussed the subject with officially designated representatives of the Association, it was under no legal mandate to do so.[43]

In another case the New Jersey Supreme Court held that a school board's decision to consolidate the chairmanships of two department was predominantly a matter of educational policy and was not, therefore, a term or condition of employment.[44]

Effect of Statutory Statement of Management Prerogatives

The determination of the scope of negotiations in the public sector does not end with a review of whether a given subject falls within the area of "wages, hours and other terms and conditions of employment." In many situations, a given topic might very well be deemed to fall within this phrase, but is nevertheless not a subject for mandatory negotiation because of a statutory reservation of management rights or because it conflicts with civil service rules and regulations. The effect of a statutory statement of management prerogatives on the scope of bargaining will be reviewed first.

Because certain matters have been deemed to be vital to the operation of government, many of the public sector statutes specifically exclude designated managerial prerogatives from the scope of bargaining. This follows the lead of the federal government in Executive Order 11491, which contains the following reservation of management rights:

> Management officials of the agency retain the right, in accordance with applicable laws and regulations—
> (1) to direct employees of the agency;
> (2) to hire, promote, transfer, assign, and retain employees in positions within the agency, and to suspend, demote, discharge, or take other disciplinary action against employees;
> (3) to relieve employees from duties because of lack of work or for other legitimate reasons;
> (4) to maintain the efficiency of the Government operations entrusted to them;
> (5) to determine the methods, means, and personnel by which such operations are to be conducted; and
> (6) to take whatever actions may be necessary to carry out the mission of the agency in situations of emergency.

The Hawaii, Kansas and Nevada statutes have similar provisions. Moreover, a number of other states provide that public employers are not required to bargain over certain matters. For example, the Pennsylvania act provides that "public employers shall not be required to bargain over matters of inherent managerial policy, which shall include but shall not be limited to such areas of discretion or policy as the function and programs of the public employer, standards of services, its overall budget, utilizations of technology, the organizational structure and selection and direction of personnel."

In the past several years the Federal Labor Relations Council (FLRC) and the various state and local labor relations agencies have been called upon to interpret the effect of a statutory statement of management prerogatives on the scope of bargaining. In *Department of the Army Corps of Engineers*,[45] the FLRC ruled that a union's request to negotiate on rotating shift work schedules was negotiable. It rejected the agency's argument that the union's proposal would be contrary to the right of management under Section 12(b)(4) of Executive Order 11491: "to maintain the agency of Government operations entrusted to them." In so ruling, the FLRC stated:

> In general, agency determinations as to negotiability made in relation to the concept of efficiency and economy in section 12(b)(4) of the Order and similar language in the statutes require consideration and balancing of all the factors involved, including the well-being of employees, rather than an arbitrary determination based only on the anticipation of increased costs. Other factors such as the potential for

improved performance, increased productivity, responsiveness to direction, reduced turnover, fewer grievances, contribution of money-saving ideas, improved health and safety, and the like, are valid considerations. We believe that where otherwise negotiable proposals are involved the management right in section 12(b)(4) may not properly be invoked to deny negotiations unless there is a substantial demonstration by the agency that increased costs or reduced effectiveness in operations are inescapable and significant and not offset by compensating benefits.[45]

This decision should be contrasted with the FLRC's earlier decision in *Plum Island Animal Disease Laboratory*, wherein it held that "the number of its work shifts or tours of duty, and the duration of the shifts, comprise an essential and integral part of the 'staffing patterns' necessary to perform the work of the agency" and, therefore, was not negotiable since the Executive Order reserved to management the right to determine "the numbers, types or grades of positions for employees assigned to an organizational unit, work project or tour of duty."[46]

The Hawaii act likewise contains a fairly explicit management rights provision. In *Hawaii State Teachers Association and Department of Education*,[47] the Hawaii Public Employee Relations Board held that a proposal concerning the average class size ratio was negotiable despite the employer's contention that this was a managerial prerogative reserved under the statute. In a subsequent decision, however, the Hawaii Public Employment Relations Board ruled that a proposal concerning work load which would fix the maximum number of students per teacher was not negotiable. After noting that the proposal involved "both educational policy-making and has a significant impact on working conditions," the Hawaii board determined "that it so interfere[d] with management's right to establish management educational policy and operate the school system efficiently as to render it non-negotiable."[48] The board's rationale was as follows:

> It is our opinion that the specific proposal on work load which is here at issue, while admittedly concerned with a condition of employment because it may affect the amount of work expected of a teacher, nevertheless, in far greater measure, interferes with the DOE's responsibility to establish policy for the operation of the school system, which cannot be relinquished if the DOE is to fulfill its mission of providing a sound educational system and remaining responsive to the needs of the students while striving to maintain efficient operations. Hence, the DOE and the HSTA may not agree to the subject work load proposal because such agreement would interfere substantially with the DOE's right to determine the methods, means, and personnel by which it conducts its operations and would interfere with its responsibility to the public to maintain efficient operations.[49]

In the *State Area College District* case, the Pennsylvania Labor Relations

Board vacillated with respect to the interpretation and application of the management rights proviso set forth in the Pennsylvania act. After initially ruling that some twenty-one proposals, ranging from class size to the elimination of the requirement that teachers chaperone athletic activities, were covered by the proviso and that a school board was not therefore required to negotiate on these matters,[50] the board reconsidered its initial decision and held that many of the twenty-one items which it had previously ruled nonnegotiable were, in fact, negotiable.[51] On appeal, the Commonwealth Court of Pennsylvania ruled that all of the twenty-one proposals in question were covered by the management rights proviso in that they concerned matters of inherent managerial policy. The court, in relevant part, stated:

> We must conclude that school boards have traditionally been given by the Legislature, under constitutional mandates, broad inherent managerial powers to operate the public schools and to determine policy relative thereto. If Act 195 represents a departure from the traditional principle of our public schools being operated and managed by school boards, it would be a sharp departure not to be presumed but the result of clear legislative declaration. . . .
> Matters of "inherent managerial policy" over which public employers are not obligated to bargain are such matters that belong to the public employer as a natural prerogative or essential element of the right (1) to manage the affairs of its business, operation or activity and (2) to make decisions that determine the policy and direction that the business, operation or activity shall pursue.[52]

The California Meyers-Milias-Brown Act authorizes negotiations over "wages, hours and other terms and conditions of employment," but exempts from the scope of negotiation the "consideration of the merits, necessity, or organization of any service or activity provided by law or executive order." In *County of Los Angeles County Department of Public Social Services v. Los Angeles County Employees Association*,[53] the California Court of Appeals upheld a decision of the Los Angeles County Employee Relations Commission that the number of cases assigned to welfare workers is a working condition and therefore a mandatory subject of bargaining. In balancing the conflicting provisions of the ordinance, the court stated: "The problem of interpreting these sections, and their relationship to each other, is that an argument can plausibly be made that *all* management decisions affect areas of mandatory service to the public *and* the working conditions of public employees; or, conversely, that all decisions rendered concerning a public employee labor dispute of necessity will determine the quality of mandated public service *and* the operation of management."[53] The court noted that it could find no reason why a public employer could not discuss the question of case load in light of "wages, hours and other conditions of employment," even though the "merits, necessity, or organization" of the service being rendered are excluded from negotiations.

The Nevada Local Government Employee Relations Act contains a fairly lengthy provision which reserves to public employers numerous rights "without negotiation or reference to any agreement resulting from negotiation." In *Washoe County School District*, the Nevada Local Government Employee-Management Relations Board held, *inter alia*, that proposals concerning class size, student discipline, school calendar, and teacher load were nevertheless negotiable. The board held "that any matter significantly related to wages, hours and working conditions is negotiable, whether or not said matters also relate to questions of management prerogative; and it is the duty of the local government employer to proceed and negotiate said items."[54]

Effect of Civil Service Laws on Scope of Negotiations

Prior to the advent of wide-scale collective bargaining in the public sector, the terms and conditions of employment for many public employees were established pursuant to civil service rules and regulations. In the public sector, these civil service rules and regulations were the counterpart to the collective bargaining agreement in the private sector. The enactment of public sector collective bargaining legislation has raised the question as to the extent, if any, to which preexisting civil service rules and regulations are superseded by collective bargaining. The legislative response has differed from state to state. The Michigan act, for example, is completely silent on the matter. As a result, the parties and eventually the courts have had to attempt to resolve the many conflicts that have arisen. The Michigan Supreme Court, noting that it had "to guess what the 1965 legislature would have done had the point come to its attention," held that the 1965 public employee bargaining law "must be implemented and administered exclusively as provided therein" and that the authority of civil service commissions was "diminished *pro tanto* by the [public employee labor relations] act of 1965, to the extent of free administration of the latter according to its tenor."[55]

On the other hand, some states have provided, in effect, that existing civil service rules and regulations should not be impeded by collective bargaining. For example, the Massachusetts act for municipal employees provides that nothing in the act "shall diminish the authority and power of the civil service commission, or any retirement board or personnel board established by law." The New Hampshire statute for state employees provides, not unlike Executive Order 11491, that "all collective bargaining agreements shall at all times be subject to existing or future laws and all valid regulations adopted pursuant thereto."

The third legislative approach is to provide that certain core essentials of the merit principle—i.e., the holding and granting of merit examinations and the appointment of employees from lists established by such examinations— are not negotiable, but with respect to all other matters where there is a conflict between the collective bargaining agreement and the rules and regulations adopted by a personnel board or civil service commission, the terms of such agreement shall prevail. This approach has been adopted in Connecticut.

The conflict between civil service and the scope of bargaining under public sector collective bargaining laws is clearly revealed in *Laborer's International Union of North America, Local 1029 v. State of Delaware*.[56] At issue was the negotiability of union proposals concerning pay for holiday work, paid union leave, premium pay for double shift work, use of accumulated sick leave for vacation purposes, hazardous duty pay, and reimbursement for accumulated sick leave upon voluntary resignation. The court, noting that the Delaware Public Sector Bargaining Law provides for negotiations on "matters concerning wages, salaries, hours, vacations, sick leave, grievance procedures and other terms and conditions of employment," stated that each of the union's proposals fell within the defined area of negotiations and therefore was a "proper subject for collective bargaining." The court noted, however, that "difficulty arises when one attempts to reconcile the Union's demands for collective bargaining with the provisions and purposes of the State's Merit System of Personnel Administration." After noting that "both the Merit System and the right of public employees to organize are of relatively recent origin," the court stated:

> *Having studied the statutes and the available legislative history, I am of the opinion that where there is uncertainty as to areas where the General Assembly has indicated a clear intention to deny collective bargaining, any doubt should be resolved in favor of the merit system.* The Merit System has been instituted to create a uniformity of protection and treatment for public employees. The sections listed in section 5938(c) are those in which uniformity of treatment would seem most essential if the system is to have meaning, particularly those which attempt to deal with classification based on ability, equal compensation for commensurate ability and responsibility, promotions and time off from work with pay. If each agency is to bargain with the bargaining representative of its employees on such things as the amount of pay for holidays and double shifts worked, the amount of authorized leave with pay, the use of accumulated sick leave as additional vacation with pay, etc., then the obvious result will be to have employees of the same classifications receiving different compensation and different leave arrangements for different purposes based solely upon the agency they work for and the success of their collective bargaining representatives. Section 5938(c) seems designed to prevent this while the remainder of the statute allows for bargaining on various other matters. I am therefore reluctant to

expand the scope of collective bargaining so as to effectively encroach upon rules adopted pursuant to the statutes protected by Section 5938(c) without clear legislative direction to do so (emphasis added).[56]

The court noted that: "[its] decision should not be taken to indicate a negative attitude in this State towards the rights of public employees. Rather it is an attempt to reconcile conflicts inherent in a public employment program which contemplates both merit system protection as well as collective bargaining rights for State employees."[57]

An example of the type of conflict that arises is indicated in the decision of the Orgeon Public Employe Relations Board in *University of Oregon Medical School and the State Personnel Division*.[58] There the Oregon State Employee Association represented 90 percent of the physical plant employees employed by the state, with the American Federation of State, County, and Municipal Employees representing the remaining 10 percent. When AFSCME requested negotiations with respect to salaries for the physical plant employees which it represented, the personnel division proposed that negotiations on economic matters be conducted jointly with both AFSCME and the Oregon State Employe Association; it refused to negotiate separately with AFSCME on salaries and wages. In this regard, the personnel division relied on a provision of the merit system law which provided that salaries of employees in any classification in the classified state service were to be uniform. In rejecting the contentions of the personnel division, the Oregon board stated:

> Even if it be true that the statute requires a single rate, this does not foreclose the obligation to bargain with the smaller unit nor does it force the smaller unit to sit by submissively while the larger group has determined its fate. We cannot catalog all of the possible results of bargaining with the smaller unit but, as examples of possible results, it might be that the smaller unit would be persuaded to accept the pre-set rates or that the Department would agree to some different and higher rates which might then become the standard for all employes. It is also possible that the parties would reach an impasse. It is also conceivable that ORS 240.235(3), while requiring a uniform rate, does not require that the rate be uniform throughout the state but only in geographical areas.[59]

Effect of Statutes, Charter Provisions and Ordinances

In addition to the conflict between civil service laws and collective bargaining, there is also a conflict with other state statutory provisions, municipal charters, and ordinances. In *Detroit Police Officers Association v. City of Detroit*,[60] one of the questions raised was whether the city of Detroit was required to bargain with respect to certain changes in the retirement system where such changes were incorporated in a city charter provision which had been approved by the electrorate. In holding that the duty to bargain under the Michigan Public Employment Relations Act superseded city charter provisions, the court stated: "It takes little insight to appreciate what a municipal employer and its electrorate could do to the collective bargaining process if this procedure were allowed to stand. Any 'Home Rule' city could merely write its pension and retirement system into its charter, and insulate any change therein from negotiations and settlement save with electoral approval. This to us is the exact converse of what the Legislature intended when it inserted bargaining rights for public employees into the statute."[61] Similarly, the Wisconsin Employment Relations Commission (WERC) in *Racine County*, ruled that whether salary increases were retroactive was negotiable, rejecting the employer's contention that retroactive payments were prohibited by a county ordinance. The WERC stated that "what the County enacted with respect to retroactivity, it can repeal if it so desires."[62]

In *Waterbury Teachers Association* v. *City of Waterbury*,[63] the Connecticut Supreme Court held that a board of education had a duty to negotiate the terms and conditions of employment of principals even though the job specifications of the principals had been established by civil service rules and regulations adopted pursuant to a city charter. The court noted that principals as certified professional employees were covered by the Connecticut Teacher Negotiation Act and that therefore the provisions of the state act mandating negotiations were applicable "notwithstanding ... the Waterbury Charter and the civil service rules and regulations adopted pursuant thereto."[64]

Effect of Legislative and Appropriation Process

In *Rutgers Council of the American Association of University Professors* v. *The New Jersey Board of Higher Education*[65] the court held that a state board of higher education did not violate the state's public sector bargaining law when it unilaterally adopted a student-faculty ratio funding formula applicable to the university, notwithstanding the union's contention that the formula imposed certain work loads. class sizes, class hours, etc., on the university's faculty. In so ruling, the court stated:

> The Board's right to make a budget recommendation for Rutgers was intended by the Legislature to be exercised freely, and in a manner that would enable it to receive an independent and analytical assessment of the budgetary needs of the University. As respondents point out, if the Employer-Employee Relations Act were construed to compel collective negotiations on the budget recommendations given to the Legislature by the Board, this obvious legislative intent would be

frustrated, for the recommendations it made each year would reflect compromise and not the Board's independent judgment. As we have remarked earlier in this opinion, any member of a public or private interest group may examine any budget recommendation made by the Board and, if so minded, submit his views and appropriate data with regard thereto to the executive and legislative branches of government. This, and not collective negotiation, is the proper avenue for interested parties to follow.[66]

Collective bargaining in the public sector is in many respects at the same stage of development as collective bargaining was in the private sector in the late 1930s. Like the private sector then, the public sector is beset with considerable uncertainty as to what the obligation to bargain in good faith means and what the scope of bargaining is. While much remains to be resolved, it is not unreasonable to suggest that as precedents are established to govern the conduct of the parties at the bargaining table and as the parameters of bargaining become more firmly established, the uncertainty and militancy that often accompanies public sector bargaining today will decrease. That, at least, was the experience in the private sector. I am not suggesting that the problems are easy or that everything will eventually work out satisfactorily for all concerned. I do suggest, that, as the parties become more experienced in their relatively new roles and as institutional changes are made to accommodate to the reality of collective bargaining, the crisis, conflict and confrontation that permeates much of public sector bargaining will begin to recede.

REFERENCES

1. Quoted *in* Smith, Russell A. *Labor Law*. 2d ed. Indianapolis, Bobbs-Merrill, 1953, p. 647.
2. *National Labor Relations Act*, 29 USCA 158(d).
3. *See generally* Edwards, Harry T. "The Emerging Duty to Bargain in the Public Sector," *Michigan Law Review*, 71:885-934, April 1973.
4. *The City of Superior*, Wisconsin Employment Relations Commission Dec. No. 8325 (1967).
5. *Ft. Jackson Laundry Facility*, A/SLMR Dec. No. 242 (1972).
6. *Barry County Board of Commissioners*, Michigan Employment Relations Commission Case No. C74 B-42 (1974).
7. *City of Milwaukee*, Wisconsin Employment Relations Commission Dec. No. 6960 (1964), reprinted *in* Russell A. Smith, Harry T. Edwards, and R. Theodore Clark, Jr. *Labor Relations Law in the Public Sector*. Indianapolis, Bobbs-Merrill, 1974, p. 173; and *Accord, City of Stamford (Public Works Department)*, Connecticut State Board of Labor Relations Dec. No. 862 (1966).

8. *City of Saginaw,* Michigan Employment Relations Commission Lab. Op. 465 (1967).

9. *See generally* Huston, Robert A. "Furnishing Information as an Element of Employer's Good Faith Bargaining," *University of Detroit Law Journal,* 35:471-504, April 1958; and Miller, Max J. "Employer's Duty to Furnish Economic Data to Unions–Revisited," *Labor Law Journal,* 17:272-79, May 1966.

10. *Saginaw Township Board of Education,* Michigan Employment Relations Commission Lab. Op. 127 (1970), reprinted *in* Smith, Edwards, and Clark, *op. cit.,* p. 544.

11. *Westinghouse Electric Corporation,* 129 NLRB 850 (1960).

12. *NLRB* v. *Truitt Manufacturing Co.,* 351 U.S. 149, 153 (1956).

13. *Town of Stratford,* Connecticut State Board of Labor Relations Dec. No. 1069 (1972).

14. *Borugh of Naugatuck,* Connecticut State Board of Labor Relations Dec. No. 769 (1967).

15. *West Hartford Education Association* v. *DeCourcy,* 162 Conn. 566, 295 A.2d 526 (1972), reprinted *in* Smith, Edwards, and Clark, *op. cit.,* p. 528.

16. *Ibid.,* p. 521.

17. *NLRB* v. *American National Insurance Co.,* 343 U.S. 395 (1952).

18. *See, e.g., West Hartford Education Association* v. *DeCourcy, op. cit.*

19. *General Electric Co.,* 150 NLRB 192 (1964), enf'd, 418 F.2d 736 (2d Cir. 1969), cert. denied, 397 U.S. 965 (1970).

20. *Ibid.,* 150 NLRB 194-95.

21. *West Hartford Education Association* v. *DeCourcy, op. cit.*

22. *See, e.g., City of Milwaukee,* Wisconsin Employment Relations Commission Dec. No. 8505 (1968), reprinted *in* Smith, Edwards and Clark, *op. cit.,* p. 560; and *Ador Corporation,* 150 NLRB 1658 (1965).

23. *Philip Carey Mfg.,* 140 NLRB 1103 (1963), enf'd, 331 F.2d 720 (6th Cir. 1964).

24. *See, e.g., Mayor Samuel E. Zoll and the City of Salem,* Massachusetts Labor Relations Commission Case No. MUP 309 (1969); and *Architectural Fibreglass, Division of Architectural Pottery,* 165 NLRB 238 (1967).

25. *Architectural Fibreglass, Division of Architectural Pottery, op. cit.*

26. *See generally* Smith, Edwards, and Clark, *op. cit.,* pp. 364-521.

27. Lane, Willard R., quoted *in* Clark, R. Theodore, Jr. "Negotiating the Public Sector Agreement." *In* Thomas P. Gilroy and Anthony V. Sinicropi, eds. *Collective Negotiations and Public Administration.* Iowa City, Center for Labor and Management, College of Business Administration, University of Iowa, 1970, p. 30.

28. Quoted *in* Clark, *ibid.,* p. 30.

29. Wellington, Harry H., and Winter, Ralph K., Jr. *The Unions and the Cities.* Washington, D.C., The Brookings Institution, 1971, p. 24.

30. *Ibid.,* p. 30.

31. *West Hartford Education Association* v. *DeCourcy, op. cit.*

32. *See generally NLRB* v. *Wooster Division of Borg-Warner Corporation,* 356 U.S. 342 (1958).

33. *See, e.g., Sanilac County Road Commission,* Michigan Employment Relations Commission Lab. Op. 461 (1969).

34. *Allied Chemical and Alkali Workers Local 1* v. *Pittsburgh Plate Glass Co.*, 404 U.S. 157 (1972).
35. *Fibreboard Paper Products* v. *NLRB*, 379 U.S. 203 (1964).
36. *Ibid.*, 379 U.S. 223.
37. *Westwood Community Schools*, Michigan Employment Relations Commission Lab. Op. 313 (1972).
38. *West Hartford Education Association* v. *DeCourcy, op. cit.*
39. *New Rochelle School District*, 4 New York PERB 4-3060, 3704, 3706.
40. *Board of Higher Education of New York City*, New York PERB Case No. U-0904, Government Employee Relations Report (GERR) No. 558, B-10 (June 1974).
41. *National Educational Association of Shawnee Mission, Inc.* v. *Board of Education of Shawnee Mission Unified School District*, 512 P.2d 426, *Labor Relations Reference Manual*, 84:2223, 1973.
42. *Burlington College Faculty Association* v. *Board of Trustees, Burlington County College*, N.J. S. Ct., *Labor Relations Reference Manual*, 84:2857, 1973.
43. *Ibid.*, p. 2858.
44. *Dunellen Board of Education* v. *Dunellen Education Association*, GERR No. 535, G-1 (Dec. 1973).
45. *Department of the Army Corps of Engineers*, Federal Labor Relations Council No. 71A-26 (1972), GERR Ref. File 21:7023.
46. *Plum Island Animal Disease Laboratory*, Federal Labor Relations Council No. 71A-11 (1971), GERR Ref. File 21:7013.
47. *Hawaii State Teachers Association and Department of Education*, Hawaii Public Employee Relations Board Dec. No. 22 (1972).
48. *Department of Education*, Hawaii Public Employee Relations Board Dec. No. 26 (1973), reprinted *in* Smith, Edwards, and Clark, *op. cit.* p. 446.
49. *Ibid.*, p. 451.
50. *PLRB* v. *State College Area School District*, GERR No. 426, F-1 (Nov. 1971).
51. *Ibid.*, GERR No. 464, B-2 (Aug. 1972).
52. *State College Education Association* v. *PLRB*, 306 A.2d 404 (1973), reprinted *in* Smith, Edwards, and Clark, *op. cit.* p. 432.
53. *County of Los Angeles County Department of Public Social Services* v. *Los Angeles County Employees Association*, GERR No. 515, B-17 (Aug. 1973), Calif. Ct. App., 2d App. Dist. (1973).
54. *Washoe County School District*, Nevada Local Government Employee-Management Relations Board Item No. 3 (1970).
55. *Civil Service Commission* v. *Wayne County Board of Supersisors*, 184 N.W. 2d 201 (1971), reprinted *in* Smith, Edwards, and Clark, *op. cit.*, p. 476.
56. *Laborer's International Union of North America, Local 1029* v. *State of Delaware*, Del. Ct. of Chan., Kent County (1973), *Labor Relations Reference Manual*, 84:2418-19, 1973.
57. *Ibid.*, p. 2420.
58. *University of Oregon Medical School and the State Personnel Division*, Oregon Public Employe Relations Board Dec. No. C-70 (1972), reprinted *in* Smith, Edwards, and Clark, *op. cit.*, p. 478.

59. *Ibid.*, p. 480.
60. *Detroit Police Officers Association* v. *City of Detroit*, 200 N.W. 2d 722 (Mich. Ct. App. 1972), reprinted *in* Smith, Edwards, and Clark, *op. cit.*, p. 504.
61. *Ibid.*, p. 507.
62. *Racine County*, Wisconsin Employment Relations Commission Dec. No. 10917-B (1972).
63. *Waterbury Teachers Association* v. *City of Waterbury*, Conn. S. Ct. (1973), *Labor Relations Reference Manual*, 84:2158, 1973.
64. *Ibid.*, p. 2155.
65. *Rutgers Council of the American Association of University Professors* v. *The New Jersey Board of Higher Education*, N.J. Super. Ct., App. Div. (1973), *Labor Relations Reference Manual*, 85:2214, 1973.
66. *Ibid.*, p. 2219.

MARTIN WAGNER
Professor
Institute of Labor and Industrial Relations
University of Illinois
Urbana-Champaign, Illinois

Grievances

In preparing this discussion on grievances I have made two assumptions. First, I assume that an established collective bargaining relationship exists. I am not suggesting that this relationship is necessarily desirable, but the assumption is important. When grievances arise in an unorganized situation, their disposition is different than handled under collective bargaining. In addition, statutorily or organizationally established grievance procedures may be different from those established through collective bargaining.

My second assumption is that the subject is not limited to the substantive matter of which types of issues and problems constitute grievances in a collective bargaining relationship. I am assuming for the purpose of this discussion that the subject concerns not only those issues but also the problem of institutional procedure for dealing with grievances. In fact, the procedural aspect of the subject may be the most important part of the entire problem.

Before turning to the specific subject of grievances, I want to direct attention to the background against which I believe our discussion must be carried on. All organizations of substantial size have procedures for establishing employment conditions and for administering them on a continuing basis. In some instances these are poorly conceived and haphazardly administered. In others they are thoughtfully constructed and carefully executed. These procedures exist in organized as well as unorganized situations—in any large organization there are some arrangements for dealing with employment conditions. In contrast to the procedure generally followed in unorganized situations, in which employment conditions are established and administered at the discretion of managers alone, under collective bargaining these

This article is an edited transcription of Mr. Wagner's presentation at the Institute.

employment conditions are established and administered bilaterally through negotiations and structured consultations with representatives of the employees to which they are applicable. Collective bargaining, therefore, is a particular procedure for establishing those employment practices and policies and the procedures for administering and executing them. Out of this collective bargaining procedure a kind of governmental process develops for dealing with these employment concerns on a continuing and structured basis. The analogy with a governmental process may be overdrawn, but it does indicate something about the nature of this activity, particularly in relation to the administration of the process. It is the nature and the quality of this governmental process that is real for most of those involved in it and affected by it, and it is central to our concern.

Like those who study other complex institutions and relationships, those who examine the entire collective bargaining situation find it useful and meaningful to examine systematically different functional aspects of the process relationship in order to get a better understanding of the whole. At times we tend to examine separately—or abstract from the whole—one interesting and fascinating part of this procedure, the negotiation process. This is the dramatic process of changing or redefining the substantive terms, the basic practices and conditions of the relationship. We look at the negotiating process in which existing employment conditions are reshaped and redefined, and we become interested in and preoccupied with the strategies and tactics used by the negotiators to yield an acceptable result. At times those of us who look at the process break that negotiating aspect of the relationship into even smaller units, and examine the different stages at which these negotiating processes or procedures take place. Then we examine the involvement and the influence of additional parties such as negotiators, factfinders, or arbitrators, or some outside governmental forces, factors or persons who step into these procedures. We also look at the use of alternative pressure mechanisms and the contributions and effects that these have on the outcome of the negotiations. The breaking down of this large chain into smaller and smaller units to try to comprehend what is going on is an important analytical device and a good intellectual approach.

Similarly, we occasionally set a different task for ourselves and examine separately the procedures whereby the same negotiated conditions that were the product of one of these negotiation sessions are put into effect at the work place and how differences, controversies and disputes about their application and interpretation are resolved. Here we are examining another facet of this continuing relationship, looking at it in great and greater detail and asking: How does it work? How do we resolve the inevitable differences and controversies that may arise under an agreement or previously established set of ground rules? What procedures are useful in trying to handle this kind of dispute? As with negotiations, we divide the relationship into smaller units and examine the mechanisms that are used to resolve those differences and those matters which the negotiating parties were unable to resolve.

The program for this institute illustrates my point. We are dealing with a whole series of topics, including the scope of negotiations, the establishment of bargaining means, grievances, the negotiating process, and the negotiation of substantive terms of a new relationship. Each of these topics is abstracted from a continuing relationship in an attempt to gain some insight or some sense of what is occurring. As useful or significant as this approach is, we need to remind ourselves regularly that each of these functions, each of these categorized aspects of the relationship, is an integral part of the total relationship. Whether deliberate or not, a change in any one of these functions has some effect or influence on the total relationship. The segments are abstractions, and it is the totality which is real and significant. It is that totality with which we should be concerned.

What happens in the day-to-day administration of the previously agreed-upon conditions, the day-to-day application of those agreed-upon practices, has a tremendous impact on their negotiation the next time. Similarly, not only the agreements reached, but also the manner in which the agreements are reached in negotiation—including the style, the respect or lack of respect, and the attitudes of the parties involved—has a tremendous effect on the daily applications of the relationship that follows. To state it simply, attitudes and sentiments are shaped in each of these segmented procedures, but they are not confined to those particular procedures or to that setting; they spill over into the others. In general, neither the substantive issues nor the procedures adopted for dealing with grievances are as visible or as dramatic as those dealt with in the negotiation for changes in conditions, as is true in many other parts of the collective bargaining process. The headlines today discuss pending negotiations, and negotiations in progress, but little is said about what has been happening at the coal face in the last two years in the daily administration of safety provisions and the contractual provisions of the previous agreement. The drama is in the negotiations, and yet the absence of drama in the handling of grievances does not mean that they cannot and do not have a significant effect on those negotiations. What takes place in the day-to-day administration of a collective bargaining relationship may lend more flavor than the actual negotiations do. It is against this background that I wish to discuss the specific problem of grievances and the grievance procedure.

What is this business of grievances about? A first major characteristic is that the establishment of a grievance procedure or the existence of a grievance is premised on recognition. It is in the application of the bargaining agreement that the meaning of the grievance procedure is realized. You can sit down in a room and negotiate a collective bargaining agreement, and include guidelines and substantive terms, but until that agreement becomes a viable, active instrument at a work place it is only a piece of paper. It is in the application of the agreement that it becomes alive and obtains its significance.

A second important point is that in any complex, dynamic organization in which collective bargaining agreements exist, differences over the application and interpretation of those agreements will inevitably arise. Because of this, it makes eminent good sense to make arrangements for dealing with those differences when the specific issues of an individual situation are not before us, to deal with the potential difference before it occurs. Once a difference arises, the feelings aroused by the difference itself are imposed on the question and we cannot resolve it. Therefore, when we recognize that differences will arise, there are two approaches we can take. One is to say that we will deal with them on an *ad hoc* basis as they arise. There are dangers in that procedure. Alternatively we can say that we anticipate them, that we expect that the resolution of those differences will be important in terms of our continuing relationship, and that we ought to devise an instrument for solving them.

It is also important that the actual parties to the relationship negotiate the grievance procedure. It is on the basis of their experience, knowledge and understanding of their situation that they decide to develop an instrument or mechanism for dealing with future differences. No one from the outside imposes these mechanisms. No one says, "This is the model, and it's the only model," although in practice there is a tendency to adopt standard models because the parties involved have not asked the question, "What is this relationship about?"

A major subject of negotiation in most collective bargaining relationships, therefore, is the grievance procedures, the mechanisms whereby we attempt in some orderly, sensible, pragmatic way to handle the differences that inevitably will arise. We can shape these procedures to our own situation, to suit our particular environment and our particular need. Those of us who have looked at grievance procedures find that a wide range of mechanisms is adopted because each is tailored to the problems at hand. The parties negotiate these mechanisms to solve their own problems, and the outcome of this negotiation is shaped by the views of the negotiating parties about what should be stressed, and by their relative bargaining power and skill. There is as much concern about grievance procedure as there is about other matters.

Now let me turn to the specific matters in this grievance procedure that require attention. Even though the particular form of the grievance procedure tends to vary with the situation—with the nature, size and character of the organization—virtually all grievance procedures have one characteristic in common. This is a kind of appellate arrangement in which there are numerous steps. The number of steps may vary. The determination of who is involved at each step may depend on the character of the particular situation, and this can and should be related to the requirements of the parties in their setting. But most grievance procedures have a kind of appellate arrangement in which problems, issues or differences are first handled at some low level—at the level of the origin of the difference—and then may ultimately be taken to the top of the organization, to some higher level in which top officials or administrative officers of both organizations who had something to do with shaping the original agreement look at and dispose of the grievance.

Another problem concerns the matters that can be submitted to and processed through this machine. This is an important and critical question, and great controversies exist. I propose two possible answers: (1) any difference that may arise between the parties during the existence of this agreement may be initiated and processed through the grievance procedure; (2) any difference over the interpretation or application of the agreement may be handled under the grievance procedure. They sound alike, but are they? This is a tremendous issue, and parties argue vigorously over it. "Any difference" is one proposition; "any difference over the interpretation or application of the agreement" is a much more narrowly defined or circumscribed matter.

Another concern is with the point in this machinery where the particular issue may be dealt with most effectively. For example, if a difference arises, where in the organizational hierarchy do you take the problem? Do you always start at the lowest level, or in some cases do you say, "This is an issue of such a nature that we ought to talk about it at an intermediate level and bypass a lower level which obviously cannot resolve it"?

A fourth problem concerns the parties to the grievance and when they become parties. When a grievance occurs, should the grieving party—whether an individual or a group of employees—deal with the supervisor or administrator directly, or is it appropriate for the organization to which they belong to become involved with the grievance immediately?

Another question is whether the employee organization has independent standing to process and pursue a grievance as an organization, or whether it is solely representative of employees and can act only as the employee authorizes, delegates or designates. This is a critical question, a matter with which the U.S. Supreme Court has had to deal. Does the organization have independent standing to advance the interest of the organization and its members, or does it derive its authority to speak for the employees only as a result of a specific delegation of authority by the employees? Both positions prevail.

Another interesting problem arises in the case of reprimand or discipline. If an employee is to be reprimanded, suspended or dismissed from the job, should the labor organization to which the individual belongs be involved at the outset in order to protect the interest of the employee? If an employee is to be disciplined, is it to his interest that he at least have the opportunity before discipline is imposed to have someone there to serve as his spokesman or representative, to look out for his interest and perhaps to protect that interest? Many labor organizations have found that in order to get maximum protection for an employee when an adverse action is contemplated, it is in the interest of that employee to be afforded the right of representation. Although arguments can be made for and against it, my bias leans toward representation before drastic action is taken to protect the rights and interests of the employee and perhaps to cool the situation before a major confrontation exists.

Another interesting problem concerns time limits for processing grievances. However we define the grievance, should there be time limits for processing it? Should there be some kind of attempt to bring the issue to the attention of those whose action is being challenged? If so, what are those time limits to be? What is the reason for the time limit? What is the function of the time limit? Should matters be allowed to ride for weeks before raising the question? That may be terribly unfair, since by the time the issue gets joined to the employer, for example, the witnesses may no longer recollect what transpired and the data and the evidence may be gone. Should the issue be joined early? The time limit may be so short that the interest of the individual or group of employees cannot be fully protected because we cannot develop data or make the necessary investigation to look out for the interest.

We now come to what I consider an extremely important part of the question of grievances: the grievance procedure itself. Who initiates a grievance? There are some cases in which employers do, but in the overwhelming majority of situations employees initiate a grievance. They contend or argue that the employer has done something improper, that he has failed to carry out an agreed-upon practice or to follow one of the established guidelines. The employees seek the redress which they believe the agreement or the guidelines provide them. Suppose we then have extended discussion through the grievance procedure. We take it through the appellate arrangement and we reach the top of the structured appellate arrangement. And the employer says, "We have heard all of your arguments and your discussions, and we're not persuaded." What do we do now? In the private sector, where the parties have the right to resort to self help, in such a situation a labor organization might say, "We have carried this through the orderly procedure as far as we can. The employer does not agree. We are not prepared to accept the employer's final answer as the final disposition, and we reserve the right to resort to self help." In the private sector this is permissible and in some cases even takes place, but the parties involved have recognized that this procedure doesn't really make a great deal of sense. Employers do not want stoppages over these differences, and unions acting on behalf of employees don't want to shut the plant down over every difference that arises. So, in 96 percent of the agreements in the private sector, they devise a procedure in which they say that, since they are not able to resolve their difference in direct negotiations and direct consultation, they shall submit that difference to an outside party, a tribunal or an arbitrator, and agree that this outside party's determination shall be final. Each side then gets a fair shake at the particular controversy. In the private sector, employers readily agree to that kind of arrangement, provided the union agrees to not resort to a strike. This is what the Supreme Court called the *quid pro quo*. The employer agrees to let this kind of problem be resolved by some agreed-upon third party, who is to judge the case on its merits as a judge would. The employer agrees to be bound by that determination, but in turn asks the union to withhold the right of self help.

When we enter the public sector we encounter some new problems. The common condition in most jurisdictions in the public sector is that the employees do not have the statutory or judicially recognized right to strike, so they cannot give up that which they do not have. In the public sector, therefore, there is an even greater reason to consider some judicial procedure in which outside parties are in a position to make some determination when a party feels that a grievance has not been handled in compliance with the agreed-upon guidelines. The procedure whereby this outside tribunal is to be brought into play is, of course, negotiable. Parties have both the right and the bargaining capacity to negotiate the grievance procedure, and they also have the authority, power, and right to negotiate what the nature of this outside tribunal will be. What shall the composition of that tribunal be? How is it to function? What shall its procedure be? Shall it be highly structured, legal and like a court, or shall it be relatively informal? Decisions on all of these questions reside with the negotiating parties, and they have the authority to shape the arbitration process on the basis of their own experience and situation. The kinds of problems which may go to arbitration may be limited, and this is an area in which great bargaining debates can take place. The employer may say, "We are perfectly willing to talk about any matter up to the point of the employer's final determination, but we submit to the arbitrator or to the tribunal only those matters that deal with the agreement or the guidelines." The union, on the other hand, may reserve the right to strike over certain issues. These practices are negotiable, and the outcome is significant.

Thus far I have described the elements of the grievance procedure and what may or may not be a grievance. I will now make a few observations about what occurs when we use and apply the grievance procedure. The grievance procedure is the mechanism for obtaining compliance with the results of negotiation—the dramatic part of the relationsip. It is the instrument whereby employees test an employer's action which they feel is not in accordance with those guidelines. If the challenge is valid and the employer does not agree, an arbitrator may tell him he has not complied. In other instances, a charge or contention may be raised and go ultimately to an arbitrator who determines that there really is no merit to the claim, and that the employer has in fact complied. The grievance procedure is therefore an instrument whereby an employer's actions and conduct are tested against that which the employer agreed upon in the negotiation. It is in that sense a compliance instrument, a most important part of the collective bargaining relationship.

The grievance procedure is also an extremely important communications mechanism. It is the instrument whereby parties are constantly exchanging ideas and issues as they arise and are testing them and talking about them. It is the day-to-day instrument used to deal with the nuts and bolts problems on a continuing basis. Employers and employees are engaged in a constant interchange of ideas, points of view and positions, in some cases not even dealing with grievances, for in the course of dealing with a grievance other issues may arise. It is that kind of exchange of ideas and sampling of views and opinions that gives continuity and flavor to the continuing relationship between employers and employees. My own predilections are in the direction of using the grievance procedure to the maximum, at least in the early stages, to share ideas, to hear what employees have on their minds, what concerns they have, and to try to explore ways and means of dealing with them. The grievance procedure can be looked upon as a legalistic device, a kind of court procedure in which somebody sits back with detachment and says "you were right" or "you were wrong." But it can also be used as a clinical device—to sound out the sentiments, ideas and attitudes that exist. It can be used not only to settle grievances in a legal way, but also to keep aware of the state of things in the organization.

This rather mundane, not very attractive, not particularly dramatic process of dealing with grievances is an extremely important matter, an extremely important element that adds character and quality to the relationship. I hope I have challenged you not to become so preoccupied with the niceties of the sub-part that you fail to recognize how important each of these sub-parts is in relation to the others, and how the integral parts of the whole which finally combine give character and quality to this kind of governmental relationship.

JAMES L. STERN
Professor of Economics
University of Wisconsin
Madison, Wisconsin

Impasse Resolution in the Public Sector

Before examining the various alternatives used to resolve public sector labor disputes, it seems sensible to set forth explicitly some of the underlying value judgments that, in effect, provide the framework within which we choose among these alternatives. Then, subsequent sections of this paper will briefly summarize bargaining systems, describe the tools for dispute resolution, examine the evolution of dispute settlement techniques in various segments of the public sector, and evaluate how these tools are working.

In a political democracy there will be continuing pressure to extend this concept to the workplace and to introduce "industrial democracy." This was nicely put by an English critic of collective bargaining who wrote in 1869: "One thing is clear ... the relation between workmen and their employers has permanently changed in its character. The democratic idea which rules in politics has no less penetrated into industry. The notion of a governing class, exacting implicit obedience from inferiors, and imposing upon them their own terms of service, is gone, never to return. Henceforward, employers and their workmen must meet as equals."[1]

In the 100 years that have elapsed since that statement was written we have in effect adopted a standard of values which says that, other things being equal, bilateral decision-making between those who direct work and those who perform it is preferable to unilateral action. Phrased another way, we can say that we have enacted legislation to promote collective bargaining over individual bargaining and in the process have created a value judgment on the part of most citizens of western democracies that collective bargaining is good.

At first, however, the public sector was exempt from the direct application of this doctrine. Instead, substitutes were found. Essentially, these were civil service type systems in which standards for judging merit were established and procedures were followed in order to eliminate favoritism. It was assumed that those who directed activities in the public sector, free from the insidious pressures of the profit motive of the private sector, would act in a fashion that would eliminate the need for collective bargaining by public employees. But this need has not been eliminated. Public sector employees have said that they want the right to be consulted, and, in many instances, the further right to bargain about the work they perform. The transfer of values from the private to the public sector is not a surprising phenomenon. Its significance tends to be overlooked, however, because it is occurring gradually, and as yet, the changes that are implied have not been fully comprehended.

Twenty-five years ago, conventional wisdom suggested that it was not appropriate for public employees at the federal, state and local levels to engage in collective bargaining. Today, conventional wisdom suggests the contrary and calls attention to the inevitability of this development. Although it may seem trite to call attention to this change in values, it should be noted that many problem areas are regarded as problem areas primarily because the methods traditionally used to resolve them are consonant with the value system of the past rather than that currently being formed.

Despite the risk of grossly oversimplifying the problem, one can characterize it as the replacement of the principle of "sovereignty" by that of "essentiality." No longer is there reliance on the idea that actions cannot be permitted because they threaten the sovereignty of the public employer. Instead, this has been superseded by dependence on the idea that actions can be prohibited in the public interest if they threaten the health and safety of the community. This new value judgment is not yet well identified and is still in the process of change.

Most threats to health and safety are being defined broadly today by judges and government officials to include any stoppage of services which inconveniences and irritates important voting blocs sufficiently to have adverse political consequences. Actions which do not endanger health or safety, but which are legally classified in that category in order to minimize irritation, may have to be endured if, in the future, the community is to be protected from stoppages that actually threaten its health or safety. A few court decisions in the past few years have reflected a less sweeping and more accurate definition of threats to health and safety, and may exemplify the position that will prevail in the future. For example, the Michigan Supreme Court denied injunctive relief in a situation in which the employer had not demonstrated that irreparable damage to the public health and safety would be caused by a teacher strike.[2]

In addition to this problem of changing values, however, there is another, distinctly different, set of problems which are relevant whether we are discussing the United States, a socialist or communist industrialized nation, or even one of the newly developing countries. These are the problems which arise out of the relationship between the individuals who perform the work and the individuals who supervise them. In all societies, decisions must be made about what work is to be done, how it is to be carried out, how hard individuals will be required to work and how much they will be paid for their efforts. Regardless of the way in which the enterprise is organized, individuals doing the work develop their own norms and, by a variety of tactics, attempt to introduce those norms into systems designed by the managers.

Essentially, the second underlying point being raised here is that, even in the absence of collective bargaining, workers have historically formulated norms of output and patterns of performance which in turn have influenced the ways in which the directors of enterprises have been able to carry out their tasks. The extension of collective bargaining to the public sector means that the framework for making such decisions has been changed and that there has been an explicit recognition that such decisions are bilateral in nature.

SUMMARY OF COLLECTIVE BARGAINING SYSTEMS

The various public sector bargaining systems for federal, state and municipal employees of different types are modeled after the private sector system, although there are significant differences. In both the private and public sectors, the ground rules for bargaining are outlined in a statute or executive order and one or more administrative agencies are created to interpret the legislation and administer its operation.

These statutes and agencies must define the classes of employers and employees to be covered and determine the appropriate bargaining units for such covered employees. Once units are determined, the agency then must interpret the provisions of the statute in regard to such problems as the scope of bargaining. For example, is bargaining to be confined to working conditions, or to wages and working conditions, but not fringes such as pensions? There are also procedural problems to be faced, e.g., whether the parties are obligated to bargain in good faith and what penalties may be imposed if it is found that one side or the other has committed an unfair labor practice.

If the parties are able to reach agreement and have negotiated a labor contract, the contract usually contains a provision for airing and resolving problems of contract interpretation. This mechanism, typically identified as a girevance and arbitration procedure, requires the use of a neutral third party if the parties are not able to reach agreement. An administrative agency generally plays a role in establishing rosters of neutrals and procedures by which the parties can select a neutral when needed.

In addition, in both the private and public sectors, there is a statutory framework and set of administrative rules for the resolution of disputes arising over the terms of a new agreement. The problems of which set of rules and what framework is appropriate for use in various portions of the public sector are the ones on which this paper is focussed and to which attention is directed in subsequent sections.

TOOLS FOR USE IN DISPUTE RESOLUTION

Before examining the present state of public sector dispute resolution, the various tools are listed and briefly explained and the situation in the private sector is summarized. Some of these tools are well known and need little explanation; others are mentioned in the literature but have not been applied in practice or, possibly, have had only limited use.

Mediation

The most uncontroversial tool is mediation.[3] To some degree its uncritical acceptance stems from the fact that it is private and noncoercive, and therefore can be safely ignored if so desired. Mediation is usually undertaken by full-time government staff who specialize in this activity. Mediation itself consists of attempting to prevent one of the parties from breaking off negotiations, persuading the parties to make or to listen to new proposals, and suggesting compromises and alternative solutions to the problems which have caused the parties to reach an impasse.

Traditionally, mediation proceedings are confidential. Each side is encouraged to give the mediator the full explanation of its position with the understanding that he will not relay to the other side any information other than that which the party wants relayed. It is also assumed that the mediator will face the general public and assuage it with statements such as: "The parties have engaged in a lengthy and profitable session but as yet have not reached agreement," but will not disclose the exact nature of the dispute. It would be considered a *faux pas* in most situations if the mediator were in any way to suggest that one side was being unreasonable. Like all generalizations, however, this one has exceptions, e.g., when a mediator sees no alternative and may endanger his long-run relationship with one party in order to bring pressure on it to change its position.

It should be noted that mediation is regarded as a minimal form of outside interference and is usually tried first or in combination with other more coercive tools. Mediation is used in the private sector as well as in federal, state and local government labor negotiations. It is also used in disputes outside of the labor field, such as in race relations, and in some instances involves *ad hoc* mediators or staff members of nonprofit, nongovernmental agencies.

Factfinding

Another widely used tool is called factfinding, although the term itself is regarded by many people as a misnomer for the actual process involved. Factfinding is usually carried out by an eminent neutral who has been appointed by a government agency on an *ad hoc* basis to help resolve a particular dispute. The factfinder has some other regular occupation such as lawyer, university professor or grievance arbitrator. In contrast to mediation, it is supposedly a public process designed to bring pressure to bear on the parties.

The usual procedure followed after the factfinder is appointed is for him to hold a public hearing at which the parties enumerate the items on which they cannot agree and present evidence in support of their positions. After the presentation of evidence, they make oral arguments or, in some instances, forego the oral argument and submit written post-hearing briefs. The factfinder studies the evidence, considers the arguments, and then issues a report discussing the issues and recommending solutions to each one. Usually, these are advisory recommendations unless the parties have agreed to be bound by them.

In many situations, factfinders engage in mediation, particularly when there are many items in dispute and it appears impractical to make recommendations to resolve all of them. The actual factfinding hearing may be formal and resemble a courtroom procedure or may be informal, depending on the wishes of the parties, the particular statute authorizing the use of factfinding, and the style that each individual factfinder prefers. The factfinding recommendations are a blend of the judicial and the practical. The factfinder is influenced by considerations of equity and criteria in the statute (if any are specified) but, since his recommendations are advisory rather than mandatory, must also take into account the acceptability of his recommendations by the stronger party. Theoretically, the issuance of the factfinding recommendations furnishes the parties and the public at large with a standard by which to judge the dispute and to bring pressure to bear to resolve it on that basis.[4]

Factfinding is used primarily in the public sector for the resolution of disputes involving municipal employees. Normally, it is not used in the private sector where the parties are free to strike. The right to strike is protected in the private sector and is the method relied upon for resolving private sector disputes about the terms of a new agreement. In the public sector, however, where for the most part strikes are outlawed, access to factfinding has been introduced as a substitute mechanism for dispute resolution.

One variant of factfinding that should be noted in passing is the use of factfinding without recommendations in the resolution of national emergency disputes. In those situations a board of inquiry ascertains the facts relevant to the dispute and submits these to the President of the United States, who in turn submits them to Congress with recommendations of his own for resolution of the dispute. In actual practice, boards tend to make recommendations and engage in mediation but, technically, the law limits the authority of the board to finding facts.[5]

Arbitration

A third tool for resolving disputes is arbitration. In a procedural sense, arbitration resembles factfinding. The arbitrator is usually hired on an *ad hoc* basis, has some other primary occupation, and is selected by the parties from candidates submitted by some government or nonprofit agency. As in factfinding, the parties attend a hearing, present evidence and arguments or written post-hearing briefs. One significant difference between the procedures arises from the fact that an arbitration award is binding whereas a factfinding recommendation is advisory. Therefore the arbitrator need not give the same degree of attention to acceptability as he might be inclined to do if his decision were only advisory.

Arbitration, like factfinding, is considered an alternative to the strike. Although it is not common for statutes to provide for the use of arbitration upon petition of either party after an impasse has been reached, arbitration is provided for in the federal statute covering postal employees and in approximately a dozen states, usually for disputes involving firefighters and policemen. The private sector statute does not provide for arbitration although the parties may voluntarily renounce their right to strike and resort instead to arbitration if they so desire. For example, the United Steel Workers Union and ten major steel companies recently adopted an experimental negotiating agreement which provided for the arbitration of certain unresolved items if it became necessary.[6]

Arbitration is usually invoked as a last resort following mediation and possibly also factfinding. For example, Congress has authorized arbitration of disputes on the railroads when all other prior attempts to resolve the dispute have failed. There are various forms of arbitration, some of which are attracting considerable attention at present. One of these is called *med-arb*, which is a contraction of the words mediation and arbitration. This is a process in which the parties: "agree in advance that all decisions, whether reached by mediation or arbitration become part of the mediator-arbitrator's award and are final and binding. None of the decisions go back to the parties for acceptance or rejection."[7]

Another form of arbitration hs been identified as final-offer arbitration. Under this arrangement the arbitrator is limited to choosing the offer of either management or labor as a whole without modification.[8] He may not select a compromise position as would be possible under conventional arbitration. A variation of final-offer arbitration was adopted by the Michigan legislature in dealing with disputes of firefighters and policemen. Under that statute, the arbitrator must choose the position of either party on *each* economic issue,[9] in contrast to the all-or-nothing situation in Wisconsin.

Other Dispute Settlement Tools

In addition to mediation, factfinding, and various forms of arbitration used alone or in combination with other techniques, several other procedures have been suggested in the literature about dispute resolution and some have been tried in the private or public sector. These include the nonstoppage strike, continuous bargaining, and the use of the referendum. A nonstoppage strike is one in which the workers continue to work but receive progressively less pay as the strike continues. In turn the employer is also penalized comparable amounts in order to increase his incentive to reach a settlement.[10]

Continuous bargaining, as the name implies, consists of bargaining during the life of the agreement and voluntarily amending the terms of the agreement prior to its expiration date. It differs from conventional crisis bargaining in which settlements are reached only after threat of a strike and at the last possible moment. This form of bargaining was attempted in the steel industry in the early part of the last decade.[11] The referendum is discussed by Wellington and Winter as a possible tool for use in resolving municipal labor disputes. They note that a group such as the San Francisco Chamber of Commerce can threaten to circulate petitions for such a referendum as a means of persuading public employees to moderate their demands.[12]

Strikes

To complete the litany of dispute resolution procedures, mention should be made of the strike. In the private sector this is the usual way in which disagreements are resolved. Except when the national emergency dispute procedure is invoked, the strike is protected in the private sector as the legitimate means to be used by workers in pursuing better contract terms. In the public sector, however, the strike is banned in most jurisdictions and other procedures have been introduced as substitutes. Even so, in a few states (Hawaii, Pennsylvania and Alaska) some categories of public employees have been given the right to strike, subject to certain constraints.

PRESENT STATE OF PUBLIC SECTOR DISPUTE RESOLUTION

At present, public sector dispute resolution is in flux. Descriptions which are accurate today soon become obsolete. Furthermore, the changes being introduced are not uniformly applied. Different paths are being followed by different government bodies, and different procedures are being devised for application to different occupations.

Police and Firefighters

Municipal law enforcement and fire protection services have their own pattern. Originally, police unionism was actively discouraged by municipal management. When this tactic did not succeed, policemen learned that, although they had the constitutional right to form unions, they did not have the right to force recalcitrant employers to bargain with them in the absence of legislation requiring the employer to do so. Firefighter unionism did not encounter the same degree of resistance and has progressed further than police unionism. But, because both groups are considered to be essential, military-type discipline organizations, regulated by the same commission, they tend to be treated alike when labor relations legislation is being formulated.

When legislation was first passed in some states it provided policemen and firefighters with the right to petition neutral third parties for advisory opinions. After a few years' experience with this procedure, protective service employee organizations became dissatisfied, and then, contrary to other groups such as teachers, rejected the use of the strike and turned instead to arbitration. Some strong firefighter or police unions have secured this right to refer disputes to arbitration.

In localities where police and firefighter unionism is weak, there is either no legislation, or legislation that culminates in factfinding. In other localities, such as Illinois, firefighter and police unions in the larger cities engage in collective bargaining without the benefit of statutory protection. A survey of the country would find thousands of police and firefighters in each of these situations. Even so, the trend in recent years seems to be toward reliance on arbitration, although only about twelve states have reached that point.

Teachers

In the last fifteen years, the legal framework for resolving disputes involving teachers has changed substantially, but teacher union attitudes have changed to an even greater degree. Only a minority of the fifty states have passed statutes giving teachers the right to form unions, request certification elections, file unfair labor practice charges, and use third-party help in the resolution of disputes about the terms of new agreements. Despite this, however, bargaining has spread rapidly.

The third-party procedure included in most statutes enacted in the 1960s included mediation and factfinding, procedures which were endorsed by the teacher organizations at that time. More recently, teachers have tended to ignore factfinding in some situations and instead have struck or threatened to strike.[13] In states in which there are no bargaining statutes covering teachers but where the teachers' union is strong, teachers have undertaken to strike in order to gain higher wages and other improvements in their contracts.

For these reasons it is difficult to characterize the present stage of teacher bargaining. In some states without legislation, strong teacher unions are solving impasses by means of strikes. In other states without legislation where teacher unions are weak, very little bargaining may take place. In still other states which have passed legislation including the use of factfinding to resolve disputes, the procedure is being ignored by strong unions and is being relied upon by weak ones. This varied situation may lead teachers to turn to the system used in the Canadian Federal Service under which employees may choose between arbitration and the right to strike, options which are considered at some length later in this paper.

Other Municipal Employees

The bargaining framework for other municipal employees is similar to the situation covering teachers, described above. Typically, there is either no legislation or legislation that provides for factfinding as the terminal step for the resolution of disputes about the terms of a new agreement. And, like teachers, strong unions of municipal employees in park, street, and sanitation departments have turned to the strike regardless of whether it is illegal or whether they are entitled instead to initiate factfinding. Weaker unions may rely upon factfinding where it exists, while weak unions in jurisdictions where there is no legislative protection may not engage in bargaining or may do so in a somewhat restrained fashion and must be prepared after relatively brief discussion to accept the management offer.

In general it can be said that municipal management has not regarded municipal employment, except in the case of police and firefighters, as sufficiently essential to warrant consideration of arbitration. Nor have the unions pressed for arbitration because they believe that they should have the right to strike instead. In those states where legislation exists, it provides for factfinding but in recent years has gone unused, for the same reasons that the teachers have abandoned it.

Federal and Postal Employees

Civil service federal employees are covered by executive orders which, since 1962, have provided them with the right to engage in collective bargaining in a somewhat limited fashion. Bargaining was first introduced as a form of nonadversary employee participation. Subsequently this approach was amended to conform more closely to the patterns followed in other jurisdictions. It is important to note that the scope of bargaining in this sector is limited and that wages, pensions and items covered by civil service are excluded from bargaining.

Insofar as impasse resolution is concerned, the initial procedure terminated with a review of a factfinding decision by the cabinet officer in charge of the department. Subsequently this system of bargaining within a department without central controls was abandoned. Impasses in negotiating new agreements could be referred to a neutral impasse panel which could make binding awards subject to appeal to a top government management body composed of the Secretary of Labor, the Chairman of the Civil Service Commission, and a representative of the President. The terminal step under this procedure is more management-oriented than some of the other procedures previously discussed and may represent a transitory arrangement which will be abandoned in favor of one patterned after the one adopted for use in the postal service.

Postal employees were originally covered by the same system as civil service employees but were given separate and more favorable treatment by Congress after they engaged in a wildcat strike that spread across the nation. These employees have been covered by the private sector legislation for most purposes but have been given binding arbitration as the terminal step in the dispute resolution procedure. As yet it has not been invoked, but it is significant to note that the largest employer in the United States is subject to arbitration in the establishment of wages if the employer and the union cannot reach agreement.

The foregoing review of the type of dispute resolution procedure that exists for different occupational groups employed by different public sector bodies illustrates the diversity of procedures that have been adopted. It further shows that the actual practices may differ from those called for in the legislation. In general, a review of existing patterns shows that, despite the present preeminence of mediation and factfinding, there seems to be a trend toward arbitration or the right to strike or both. Before examining these two more extreme alternatives, the possible explanations for the declining use of mediation and factfinding are explored.

EVALUATION OF DISPUTE RESOLUTION TECHNIQUES

Mediation

For mediation to succeed, a corps of knowledgeable mediators is needed. They must be individuals with the personality and skill to persuade the parties to settle. One theory of mediation is based on the idea that the parties want to settle but that there is faulty communication between them and they are therefore unable to reach a mutually satisfactory point. Under these circumstances, the mediator is able to help by making the proposal as if it were his own suggestion; both parties can then agree to it without feeling that they had given into the other side. This fortuitous outcome does not happen too often except in new, small negotiations in which the bargainers are relatively unsophisticated.

More frequently, the mediator has the task of persuading one or both of the parties to reduce their actual goals and to come up with a new solution. He knows that the position of each side represents an amalgam of differing views and that in effect he has some support from some members of each team who are not enthusiastic supporters of the majority view. For example, some members of management who are concerned with hiring in a tight labor market may be pleased to make a further concession in the hiring rate—raising it may increase costs, but at least it makes hiring easier. The same spectrum of views exists on the union side—older workers may have different preferences than younger workers.

Also, the mediator must have a pocketful of new solutions that will permit the parties to gracefully slide from their present positions to ones that lead to settlements. For example, mediators can suggest that past service pension credits be funded over thirty years instead of twenty and that the money saved be used to provide extra vacation and holidays.

Over the years the task of the mediator becomes more difficult for several reasons: (1) the parties learn more about the process and eventually there are very few new solutions that a mediator can offer; (2) the parties may be communicating perfectly and do not need the mediator as a go-between; (3) for their own internal political reasons they may not want to reach a solution voluntarily; (4) most mediators have extensive private sector experience but limited public sector experience and are handicapped by lack of knowledge about the industry. Probably the most important reason, however, that mediation will not be accepted as the terminal step of a procedure is that the mediator lacks power and the procedure itself lacks finality.

There appears to be a continuing role for mediation in the public sector similar to the one that it fills in the private sector. It is a way of assisting smaller, less knowledgeable managements and unions. Also, mediators are able to serve as face-savers in situations where neither management nor union negotiators can afford to initiate compromises. But mediation, standing alone, is insufficient. In the private sector, it is followed by strikes when agreement is not reached. In the public sector there must also be some additional tool which follows mediation and can be used to resolve disputes which could not be mediated.

Factfinding

Factfinding is the dispute resolution tool that usually is invoked in the public sector after mediation fails. Unfortunately, factfinding also suffers from the same lack of finality as does mediation. Typically, it has been found that unions and managements in the public sector accept most recommendations of the factfinder. Initially, partial acceptance of the recommendations was not of great concern to unions or managements who attempted in turn to bargain up or down from the recommendations but found them useful as a basis for settlement. Over the years, however, some unions have claimed that management acceptance of factfinding recommendations was diminishing and that it was pointless to use the procedure if management would not abide by the results.

Management, in turn, would point to strong unions that struck instead of initiating factfinding procedures as provided for in the statute. In any event, without assessing where the blame lies, it is fair to conclude that factfinding is a tool with limited life and that its lack of finality will lead to its abandonment. The fault may not lie in the technique, per se, but may flow from the fact that it only fits in an environment in which unions are not militant and public employers regard factfinding recommendations in the same light as judicial findings.

It also should be pointed out that unions have found that the cost of going to factfinding is about the same as that of going to arbitration. Therefore, if they pay the same amount for each type of third party judgment, they might as well seek a judgment that is binding on management. If they win, management must comply instead of bargaining down. Management, in turn, would prefer a less restrictive advisory decision to a binding one.

It should be noted that, despite its lack of finality, factfinding may play a significant role when it is coupled with either the right to strike as in the recently enacted health care industry legislation, or where it is followed by arbitration, as is the case in the amended New York City procedure. This suggests that the importance of an advisory tool such as factfinding is increased by being put into the next-to-last position in contrast to being the terminal step.

Traditionally, however, it has been thought that the addition of an extra step tends to diminish the importance of what was formerly the last step. It appears, however, that this generalization is one that should be reconsidered. For example, if a school board in a rural area in which the union is weak decides to reject most of the factfinder's recommendations, and this is the last step in the procedure, there is little that the union can do about this board action. If, instead, the union had the right to petition an agency to appoint an arbitrator to decide whether the previously issued factfinder's recommendations should be made binding on the parties or amended in some fashion, the board might have been willing initially to accept the factfinder's recommendations more fully.

Critics of such a multi-stage hearing procedure might suggest that the parties would agree to omit the factfinding step and proceed directly to arbitration. It is doubtful that public managements would find such a step desirable and probably would resist it. Also, by statute or administrative rulings, the procedure can be arranged so that access to arbitration requires that the parties first try to resolve the dispute through factfinding. Finally, it should be noted that, to the degree the arbitrator takes cognizance of the factfinding recommendations issued in the case before him, he can be expected to follow along the same path rather than to carve new ground. This tendency would further increase the significance of factfinding. (The recently enacted Massachusetts statute covering police and firefighters provides a multistep hearing procedure of this nature in which binding arbitration follows factfinding if a dispute is not resolved.)

Arbitration

The usual charge against the use of arbitration to resolve disputes about the terms of new agreements is that it causes collective bargaining to atrophy. In effect, it is seen as a substitute for bargaining—one to which the weaker party will turn quickly and repeatedly in preference to bargaining. Many years ago Secretary of Labor Willard Wirtz said, in support of this line of reasoning: "experience—particularly the War Labor Board experience during the '40s—shows that a statutory requirement that labor disputes be submitted to arbitration has a narcotic effect on private bargaining, that they turn to it as an easy—and habit forming—release from the obligation of hard, responsible bargaining."[14]

More recent experience, however, challenges this conclusion. Although it may be premature to call any of the arbitration experiments successful, the so-called "narcotic" effect has not emerged as a significant problem in such states as Pennsylvania, Michigan and Wisconsin in the three or more years that each of these states has permitted arbitration as a means of resolving firefighter and police disputes. Furthermore, it should be noted that for some time several scholars have questioned on theoretical grounds the ready acceptance of the idea that arbitration spells the end of bargaining.[15]

Even though there is not current evidence to support the charge that the advent of arbitration spells the end of bargaining, there is the question of what mixture of bargaining and arbitration is best. Is it better if only 1 percent of the disputes are resolved by arbitration, rather than 10 percent, or 20 percent, or is the 1 percent figure too low? For example, it could be argued that the process is too costly and that a record of 1 percent suggests that small unions do not use arbitration because of cost considerations. To the degree that a high value is placed on self-settlement, it can be argued that a low percentage is superior to a higher one. But, such arguments probably apply to comparisons on the order of 10 percent usage in contrast to 30 percent usage.

One possible standard against which to measure the use of arbitration is the use of the strikes in the private sector. There, it is believed that a few strikes are needed to make the threat of a strike credible enough to force the parties to agree. In the private sector, there are about 3,000 such strikes in the negotiation of about 50,000 agreements annually—the strike occurs in approximately 6 percent of the situations. This is a rough estimate and it is preferable to suggest that in the private sector, strikes occur in about 5 to 10 percent of the annual contract negotiations.

In a forthcoming study of the impact of arbitration on the bargaining process and outcome, based on a sample of police and firefighters in Pennsylvania, Michigan and Wisconsin, it was found that arbitration was used to resolve disputes in 10 to 30 percent of the negotiations, depending on the year, the state, the type of arbitration involved, and the nature of the processes that preceded it.[16] This utilization rate exceeds the strike rate and quite possibly means that the effect of arbitration on the process and outcome of bargaining differs from that of the strike. However, research efforts have not yet enabled us to make a definitive statement about such differences. Remarks about this point are therefore limited to speculative generalizations which may not hold up when further information is obtained. With that caveat in mind, attention is directed to further criticisms of arbitration.

Another alleged defect in arbitration is that it takes authority away from appointed or elected managers and as such is inefficient. This criticism differs from the old saw of improper delegation. Presumably, that question is settled—governments can legally delegate wage setting authority to arbitrators and give them statutory standards for guidance. The question posed here is whether or not this delegation to an arbitrator so weakens the management authority structure that it causes inefficiency.

Despite claims of management that it may do this, there is little evidence offered in support of the claim. It should be kept in mind that once the concept of collective bargaining has been adopted, the authority pattern is modified and arbitration only involves a further minor shift. The authority of management is subject to challenge by the union under a system of collective bargaining and the granting of the final word to an arbitrator may not represent a further erosion. It may even strengthen management in situations where it faces a very strong union.

One question frequently raised about arbitration is whether unions will comply with awards. On the whole, the answer seems to be that they will.

Noncompliance is rare and where it has occured it has taken the form of avoiding the arbitration procedure, rather than striking in defiance of an award. Possibly this excellent record is attributable to the fact that unions usually have been the driving force in securing the adoption of the arbitration system by state legislatures and therefore have felt morally bound to go along with the results of the system. If arbitration were imposed over the objections of the union covered by the procedure, they well might not go along with it and noncompliance would then be a serious problem.

Another criticism of arbitration is that it might change the wage patterns and possibly raise wages more than would otherwise be the case. One possible effect is that arbitration will not affect wages on the average very much, but it will reduce the dispersion. The existence of arbitration may make it more difficult for pattern setters to establish new patterns and to innovate—because of the weight given to comparisons of wages and fringes paid elsewhere—but it also will help unions in situations where they have lagged behind the pack. It should be noted at this point that there are a variety of arbitration arrangements and they may have different consequences.

Final-offer arbitration on individual economic issues—which is carried out on an issue-by-issue basis—should deter usage of arbitration to a greater degree than conventional arbitration. The all-or-nothing effect associated with unmodified final-offer arbitration should, at least theoretically, pose the greatest deterrent to the use of arbitration. Initial applications of the three systems in Wisconsin, Michigan and Pennsylvania lends some support to this theory. It should be noted, however, that other differences in the procedure make it impossible to determine how much of the greater deterrent effect is associated with the form of arbitration and how much is associated with other differences in the procedures.

A further question about final-offer arbitration is whether it brings the parties closer together than conventional arbitration. A charge leveled against conventional arbitration is that it encourages the parties to hold firm, make no compromises and maintain a large gap between their positions with the hope that the arbitrator will favor a position in the middle—and the more extreme your position, the closer the arbitrator's position will be to your actual goal.

When the parties are faced with an arbitration in which the arbitrator must select that final offer which he believes to be the more reasonable, the pressure is on each party to come a little closer than his opponent to the solution which he thinks the arbitrator will regard as the more equitable. If the management thinks that the arbitrator would find a 6 percent wage increase to be proper, and the union is asking for 10 percent, it might decide to defend 4½ percent, calculating that it could safely win at that level.

If the union, however, were asking 8 percent, the city might decide to argue for 5 percent, and if the union were asking for 7 percent, the city might well want to offer 5½ percent. Theoretically, this pressure to converge will lead the parties to settle without arbitration. But even if they do not settle, the nature of the process should make the gap smaller than in conventional arbitration where just the opposite pressure prevails.

Under some circumstances, final-offer arbitration by each issue may not differ appreciably from conventional arbitration, while in others it may not differ from final-offer package arbitration. Where it stands depends on the number of issues and the degree to which tradeoffs are possible between issues. For example, if the union is asking for more holidays and more vacation time, the arbitrator in a final-offer-by-issue case could grant one of the two demands and thereby make an award that had identical financial consequences as a conventional arbitration award in which the arbitrator reached a compromise position on each issue. On the other hand, if there were only one issue at stake, there would be no difference between a final-offer package and final-offer by each issue, but both would differ substantially from conventional arbitration.

One criticism voiced about final-offer arbitration is that it may force the arbitrator to choose between two unreasonable positions—or at least between two offers which each contain undesirable items.[17] There does not seem to be a ready answer to this defect except to note that it is the price the parties pay for failure to resolve the dispute themselves and thereby avoid the use of arbitration. And, the higher the price of failing, the more likely the parties are to avoid the use of arbitration and the situation in which this problem can arise. In Wisconsin, for example, this problem has arisen in fewer than six cases in a three-year period, during which about 400 police and firefighter contracts were renegotiated under a final-offer arbitration system. This suggests that the problem, although perplexing when it appears, is not likely to appear very often.

Another form of arbitration which has occasioned comment in recent years is "med-arb." As explained previously, when med-arb is used in the private sector, it means that at the outset of negotiations the parties have voluntarily agreed to forego the strike or lockout and instead to be bound by the terms of an award made by a neutral person whom they have selected. This format excludes the rank and file from participation through the ratification procedure because the award is binding upon the parties and does not require membership approval to become effective.

Med-arb is a powerful tool and is rarely used in the private sector for several reasons. The parties are reluctant to give up their right to use economic pressure and to reduce membership participation in negotiations. Also, few neutrals have sufficient experience and acceptability to be granted this power by the parties. It was used successfully in the 1970 San Francisco Bay area nurses negotiations and perhaps will turn out to be particularly suited for use in essential industries in which there have been strikes in the past and in which the parties wish to avoid another round of strife.[18]

Med-arb differs from voluntary arbitration in that the parties expect the arbitrator to mediate most issues and to issue an award which reflects, for the most part or entirely, agreements reached by the parties themselves. The mediator is able by judicious hints and prompting to persuade one or both of the parties that a particular position should be abandoned and that the arbitrator would be more inclined to support one of the parties if it took a more moderate position. Sam Kagel, the neutral most closely associated with the development of this procedure, stresses that it is primarily mediation and works because the mediator has clout—that is, the ability to make a binding award gives the mediator sufficient authority to be persuasive on most issues.

Med-arb in the public sector could be carried ou in the same fashion as it is in the private sector if the parties agreed to try the procedure. It is more likely to occur, however, in jurisdictions in which the statute calls for binding arbitration. Under that situation, med-arb only means that the arbitrator spend some time attempting to persuade the parties that they should work out some or all of the issues themselves rather than force him to issue an award. Theoretically, agreed-upon awards are superior to imposed awards because the parties are more likely to agree upon solutions which cause no subsequent administrative problems and because the parties are thought to be more willing to abide by solutions which they helped to devise, rather than solutions designed by a third party.

The success of med-arb when tried in the public sector in a situation in which the statute calls for arbitration and makes no mention of med-arb will depend on the degree to which one values agreed-upon settlements relative to imposed settlements. By mediating, the arbitrator may be weakening the bargaining process that preceded the *ad hoc* med-arb effort. The parties may not try as hard as they otherwise might if they know that the arbitrator subsequently will be conducting confidential mediation sessions at which they make concessions in order to gain their objectives on other items.

An interesting variant of med-arb has been tried in a few instances in Michigan where the statute covering police and firefighters provides for final-offer arbitration by economic issue and also for a tripartite panel. In that situation the panel members representing each side have the opportunity to sound out the neutral arbitrator in an executive session and then amend their final offers to conform more closely to a position favored by the neutral.[19] Although this same format could be followed if conventional arbitration were involved, the neutral arbitrator seems to have greater mediating power when he is prevented by statute from selecting a compromise position and can only select such a position if one of the parties adopts it as its amended final offer.

Med-arb also could be tried if the statute calls for final-offer package arbitration and permits amendment at the hearing. It may be difficult to amend final offers at a public hearing, and it should be noted that the tripartite panel arrangement facilitates mediation by the panel members in executive session. Theoretically, the neutral has even greater mediatory power in dealing with the partisan arbitration panel members under a system which requires that he must choose between one package or the other, rather than do so for each issue, or compromise as he sees fit as under conventional arbitration. The partisan panel member runs the risk of losing everything if he is not responsive to the hints of the neutral when the system requires the neutral to pick one final offer in its entirety without modification.

A quite different approach to the question of how well the various forms of arbitration work emphasizes their nonuse and gives little weight to whether the settlement is an agreed-upon one as in med-arb, or an imposed one, as is the case when the arbitrator does not mediate but functions in a judicial manner. From this point of view, an arbitrator should not mediate. If the parties have not resolved their dispute and have referred it to him, he should protect the integrity of the procedure and render his award in arm's-length proceedings based on evidence presented in open session. If the award turns out to be punitive because the arbitrator must choose the final offer of one of the contending parties, and both offers contain unsatisfactory elements, the party that loses presumably will learn a lesson and in the future will bargain more effectively and be less likely to go to arbitration again; if forced to arbitration again this party may formulate a much more sensible final offer that will be devoid of unreasonable elements.

Considerable attention has been devoted here to various potential problems associated with the use of arbitration. It should be noted, however, that in actual current practice experience with these procedures is rather limited, and many of these potential problems have not emerged or only rarely have been troublesome. An overall judgment on the use of arbitration, however, will not be attempted here until the alternative to it—the right to strike—has been explored. The question facing society is not whether arbitration is a good tool to use but whether it is better than alternative tools to resolve disputes in particular public sector industries and occupations. We now turn, therefore, to a consideration of the use of strikes to resolve public sector disputes.

Strikes

The basic theoretical argument for the strike is that the threat of a strike is needed to compel agreement of the parties. This is the private sector model. Advocates of it simply argue that it can be transferred intact to the public sector. Opponents of this position argue that this is unsound because of the differences between the public and private sectors. The primary difference cited by those who would not adopt the private sector model is the absence of the profit mechanism. A strike in the private sector reduces the income of the entrepreneur while leaving him with some fixed costs. His loss of sales and profit may make him more ready to settle, just as the workers' loss of wages may make them more tractable.

In the public sector, closing down a public facility may inconvenience the public and in some instances may have substantial economic side effects, but usually the employer does not suffer loss of income. In fact, just the reverse occurs; he saves money. A teacher strike, for example, may balance a budget that was in a slight deficit position.

Another argument raised by those who oppose the use of the private sector model is that the government service is more likely to be a monopoly, a service for which there may not be alternative sources—police and fire service for example. This argument is not as persuasive as the first. There are also many services provided by private employers for which there may not be easily substitutable sources. For example, some cities rely on private firms for local transportation and for garbage disposal.

Also, the substitutability argument is in part intertwined with the question of essentiality. There are no close substitutes for a public library, but there is little objection raised to suggestions that librarians be given the right to strike. It seems more likely that the willingness to give librarians the right to strike stems not from any considerations of substitutability but rather from considerations of nonessentiality.

If one directly faces the question of essentiality, the conclusion may well be the one adopted in Alaska in which employees in those services deemed nonessential are given the right to strike. But essentiality is difficult to define. In Montana, nurses at a public hospital can strike provided that there are alternate hospitals to which patients can be referred. Also, essentiality will depend upon the degree to which a skeleton labor force of supervisors can maintain a minimum level of service which will eliminate the danger to the health and safety of the community even though the reduced services will cause a good deal of inconvenience.

It should be admitted, however, that even if it were possible to make distinctions among vital, less essential, and nonessential services and to give those in the last category the unrestricted right to strike, those in the middle a limited right to strike, and those in the first category no right to strike, such a system might be inequitable. In effect, society would be saying to individuals in the last group that their services would not be missed and therefore they may have the right to strike. But such a right is meaningless if the effect of withholding their services makes little or no difference. Finally, it should be noted that, conceptually, the granting of the right to strike is an admission of a failure to devise a satisfactory substitute and quite possibly establishes a more adverse model of bargaining than is necessary.

Proponents of the right to strike in the public sector raise a quite distinct and separate argument which needs examination. They argue that if public employees have the right to strike, they will be less likely to use this right for two reasons: (1) they will be aware that they will not be rescued by a judge who will order them back to work; (2) an employer will be more willing to make a fair offer if he knows that his employees can strike. The first consideration may be more than compensated for by eliminating the deterrent effect of breaking the law. That is, the fact that the strike is illegal may prevent a greater number of strikes than are created in instances where workers undertake them, secure in the knowledge that they will be ordered back to work by a judge. In any event there is no evidence on which to judge the merits of these two positions.

As for the second argument, it is quite possible that the threat of third party arbitration may make an employer more willing to make a fair offer than the threat of a strike. For example, the negotiator for New York City said that in disputes involving what are known as management perogatives "the threat" of arbitration is an even greater spur to management's settlement motivation than a strike: "my fear of itinerant philosophers making judgments on policy determinations will likely keep my feet to the fire even longer than my fear of a walkout."[20]

Other Techniques

The use of "nonstoppage strikes" intrigues scholars but has little appeal to practitioners. A few instances of its use in the private sector have been reported, but the idea has not gained even limited acceptance. Its defect seems to be twofold. First, there are problems in designing penalty scales for each side which are comparable. How much revenue must be given up by an employer to match, for example, a 20 percent wage forfeit by employees? Second, if the escrow account into which penalty funds are diverted is one from which the parties cannot subsequently recapture all or part of the penalties when they eventually settle, they may be quite unhappy about making large donations to some third party, no matter how worthy it may be. If the funds can be recaptured, however, then the force of the penalty is greatly diminished and the plan no longer provides a powerful incentive to settle.

Continuous bargaining appeals to the rational side of all individuals—it is clearly much better to make decisions deliberately with full thought of their consequences than to make them in haste under pressure. However, very few adversaries will make the necessary concessions to enable them to reach agreement without such pressures. The ritual of bargaining is built on the notion that it takes the threat of an imminent strike to persuade both sides to finally retreat from positions that they have firmly advanced for many weeks.

A change from the customary, adversary type of crisis bargaining to a problem-solving, continuous-bargaining framework requires a basic change in attitudes on the part of both management and union. This has come about in some industries after extended strikes and the growth of the idea that there must be a better way of resolving disputes. If the change to continuous bargaining is made, however, there still must be some method of resolving disputes. In this framework, that method would appear to be arbitration. The ten major steel companies and the United Steelworkers Union have adopted such a system and, at least at present, it seems to be working well.[21]

Continuous bargaining has several drawbacks which should be noted. It requires that the employer be willing and able to suffer additional costs in return for the willingness of the union to settle early. For example, in the 1970 negotiations, Armour & Company and the Amalgamated Meatcutters and Butcher Workmen's Union agreed through informal, early, noncrisis bargaining to a settlement which was made effective about six months in advance of the scheduled contract termination date. In the steel industry, workers received a cash bonus payment for agreeing to forego the strike and to resolve matters by noncrisis negotiations subject to arbitration. The costs of advance settlement do not seem to be inordinate, however, and this should prove no barrier to wider adoption of this procedure.

Another problem is that the negotiators do not wish to bargain continuously, or at least they do not wish their constituencies to adopt a frame of mind which would require negotiators to resolve each problem as it arose by negotiating a change in the labor agreement. Both sides recognize that problems are constantly emerging and that there will always be some groups of workers who wish to renegotiate the contract. It is probably impractical to attempt to meet these constantly emerging and changing demands; yet if the fixed term agreement does not exist as a barrier to consideration of implementing changes immediately, rank and file groups can be expected to continually press for changes and in the process may promote a good deal of unrest on the shop floor.

Both of the above problems, however, seem minor compared to the basic one: bargaining today is a distributive problem—one side taking something from the other—rather than a mutually profitable problem-solving exercise. Until this basic attitude is modified, continuous noncrisis, nonadversary type bargaining will have only limited acceptance.

The current consensus about the use of the strike as the normal dispute settlement procedure is that most people regard strikes as wasteful and unwise. Politically, it does not seem to be acceptable today to most citizens.

In two instances where it has been adopted (Philadelphia and Hawaii school teachers), judicial interpretations of the law have been so restrictive that we really have not learned whether such a system is politically viable.

Factfinding seems to be falling out of favor because of its lack of finality. Nonstoppage strikes and possible use of the referendum are ideas which are not considered ready for center stage on grounds of impracticality. Continuous bargaining also falls into that category of interesting ideas that few people want to try.

For lack of a better alternative, it appears that arbitration of different types will be getting more and more attention in the coming years. In its few uses today in the United States, arbitration is working well; that is, compliance with awards is almost universal and its economic impact seems to be that of reducing wage dispersion in the way that the free market supposedly does when it is working well.

This does not mean that arbitration will be satisfactory in the long run. It is quite possible that there is no one ideal solution. Instead, we may oscillate between solutions. Strikes will be tried for a period, followed by arbitration for a period, and then, quite possibly, back to strikes or to some other substitute. Negotiators change, constituencies change, circumstances of management change, and the dispute resolution method that is appropriate today may be unsuitable tomorrow.

In any event, just as we sought substitutes for the use of the strike to settle questions of union recognition and grievances which arose during the life of an agreement—and to some degree we have been successful in that search—it seems we should continue to seek substitutes for economic strife in resolving arguments about the terms of new agreements in the public sector. Finally, it should be noted that there need not be a single solution: small cities may use different procedures than big ones; solutions that work for fire and police workers may not work for teachers, and procedures followed by counties and states may not be acceptable for application to federal employees.

REFERENCES

1. Quoted *in* Webb, Sidney, and Webb, Beatrice. *Industrial Democracy*. London, Longmans, Greens, 1920, p. 841.
2. *Holland School District* v. *Holland Education Association*, 380 Michigan 314, 157 N.W. 2d 206 (1968).
3. *See* Simkin, William E. *Mediation and the Dynamics of Collective Bargaining*. Washington, D.C., Bureau of National Affairs, 1971.
4. *See* Stern, James L. "The Wisconsin Public Employee Fact-Finding Procedure," *Industrial and Labor Relations Review*, 20:3-29, Oct. 1966.

5. Cullen, Donald E. *National Emergency Strikes* (ILR Paperback No. 7). Ithaca, N.Y. Cornell University, 1968.

6. Abel, I.W. "Basic Steel's Experimental Negotiating Agreement," *Monthly Labor Review*, 96:39-42, Sept. 1973.

7. Kagel, Sam. "Combining Mediation and Arbitration," *Monthly Labor Review*, 96:62, Sept. 1973.

8. Stern, James L. "Final-Offer Arbitration—Initial Experience in Wisconsin," *Monthly Labor Review*, 97:39-43, Sept. 1974.

9. Michigan Police-Fire Fighters Arbitration Act, Act 312 of Public Acts of 1969, as amended by Public Acts 1972, no. 127.

10. Sosnick, Stephen H. "Non-Stoppage Strikes: A New Approach," *Industrial and Labor Relations Review*, 18:73-80, Oct. 1964.

11. Healy, James J., ed. *Creative Collective Bargaining*. Englewood Cliffs, N.J., Prentice-Hall, 1965, pp. 192-243.

12. Wellington, Harry H., and Winter, Ralph K., Jr. *The Unions and the Cities*. Washington, D.C., The Brookings Institution, 1971, p. 200.

13. See, for example, Gatewood, Lucian B. "Factfinding In Teacher Disputes: The Wisconsin Experience," *Monthly Labor Review*, 97:47-51, Oct. 1974.

14. *Daily Labor Report*, Bureau of National Affairs, Washington, D.C., Feb. 1, 1963, p. F-2.

15. See, for example, Phelps, Orme W. "Compulsory Arbitration: Some Perspectives," *Industrial and Labor Relations Review*, 18:81-91, Oct. 1964; and Stevens, Carl M. "Is Compulsory Arbitration Compatible with Bargaining?" *Industrial Relations*, 5:38-52, Feb. 1966.

16. Stern, "Final-Offer Arbitration. . ." *op. cit.*, pp. 39-43.

17. Witney, Fred. "Final-Offer Arbitration: The Indianapolis Experience," *Monthly Labor Review*, 96:20-25, May 1973.

18. Kagel, *op. cit.*, pp. 62-63.

19. Rehmus, Charles M. "Is a 'Final-Offer' Ever Final?" *Monthly Labor Review*, 97:43-45, Sept. 1974.

20. Haber, Herbert L. "Alternatives in Public Sector: Factfinding with Binding Recommendations," *Monthly Labor Review*, 96:44, Sept. 1973.

21. Abel, *op. cit.*, pp. 39-42.

ROBERT E. BROWN
Assistant Director
Graduate School of Library Science
University of Illinois
Urbana-Champaign, Illinois

Negotiation Simulation

According to many participants at the 1974 Allerton Park Institute, perhaps the most memorable part of the conference was a seven-hour session simulating labor-management contract negotiations. In planning the Institute, we realized that there should be a portion of the conference which would give participants some kind of "hands on" experience in the collective bargaining area. Of all the activities in collective bargaining, the actual bargaining session lends itself best to simulation activity, and we were very pleased to be able to locate an existing project which could be adapted for use at the Institute. This project was an industrial contract negotiation simulation developed by the Division of Public Employee Labor Relations, Labor Management Services Administration, U.S. Department of Labor (U.S.D.L.). The U.S.D.L. not only agreed to let us reproduce their material free of charge, but also sent specialists to a preconference training session and to the actual conference.

The simulation session took place at the same point in the Institute as it appears in this volume—after the introductory papers and the papers dealing with special topics in collective bargaining, and before the concluding papers examining the implications of unionization for various types of libraries. By waiting until this point in the proceedings, we gave each participant time to develop a maximum knowledge of the nature of collective bargaining, and also provided a change of pace at a time when people might have been getting tired of sitting and listening.

The U.S.D.L. negotiation simulation was designed to utilize groups of approximately ten participants (five management and five union negotiators), each supervised by a moderator-facilitator. Since approximately 100 participants were expected at the conference, ten negotiation sessions would have to be held simultaneously. Since the U.S.D.L. could not be expected to provide a team of ten moderators, a group of Illinois librarians, administrators and doctoral students were trained to serve as moderators in a special two-day preconference training session three weeks before the Institute. This "each one teach one" prep session was supervised by Morris Sackman of the U.S.D.L., who guided us through the simulation session while sharing with us his vast experience in labor affairs. The training session ended with wrap-up discussion sessions for each negotiating team and a final plenary session. A problem became apparent during this session—the total negotation simulation took longer than the time allotted in the conference program. To resolve this problem the committee limited the number of issues to be negotiated, informed the participants that all of the issues listed need not be resolved if both negotiating teams agreed to the delay, drastically reduced the amount of planning time allowed the teams, and shortened the actual negotiating time somewhat. The simulation materials were to be given to the participants at registration two days before the simulation; several times during the conference they were reminded to read the materials. The committee felt that this procedure would make the participants better prepared than usual and would compensate for the shorter game time.

The simulation materials provided by the U.S.D.L. were reproduced and assembled into packets which included:

1. "Settle or Strike"—the basic document which describes the situation, provides extensive information, and sets the stage for the negotiation session. The information in this document will be paraphrased and quoted widely in this article.
2. Information privy to each negotiation team, which provided information about the five negotiators, outlined the company or union position on various issues, and presented other confidential information.
3. "Negotiation Issues"—this list included the following ten issues to be negotiated: contract duration, contracting out, grievance procedure, holidays, leaves of absence, management rights, seniority, union security, vacations and wages.
4. "Selected Contract Clauses"—a 28-page listing of recent contract clauses in seven of the above areas.
5. "Glossary of Collective Bargaining Terms"—listing 107 terms used in bargaining (prepared by the Labor Relations Training Center, Bureau of Training, U.S. Civil Service Commission).
6. "Background Profile"—each participant received a description of the particular role he was to play on his negotiation team.

Each institute participant received a total of sixty-seven pages of material on Sunday evening, with instructions asking that it be read before negotiations started at ten o'clock Tuesday morning. Although during this same period the participants were also exposed to five of the regular institute sessions, most people read the background information and were ready to play an active role in the negotiations. The following paragraphs summarize the simulation materials distributed and the general nature of the simulation process.

SIMULATION

Lastik Plastik, Inc. (LPI) is a small manufacturer of a variety of plastic products in Rapid Junction, a small midwestern city with a population of 20,000. LPI has 104 employees and is the smallest of nine light manufacturing factories in the city. Like most of the other companies, LPI had been without a union since it opened twelve years ago. Recently the company employees voted, by a small majority, to have the Amalgamated Workers Union (AWU) represent them in future negotiations with the company.

As the simulation begins, the two negotiating teams are preparing for their first face-to-face meeting following the election of union representatives. The management negotiation team consists of five men appointed by J. B. Swope, founder, president and chairman of the board of Lastik Plastik. These include:

E. B. Whitz, team spokesman and vice-president for administration and personnel, who has been with the company since its founding. Whitz is an engineer known among his coworkers as "the diplomat." He aspires to succeed Swope as president.

R. A. Artsworth, comptroller of LPI, a CPA and lawyer who has been with the company for five years. His concern with the negotiations is strictly economic; he has developed a reputation as being aloof and a cost-cutter (almost a skinflint). He may also be aspiring for advancement to president.

Bart Trab, production manager, who rose from a general shop operator to his present position at LPI in three years. Trab is an ex-Marine sergeant who tolerates no nonsense in the plant and who is not well liked by the employees.

J. C. Hitower, general foreman, who has spent eight years with LPI and is a life-long resident of Rapid Junction. He maintains excellent rapport with the employees and sees some positive influences of the union.

R. J. Russell, a line foreman who has spent five years with LPI. He is reserved, but articulate. He is company oriented but has no strong feeling about the union.

The negotiating team consists of three locally elected representatives plus two outside representatives of the union. These include:

C.B. Halloway, team spokesman, a lead machine maintenance mechanic with ten years service at LPI. He is a quiet person but an effective speaker, and he has worked for the union during the organizing campaign. He is respected by others.

L. M. Steinway, international representative, AWU. This is his first visit to Rapid Junction; he knows little about the plastics industry or LPI but is experienced and knowledgeable in negotiating union contracts. He is not opposed to a strike at this time.

P. King, district director, AWU. King has had twenty-eight years of union experience and is very familiar with other union contracts in the district, many of which he negotiated. He aspires to be president of the international union.

Wilbur Rosen, chief shop steward. Rosen is young, aggressive, strong and ambitious. He is the leader of the more militant group in the union. Rosen has been passed over twice for promotion, and this has turned him against the company. He favors a strike to strengthen his position.

A. Walker, department steward, 23 years old. Walker is active in church and 4-H work and admires Rosen for standing his ground. He is critical of the company management because of their lack of social conscience.

The following instructions were given to the participants:

This simulation has specific learning objectives, of which the primary one is to experience the dynamics of collective bargaining negotiations. Reality must be accomodated to these, and to the constraints of time. Consequently, certain assumptions must be made. For example, the number of issues which will be negotiated has been limited to conform to the limited time frame which is available to this seminar, and they have been generally identified. The assumption is that these are the critical issues which must be resolved if a strike is to be avoided. While this may, for example, diminish the reality of how the parties determine their proposals, it is a necessary trade-off.

Also the simulation is set in the private sector. There are two major reasons for this. One is to remove participants who are public sector oriented from that specific orientation. The other is to demonstrate the universal application of the principles, techniques and dynamics of negotiations. The primary purpose of this simulation is to expose participants to the dynamics of collective bargaining negotiations, not to prepare them for negotiations in which they will actually be participating. The issues that have been identified are, furthermore, equally applicable to most public sector bargaining.

Each team is permitted to make any reasonable use of the data and information to enhance its positions, as long as it does not contradict that data and information. As occurs in real-life collective bargaining, the interactions between the management and union teams and within the respective teams often determine whether the parties can reach agreement without a strike or lockout as they seek to resolve conflicting positions over critical issues. While both teams generally seek agreement without having to resort to strikes or lockouts, the ultimate outcome is an agreement except in rare cases where the relationship between the parties is totally terminated.

Strikes and lockouts, although occasionally unavoidable, are costly to both parties and to the public. Where the parties are unable to reach agreement directly by the parties themselves, there are three modes of neutral third party intervention available to assist them to reach agreement without resorting to strikes or lockouts. These are: mediation, factfinding and arbitration. This simulation provides for only one type of neutral third party intervention—mediation. The mediator role is incorporated in the Data Bank, and the mediator is known to the parties. A simulation leader will act as the mediator. Either or both parties may request the mediator to intervene, or the mediator may seek to determine the need for intervention and, if necessary, to suggest mediation without waiting for a request by either or both parties.

The Negotiations

Each of the twenty negotiating teams (ten union and ten management) were assigned a caucus room or area to which they were to return whenever it became necessary to discuss matters among themselves. Ten larger rooms with tables were designated as negotiating areas; seats around the tables were reserved for the team members and large name signs identified each negotiator.

Final instructions to the team informed them of a pending strike with a one o'clock deadline. Negotiations were to continue until the ten issues had been addressed and the differences between the negotiating teams resolved or until a strike occurred. The twenty teams of five immediately went to their caucus areas to plan their opening moves.

In caucus the teams ranked the ten issues to be negotiated in priority order and prepared their first offers. The simulation materials had provided the negotiators with extensive information concerning the present policies, salaries and benefits at LPI, as well as in the community and the plastics industry nationwide. Using this information and the sample contract clauses provided, all teams were able to present the opposition with numerous contract proposals.

Negotiations began when both teams had agreed on a time and usually started with simple statements of position and the introduction of the first offers by each team. This first step was followed by a return to the caucus areas, after which new across-the-table negotiating resumed. In general this process continued for the next three hours with only minor variations, although one labor team walked out of their negotiating room and stayed out for over an hour, returning only after an outside arbitrator was brought in.

E. B. Whitz and C. B. Halloway served as the primary spokesmen for their respective teams in nearly all cases. The other members of the teams made comments spontaneously or upon the request of the spokesmen. Occasionally other team members (especially Trab or Rosen), dominated a session or a caucus discussion. As time passed and the negotiation tended to center on the questions most difficult to resolve, arguments occurred more frequently between and within the teams. Most participants were able to stay in role and project the image intended.

The moderator-facilitator (simulation leader) assigned to each team played many roles—arbitrator, news media reporter, and various union and company figures. His primary function, however, was to keep the action moving (or to slow it if necessary) by injecting elements of change and reporting on hypothetical happenings outside the negotiations room. The moderator used a "media board" in each room to post newspaper articles, inflammatory statements from union members and company staff, and other items of public information. He also provided each team (or particular team members) with confidential information in the form of notes, letters or telegrams. Included in the typical messages to the teams were: a letter of encouragement from the president of the international union urging the team to go after a strong contract which would be helpful in organizing other plants in the industry and offering support from the union's well-endowed strike fund (used to strengthen the union team's position); a similar letter warning that another large local had just gone on strike and would probably drain the strike funds (used to weaken the union line); a note to Bart Trab (the tough production manager) from a shop foreman telling of suspected sabotage of shop machines and urging him to shut down the assembly line (used to antagonize the union team); two letters to the management team from a large buyer for a new line of faddish plastic toys (hulahoop-type items), the first offering a contract if production can begin at once, the second threatening to withdraw the offer if labor troubles develop (used to stimulate management to settle); an offer from a competitor to buy the company (Lastik Plastik) and hire the company officers (used to slow negotiations). These messages were limited only by the creativity of the moderator-facilitator and were used effectively in all teams.

The moderator-facilitator could, as mentioned earlier, assume the role of an arbitrator, offering his services to help resolve the issues if the teams reached a stalemate. Several teams used the services of the arbitrators toward the end of the session.

As the strike deadline drew closer the negotiations became more harried and the pressure for settlement increased. Some teams made concessions on formerly unresolvable issues and others reduced the tension by referring less pressing issues to joint committees—usually to report back within a month. A couple of teams settled tentatively with such vital issues as management rights and union security unresolved. Only one team (Team J) became hopelessly deadlocked—on wages and contract duration—and went on strike.

The contracts negotiated by the tem teams varied widely, as can be seen in Table 1. Ray Gilbert, the U.S.D.L. representative at the conference, told us this phenomenon occurs regularly, even when the teams are as heterogeneous and randomly assigned to roles as they were at the Institute. The issues in Table 1 marked "no change" are those for which both teams agreed to remain with the present company policy; "postponed" issues are those which were referred to a committee for later resolution.

Wrap-Up

At the end of the negotiating session the teams assembled in larger groups (three pairs of teams) to discuss the experience. Most participants were either exuberant and anxious to discuss the experience or were exhausted and ready to retire. An atmosphere of bedlam existed at the beginning of the discussion period, when the participants shed their role identities and were able to express their real feelings. There was great interest in what others thought and in why they had acted in certain ways. The discussion leaders were able to start organized reviews of the negotiation procedure only after the participants were allowed to "let off steam" for about twenty minutes. In this plenary session the positions held by the two opposing teams were analyzed, and the following questions explored: Which issues were most important to the union and which were vital to management? Why was this so? Why did one team give in on one issue and dogmatically cling to another? Which issues might apply directly to libraries, and how might the negotiations have differed in the public sector? The recapitulation period helped to pull together the various loose ends and provided an appropriate finale to this session.

I feel that involvement learning of all types is particularly useful. The particular simulation-role-playing experience employed at the Allerton Park Institute was especially effective and can be recommended as a primer in labor negotiations. Any group faced with the prospect of negotiating a first contract should consider using this or a similar training device. Among the advantages of simulation exercises in general are:

1. This method stimulates learning by creating an immediate need for specific knowledge and producing equally immediate feedback to the participant. The impending need created by the simulation motivates the participant to learn specialized vocabularies and to acquire new skills in a way nothing else can.
2. Simulation learning involves people; everyone becomes a participant and must contribute to the game. This encourages two-way communication

Team	Wages	Union Contract	Vacations	Management Rights	Grievances
A	8.2% across the board	Agency shop Check off	No change	Except as limited by union contract	48 hour cooling off 2 week filing limit 3 day response limit 2 step thru vice pres. Binding arbitration Shared cost
B	7% 1st year 7% 2nd & 3rd year if c.o.l.* exceeds 9%	Maintenance of membership Check off	No change Average weekly salary	Unchanged	3 step—union in 3rd step
C	8 % across the board	Modified union shop language to be agreed upon within 30 days	1 wk. after 6 mo. 2 wks. after 2 yrs. 3 wks. after 10 yrs.	Except as limited by this contract	2 step Step 1 on company time
D	c.o.l.* + 4% 1st year 4% 2nd year 2% 3rd year	No agreement reached	1 wk. after 6 mo. 2 wks. after 3 yrs.	Contract rights but shall not discriminate against union	2 step 96 hrs. released time to process Cost of arbitration decided by arbitration
E	19¢ across the board Reopen 2nd year for c.o.l.* 5¢ 3rd year	Agency shop Check off	No change	Except as limited by this contract	3 step with time limits Stewards involved at each step Arbitration with shared costs
F	15¢ across the board	Agency shop	No change	Postponed	3 step Unlimited steward time Arbitration costs paid by loser
G	10% across the board 4% c.o.l.*	Modified union shop	Average weekly salary	To be worked out by joint committee	5 step plan
H	25¢ 1st year Reopen 2nd year	Maintenance of membership Check off	2 wks. after 2 yrs. 3 wks. after 10 yrs. 4 wks. after 20 yrs.	Except as limited by union contract	4 step Binding arbitration Shared cost
I	15¢ across the board	Modified agency shop	2 wks. after 1 yr. 3 wks. after 10 yrs. 4 wks. after 15 yrs.	Except as limited by union contract	4 step Binding arbitration Loser pays costs
J	Impasse Union 20¢ Management 15¢	Agency shop Check off	2 wks. after 1 yr. 3 wks. after 10 yrs.	Except as limited by union contract	To be worked out by joint committee

*c.o.l. = cost of living

Table 1. Negotiated Contracts

NEGOTIATION SIMULATION

Contract Duration	Holidays	Leaves	Contracting Out	Seniority	Team
1 year	No change	No change	No job loss guarantee	Layoff, rehire, and promotion on seniority	A
3 years with wage reopener	No change	No change except union business	No job loss guarantee	Plant and dept. seniority	B
1 year	No change	No change	Postponed	Agency-wide basis for promotion and layoff	C
3 years	1 extra day	Postponed	Postponed	Postponed	D
3 years with wage reopener	No change	Postponed	Limited to major construction No layoff Can't undermine union	Postponed	E
To be settled later	Postponed	Postponed	Postponed	Postponed	F
2 years	8 days per year	Pregnancy 1 day mo. sick leave 3 day funeral	Full employment only	Joint committee to work out	G
2 years with wage reopener	1 extra day	Maternity	No job loss 6 month probation on new products	Layoff and promotion based on seniority	H
1 year	7 plus birthday	Maternity Sick leave to 60 days	Limited areas No job loss	Layoff and rehire on seniority 10 day posting	I
Impasse Union 1 yr. Management 2 yrs.	Postponed	Postponed	Postponed	Joint Committee to work out 50-50 productivity	J

and social and intellectual interaction, which helps participants learn from one another. The element of stress introduced by the adversary arrangement and the pending strike facilitates this learning.
3. "Learn by doing" techniques tend to aid retention of knowledge. Something learned and immediately reinforced by use (often repeated use) becomes more indelibly impressed on the mind.
4. Time can be controlled to suit the learning process. The developer of a simulation project can concentrate on certain time periods, prolonging or contracting them as best fits the needs of the project. In the labor negotiations simulation the time spent in face-to-face, across-the-table negotiations was, of course, much less than it would have been in actual practice, and time between the breaks to caucus and the subsequent return to the negotiation table could well have been weeks rather than minutes. However, the essential elements involved in hammering out a labor contract were present, even to the speeding up of progress as the remaining time diminished. It was evident that 90 percent of the progress toward a contract occurred in the final 10 percent of the time.

There are some inherent problems in simulation learning. These include:

1. Simulation learning requires preparation; those who enter the game without doing their homework cannot be worthwhile participants.
2. All people do not learn well in this way; for some, simulation exercises may not be effective. It is difficult for some people to change their learning mode; those who have always learned by the traditional methods of reading and lectures may have some adjustment problems.
3. The personality of the participants may limit the effectiveness of role-playing exercises. Not everyone is outgoing enough to actively participate, and we know that some people are better actors than others. Practice, however, is helpful in developing the necessary skills and in encouraging participants to loosen up.

Most participants at the Allerton Park Institute seemed to enjoy the negotiation session and felt that it provided a nice contrast with the other conference sessions. Some even saw it as a good social mixer and wished it could have been held on the first day.

MILTON S. BYAM
Director,
Queens Borough Public Library
Jamaica, New York

Implications for Public Libraries

There is evidence of unionization in the field of public librarianship as early as 1917, according to *Library Literature*. One attempt occurred in New York and another in Detroit. Given the infancy of public librarianship at the time and the fact that staffs were often made up of women just out of high school and trained by the public libraries themselves, there was little hope for a successful conclusion to such efforts. The social class from which these young ladies had been selected, their complete identification with their public libraries, and their genteel surroundings gave them little reason for identification with the labor movement. The labor movement was not something that one thought well of in those days anyway.

The real impetus for labor unions in libraries came at the time of the replacement of the last of the library-educated librarians by their master's-degree-holding colleagues, and at the time of the major movement of unions into the white-collar field. In the case of New York this white-collar movement was helped by the establishment of the Public Employees' Relations Board (PERB), which dealt with labor unionization and made unions of public employees legal for the first time in the state of New York. In New York City, in which there are three private corporate libraries, the staffs saw benefit after benefit extended to city employees while their administrators had to fight to have them extended to libraries. When, for example, pensions were given to other city employees, the librarians were not included. The same thing occurred in the extension of Social Security, hospitalization, health plan, and career-salary plan benefits to librarians. Under the prevailing system, library employees not only lacked the benefits of a civil-service-protected tenure, but also suffered from a weakened bargaining position when benefits were handed out to other city employees.

Of course, long before the institution of unions, staff concerns in many libraries were expressed through a mechanism called a staff association. The actual name varies from library to library, but generally a staff association is an organization of staff members who seek to bring the interests of the staff to the attention of the library administration. Since their positions are not

This article is an edited compilation of Mr. Byam's presentation at the Institute and a subsequent written report.

legally enforceable, these staff associations exist through the sufferance of the administrators of those libraries. And because these staff associations often use the library mail, library paper, and library time for meetings, they are in fact organizations which have to be responsive to the administrators. One of the reasons, for example, that the staff of the Brooklyn Public Library went outside the library to look for a union was that the staff association was unable to get the administration to act on the question of a thirty-five hour week.

The success of the staff association mechanism, therefore, depends to too great an extent on the responsiveness of the library director. And library directors who are perfectly willing to recognize staff demands found themselves unable to react by reason of trustee adamancy or city refusal to take action.

There are now unions in almost every large city public library, but library governance is so varied and different from city to city that one cannot point to a typical library union. Indeed, one can go further and say public library governance makes unionization a special problem in public libraries.

One public library, for example, may be governed as a private corporation by a board of trustees, as in New York City, with no ties to the city except those surrendered by contract. It may be governed by an entirely free self-perpetuating board of trustees supported by an endowment, as is the New York Public Library, Astor, Lenox and Tilden Foundations. Even though it has a board of trustees, a public library may operate as a direct city department, with its employees gaining benefits at the same time as other city employees—as in Los Angeles, Philadelphia and Chicago—with full civil service status. A public library may be a school district based public library with an elected board of trustees or trustees appointed by the board of education, as is true of Cleveland and of many of the libraries on Long Island.

It should be obvious from this discussion that the library-union relationship is simple only for an organization with an autonomous governing body which controls the funds to carry out its power. In all other situations the public library finds itself in the position of adding by unionization yet another layer of governance to an already confused picture. An interesting case in point is the District of Columbia, where the library is responsible to a board of trustees, to both houses of Congress, to the District of Columbia government, to the U.S. Civil Service Commission, to the Commission on Human Rights, etc. With whom do you bargain in a situation like that? How does the public make its needs felt? How do you give library service under those conditions?

Look at the school district public library for example, with a board of trustees appointed by the board of education. With whom does the staff negotiate a salary increase? It could be with the board of education, which might overlook essential library needs, with the board of trustees, which might have to seek the approval of the board of education and then negotiate with the city to get the funds to implement the increase, or with the municipality itself. In some cases, it could well be with all of these.

But already the public libraries in all jurisdictions are beset and besieged by an astounding plethora of city regulations, state laws, federal regulations, and their own rules and regulations. These rules and regulations may say that there must be a bathroom in a building of given size, or that there must be a couch in a given place. In the state of New York there must be a librarian on the premises in any professionally run library at all times that the library is open. At least forty-two hours of service must be given weekly in a public library in the state of New York. Federal regulations determine how we will spend Library Services and Construction Act funds. And libraries have their own rules and regulations, which are approved by the board of trustees and must, of course, be legal under the existing state, city and federal statutes. To this tangle of laws and regulations, unionism adds yet another layer.

The result is that the needs of the federal government for financial probity are met. The state rules governing education are met. The city's need to parcel out funds with care is met. The need of the staff to have a voice in their own future is met. The one end that these many invaders of public library governance do not strive to meet is library service.

We have a very interesting situation in New York. In the Queens Borough Public Library the city is in fact doing a lot of negotiating directly with the union. We have representatives who sit in with the city on these discussions, so it is not likely that the needs of service will be overlooked in this particular type of arrangement, nor in the many similar types of arrangements which are possible here. In the case of the Brooklyn Public Library the employees negotiate with their board for those benefits—such as certain types of leave or breaks—which the trustees have not already given under the contract. All of the money questions, on the other hand, must be negotiated with the City of New York at the bargaining table. The trustees really get lost in this process. In spite of the fact that they are the titular heads of the corporation and presumably have all the power of that corporation—and these are corporations in a very real sense—they have in fact nothing to say about the negotiating process when money is involved.

My negotiating experience has included both sides of the table. I was president of the staff association of the Brooklyn Public Library at one time, although our negotiations were just minimal since they were then at the sufferance of the administration. As a member of the union executive team at St. John's University, I negotiated with the administration. I can't say that I enjoy this kind of thing, mainly because the situation is and has to be an antagonistic one. In many cases, for example, there will be members of the staff who will be more militant than the union leader, and as a result he has to take a very strong position vis-à-vis the administration to show that he is not taking any guff. As a result a lot of the negotiations are simply and purely play acting and for effect. It is only when you get past that stage and start putting things down on paper that you will find you are really moving forward.

Unionization has brought another disturbing element into the governance of public libraries: the impartial arbitrator. This is a person who stands above the city, state, library, and union and renders judgments on the appropriateness of given actions taken by the library. What happens if some arbitrator says public libraries can't be open at night or at times when the public can use them? This can be effected, simply, by requiring that given numbers of staff in certain classifications—e.g., custodians—must be on the premises during given hours, and then denying you that staff. We had exactly that situation in the District of Columbia, where the arbitrating team decided that no library could be open without a custodian on the premises. No staff member other than the custodian could be asked to lock the door. In the case of illness or absences we had to close the library until we could get a custodian on the premises. If an arbitrator says that Sabbath observers must be hired and placed in assignments, that means there is no staff in some cases on Saturday and Sunday. My concern may be unreasonable, but there are dangers when persons totally unaware of the needs of library service make decisions that concern libraries.

In the first union experience I had in Brooklyn we anticipated that we would be spending an awful lot of time handling grievances, and we were right. Everybody who feels that he has been somehow wronged files a grievance, and that ties up you, your staff, and everybody along the line while it is being resolved. The union leaders have not been very responsible in this area. They do not say to their members that they think something should not go forward. They permit anything to go forward as an example of what the union can do for its members, and hours are spent handling formal grievances over questions which could easily be settled informally. Grievances multiply and they continue to come. If people are not supposed to be able to grieve about something, they grieve about not being able to grieve about it. And you find yourself then going through the whole process, up to an arbitrator, to get a question resolved about whether or not the contract does indeed say you can grieve about a particular issue or you cannot. Even when the arbitrator has decided the issue it will come up again another way.

Most arbitration proceedings take at least a full day, and they may take several days. We had a case recently where a library staff member was found to be off the library premises when he should have been at his branch. He was suspended on the spot for being away from his assigned post without prior approval. He grieved. It went up the whole ladder to the arbitrator, and we spent three days with witnesses, testimony, and paid lawyers to get the arbitrator to tell us we did the right thing.

Generally, administrators don't go to arbitration; arbitration is usually employed by the union. We try desperately not to take cases that we are going to lose, unless there is some principle involved that requires arbitration. We try to get things settled beforehand if at all possible.

While the library press is wont to be excessively promotive of library unionism, and the spokesmen for these unions are often professional librarians, the public library unions are hardly professional in their stance, since they generally include all grades and classes of staff. In seeking the lowest common denominator to satisfy its entire constituency, the union tends to be conservative in its policies on extended hours, Sunday hours, and late night service, which the public and city officials would like to see libraries provide.

The manpower cost of the unionization of libraries has been enormous. Negotiations, grievance handling and arbitration are expensive and interminable. In a situation like this we pay all the costs, because even the union leaders are paid for by the library. We currently have a case in which the city of New York is refusing to recognize the right of a staff member who is party to the grievance to appear at an arbitration session on library time. The union is taking us and the city to the highest court in the land, in this case PERB, to argue this issue. They ask that every employee be able to appear at arbitration sessions on library time. This is public time, and it is not our time to give away. We can't just say that someone can take a couple of weeks off for union business, or for any business for that matter.

Unionization has, however, been less of a problem than anticipated by prognosticators of gloom and doom in the recent past. Unions have resulted in more evenhanded treatment of staff by municipalities, trustees and administrators. Union leaders have on the whole been aware of and responsive to the library and its needs.

Many libraries have awakened much too late to the need to be concerned with responding to the needs of staff. It is really too bad that administrators and trustees did not have the will, the ability, or the skill to get it done earlier. On the other hand, this may be an unfair comment, for today's mood favors unionization. It would be a staff which did not care much for itself which did not unionize in the face of unionization by the police, firefighters, school teachers, and everybody else. This is a movement that is going on and will go on in the future, and I expect that more and more different kinds of staff will become members of unions in the library field.

MARGARET BECKMAN
Library Director
University of Guelph Library
Guelph, Ontario, Canada

Implications for Academic Libraries

This paper may present a more restricted view of the academic library interface with collective bargaining than might have been anticipated, primarily for three reasons. First, I am more familiar with the Canadian academic library situation than with the American, although I have studied the pattern which appears to be emerging in American libraries. In addition, I am convinced that if academic library administrators had realized at any point within the past ten years that library management is a unique and demanding scientific discipline and had borrowed some of the techniques and methodologies being practiced in the business community, they could have been in a position of bargaining from strength rather than from weakness. Finally, I am firmly committed to the belief that academic librarians should achieve their status and any ensuing rights and privileges through their own merit, and not by accepting a system designed for another profession with similar, but not identical, objectives and requirements.

There is little doubt that collective bargaining will be the normal pattern for the majority of academic library staffs within the next decade. The question is not: What are the implications if we become involved? The question is: What do we do when, or hopefully before, we become involved? There are still steps which library administrators can take to ensure that their libraries will be in a relatively strong position in relationship to a union. The implications of collective bargaining for academic libraries are identifiable and positive. They are that we must achieve, in as short a time as possible, effective consultative (or participatory) library management systems, using the principles of library management so well defined by the Management Studies Office of the Association of Research Libraries (ARL).

Collective bargaining in academic libraries usually involves two groups: the professional staff and the clerical or support staff. In some instances one union or bargaining group negotiates for the support staff and some of the professional staff, but this is probably the exception. For instance, of nine unionized academic libraries in Canada, six include only clerical and other sub-professional staff, while only three include some of the professional librarians with the clerical or support staff.[1]

In June 1974, 41 percent of ARL libraries had union representation for at least some of their employees,[2] but few include many professional librarians.

This dominance of support staff in unions may not long continue, as movements for collective bargaining among the faculty on university campuses gain momentum. If university faculties unionize, the librarians, whether assigned full faculty status or not, are bound to be involved.

Therefore, the implications of collective bargaining for academic libraries follow the particular pattern which the unionization takes on the individual campus and involve both support staff and professional staff. Although there are many factors in common, and certainly we have much to learn from the unionization of clerical or support staff, these will be discussed separately, after an examination of some overriding implications fundamental to the discussion.

GENERAL IMPLICATIONS

Emphasis on the Management Function

A recent *ARL Management Supplement* phrases the immediate emphasis on management resulting from unionization in this fashion: "The art of writing a union contract serves to itemize and clarify management's options. Each provision of a collective bargaining agreement is, in effect, a limitation where none had formally existed before. In order to operate effectively, let alone to make changes or experiment within such a framework, management needs to be imaginative in planning and attentive to detail. Managing will require more time than before and will require considerably more attention."[3]

Instead of accepting what passed as library management a decade ago— and that appears to have been an adherence to whatever traditional hierarchical pattern existed, patched as necessary to meet particular or peculiar circumstances—a library must define its system of management within an intelligently organized structure. This management system must have both long-range objectives and short-term goals, determined and understood within the framework of the institution's objectives and budgetary constraints.

In order to provide the environment in which the library management system can be effectively operated, and meet its primary objectives of providing library and information services, all library management and supervisory staff must be given the opportunity to acquire the necessary knowledge and skills. Effective methods of providing the library with an effective and consciously managerial staff include: library in-service training programs for different levels of staff; seminars conducted by management experts provided by the library or university administration; and participation of both professional and nonprofessional staff in external seminars, institutes or formal courses.

The library management system must also define decision-making procedures and levels, and must provide structured vehicles for communication of all decisions to staff members. This is best provided through a participatory, or consultative, management system, with policy decisions officially taken at a level of staff involving more than just the senior administrators. This is discussed in more detail later.

Necessity for Formalized Personnel Function

A second general implication of collective bargaining for academic libraries is that the personnel function, even as the management system itself, must be formally organized. As stated in the Booz, Allen and Hamilton study of the Columbia University Libraries, "the human resources of the libraries are so important that the highest level of attention should be given to the personnel function: the Personnel Office, headed by an Assistant University Librarian, should operate as an integral part of the top management."[4]

The responsibilities of such a personnel office include coordination of library personnel policies throughout all departments; recruitment, selection, evaluation, promotion and termination routines must be consistent within the library system. A constantly updated library personnel manual is the most effective tool for achieving this result.

Job classification schedules meeting the particular needs of the library and related to detailed (and again, constantly updated) job descriptions are also part of the personnel function. The unique character of coding bibliographic data as compared, for example, to payroll coding, must be established and defined, as must be the wide-ranging activities of a science librarian with cataloging, research assistance, and collection development responsibilies. (Examples of classifications and some generic job descriptions are included in the Appendix.)

Staff development plans for support staff, specialists and librarians— including both in-service training and personnel programs, liaison with the university personnel department and the union, or the planning of new personnel policies (e.g., variation of the compressed or flexible work week)— are all part of the many functions which will be coordinated and emphasized by assigning the proper attention to the personnel function.

Threat to the Service Function

The third broad implication of collective bargaining for academic libraries is the threat to the service function. Library unions in Canada have existed longer in public libraries than in academic ones and we have been able to study, with growing alarm, the effects of such organizations on our common objective: effective library service. Specific examples can be cited in Canada of libraries which must be closed several evenings or on Sundays; where automation cannot be introduced; where staff members with seniority, but not necessarily with adequate qualifications can be transferred to public service jobs rather than filling the position with a more desirable outside candidate. All of these are the results of unions having prevailed over management in arbitration proceedings.

Academic libraries would be seriously hampered if they were not capable of meeting the changing needs of the user by restructuring departments, shifting or re-allocating personnel, introducing new technology, or entering into cooperative systems and regional or national networks. Union action need not be a threat to the service function if a library has already established its policies, objectives and organizational system consistent with the needs of both library users and staff. The implication is that each library must define those objectives, policies and organizational systems now, before collective bargaining is a reality in that library.

SPECIFIC IMPLICATIONS: SUPPORT STAFF

In speaking of specific implications of collective bargaining in relation to support staff in academic libraries, I am to a certain extent basing my observations directly on the fact that the University of Guelph has a union for all nonprofessional staff on the campus. Fortunately, that union has not been a militant or aggressive one and the library has been able to establish a management system and personnel policies which, although within the constraints of a union, can still focus on the library's service objectives.

In my experience, the most important areas on which a support staff collective agreement concentrates are discussed below.

Job Posting and Staff Transfers

As soon as a vacancy occurs in a library the position must be posted, internally to the university, usually for a period of five working days. The job classification or grade and necessary qualifications are stated briefly.

Advantages in such a system are the increased potential for staff mobility which can accrue. A clerical assistant at a Grade 2 level in the cataloging department may be locked into an unchallenging situation because of the relative stability of all the senior positions above her in the same department. The posting of a Grade 3 clerical position in the acquisitions department may provide the opportunity for both advancement and more challenging work, which can result in a more productive staff member.

There are disadvantages, however, particularly if the collective agreement stipulates that library seniority is an important factor in a transfer choice. This will result in loss of flexibility for library management, limiting its ability to promote those employees it judges to be best qualified for the job.

This internal transfer after a job vacancy posting need not necessarily involve a promotion. As long as an employee deems that a job of similar classification and requiring similar qualifications is better for her, she may apply for the transfer. This situation can impinge on effective library service, and library management may be deterred by a union contract from selecting the best person for a position.

Some actual examples of the results of union contracts, from the library's point of niew, may be helpful. The University of Guelph Library system offers service through subject divisions, with a general information division responsible in the central library for quick reference, information, and instructional services. In addition to professional staff in each division there are support staff—called library associates—with academic degrees in the subject of the discipline.

Within a period of two months, two library associates and the division head of one of the subject divisions resigned—all for valid and personal reasons. Meanwhile, the professional librarian in charge of orientation in the information division resigned at the end of a maternity leave prior to the beginning of the fall semester. The senior associate in the information division asked for a transfer to the vacancy in the subject division, with no promotion involved. This transfer, although not received with enthusiasm, was processed.

Then the second library associate in the information division asked to be transferred at her existing classification to the same subject division. This would leave the information division with no experienced staff except the division head. Although the employee is acting correctly within the terms of the contract in requesting a transfer, at some point the interests of the library and the needs of the user must be considered.

Another aspect of the problem is discussed by Donald Redmond, Chief Librarian of Queen's University at Kingston, Ontario. In his 1973-74 annual report he states that: "[the] mobility of nonprofessional staff has been simultaneously a benefit and a burden to the library system. Promotions and lateral transfers increase the value of a given employee to the university by broadening knowledge and familiarity." But he goes on to say that:

promotions and transfers mean a heavy burden on supervisors and colleagues, in training, monitoring and review.... The pattern of mobility has immediate effect on the units from which the staff move. Delays occur due to the paperwork procedures required by the University's tight budget and the collective agreement with the non-professional staff union—in job justification, posting and application. The resulting loss of working days increases the burden on staff remaining in the units.

In 1973/74, 76 movements (73 per cent of all mobility) caused the loss of 943 working days—the equivalent of five full time employees. On the average, each resignation caused one other internal movement, and the two movements together deprived the library system of 25 working days....Further, there is a hidden cost of time involved in training, particularly at the Library Technician I level which suffers both most mobility and most days lost in consequence.[5]

Promotions

Promotion of support staff can also create difficulties if a library insists that skill and proficiency, in addition to seniority, be considered. We have found that detailed job descriptions linked to regular formal evaluations are the best documentation to support promotions with the least likelihood of grievance.

One of the most difficult tasks at Guelph has been to impress on department heads the extreme importance of the evaluation procedures. An employee's performance cannot be rated satisfactory at several evaluation reviews and then, with the same documents, be assessed as not meriting either promotion or a merit increase. This area of evaluation and promotion enforces the necessity of and emphasis on the personnel function discussed earlier.

Termination

All union contracts contain clauses outlining the conditions under which an employee may be terminated, both before and after the probation period. Dismissal for disciplinary reasons—consistent lateness, extended lunch breaks, absence without sufficient cause given—is easier to handle than dismissal for inadequate work performance. Again, the detailed job description and an evaluation form which outlines all areas of job performance causing concern— inaccuracy, continuing errors, etc.—are the only protection which the library has.

A probationary period of six months is usually long enough in which to judge an employee's performance: it is far better to release an unsatisfactory or borderline employee prior to that period than to assume that an extension of the probationary period will result in improvement. Even though the evaluation procedures are well organized and effective, documenting the reasons for an employee dismissal after the probationary period are time consuming, and such a termination can create an unpleasant environment in a particular department or throughout the entire library.

Library-Initiated Transfers

Budgetary cutbacks caused by severe inflation are forcing many Canadian libraries to reduce positions. In most libraries this is done by attrition, so that positions terminated for natural causes are not filled and the necessary positions can be cut. This makes it crucial that transfers to meet service needs within the library are possible under the contract. Otherwise, the entire catalog support staff might be eliminated and the library would not have the ability to transfer personnel from other departments to equalize the total library staffing.

Job Classification

It is essential that a library have clearly defined job classifications and descriptions prior to their becoming a matter for union negotiation. It is much simpler if such schedules and descriptions remain a prerogative of library management. Most union contracts state that a union representative has the right to review such descriptions and to make suggestions. Any stronger union right in this matter—e.g., each position negotiated and described in the contract—will greatly diminish library flexibility. This would be particularly serious if new technology or changing use patterns demanded different library responses, and new or changed job classifications and descriptions had to be arbitrated on an individual basis.

Technological Advances

The problem of technological advances should be discussed in some detail for, except in a few of the smaller colleges or universities, automation of library processes, multi-media services, and mechanized information retrieval are all considered normal aspects of library service. As previously mentioned, flexibility is required within the library management system so that innovative services can be introduced, certain jobs can be virtually eliminated, and complete operations changed. Most union contracts allow for such changes, but often within very time-consuming constraints. Clauses within a contract stating that no employee be demoted or terminated because of automation, that such changes be discussed in advance with the union, and that a retraining program be the responsibility of the library are quite common.

There is at least one instance in Canada of a much more serious situation resulting from an unfortunate union contract, which states, to all extents and purposes, that automation may not be introduced into the library since job content may not be changed as a result of mechanization. This library is further hampered in that it may not join a cooperative regional processing system and receive the benefits of automation in that manner, because "contracting out" is also forbidden by explicitly expressed terms of the contract.

Work Schedules

For the most part, work schedules to meet service requirements need not be adversely affected by union contracts, if such schedules are defined as a normal part of the job content, and are so identified in the agreement.

Salaries and Benefits

The overall effect of unions is probably a rise in wages, and therefore an increase in that part of the library budget which goes to salaries as opposed to books. Another common result very apparent at the University of Guelph is the decrease in the amount of money available for merit or selective increases. With the union negotiating for large, across-the-board, basic increases, the university cannot afford additional allocations for the merit category.

In July 1974, the Guelph basic increase was 11 percent, with 2 percent made available for merit increases. This amount was so small that it was difficult to award it in any way that would be meaningful. This does not necessarily discourage the superior employee from continuing an excellent performance, but the lack of incentive does lead to a more standardized work environment.

SPECIFIC IMPLICATIONS: PROFESSIONAL STAFF

The implications of collective bargaining for professional librarians are much more complicated, both in the United States and Canada. Moreover, the Canadian environment is somewhat different in that Canadian librarians have not been, at least up to now, enthusiastic supporters of the concept of faculty status. The statement of the Canadian Association of College and University Libraries, for instance, makes a clear distinction between academic status and faculty status. Canadian academic librarians ask for the same basic recognition as do American librarians, but do so on the basis that their work is academic, not linking themselves to teaching as the requirement for faculty status, and not asking for collegial governance, rank, tenure, or other privileges traditionally associated with teaching faculty.

Whatever the terminology, the results have been quite similar. It would appear that approximately the same percentage of American universities as Canadian—10 percent in June 1974—already have agreements with faculty members and librarians.

The pattern at such universities so far has been collective bargaining for both faculty and librarians through the local faculty association. At Wayne State University the bargaining unit includes, in addition to teaching faculty, all "academic staff employees"[6] such as academic advisors, librarians, etc. It excludes all faculty and academic staff who have supervisory responsibility, so that in a smaller academic library, at least, only a small proportion of the library professional staff would be eligible for membership. This depends, of course, on the organizational structure of the library, but in the University of Guelph Library, approximately 60 percent of the professional staff engage in some supervisory or management duties.

In spite of the fact that librarians were members of the faculty association and therefore members of the Canadian Association of University Teachers (CAUT), on two Canadian campuses in 1973-74 the university administration refused to recognize a community of interest between faculty and librarians, and would not accept the librarians within the faculty bargaining unit. Librarians have been recognized as a separate bargaining unit within CAUT on both of these campuses, but their contract reflects the "second-class citizen" rank which the university obviously applies to them.

This situation also obtains in the United States. "The University of Delaware, Saginaw Valley, Youngstown State and Ashland have also excluded librarians by agreement."[7] The majority of American universities and four-year colleges covered by collective bargaining agreements are in the various statewide higher education systems which bargain on a system basis. It is anticipated that this pattern will be followed in Canada, as provincial governments tighten their control over once-autonomous universities.

Before discussing the actual implications of collective bargaining it might be useful to analyze the supposed advantages and disadvantages for academic communities. Factors which have particular significance in the library context have been selected from an Academic Collective Bargaining Information Service statement,[8] and are discussed below.

Advantages
1. Legal force—collective bargaining contracts are enforced by law, and their provisions "cannot be ignored or changed informally or unilaterally."[9]
2. Communication—better communication may result between faculty or academic employees and administrations because a continuous dialog and sharing of information is guaranteed under the terms of the labor laws.

3. Understanding of the institution—the collective bargaining process often allows the faculty and academic staff to gain a better understanding of the institution and its administrative processes and its policy and financial restrictions.
4. Definition of policy—collective bargaining supports a clear statement of administrative policy and procedure, minimizing misunderstanding.
5. Guarantee of employee rights—abuse of administrative power is reduced because the written contract guarantees employee rights, and the arbitration of a third party if a dispute should arise.
6. Compensation—there is little doubt that collective bargaining has increased the salary levels for employees at unionized universities.
7. Minorities—this is an important concern in libraries; it is believed that collective bargaining helps women and minority groups through equal pay schedules and standardized performance evaluation, recruitment, evaluation and promotion policies.

Disadvantages

1. Costs—collective bargaining increases administrative costs (both within the university and within the library, or other academic unit), because of the necessity of assigning more specialized staff to personnel and senior negotiating matters.
2. Inflexibility—as mentioned earlier, institutional and unit (i.e., library) flexibility and decision-making capabilities are diminished.
3. Individual freedom—freedom of action for the individual is also diminished.
4. Adversary relationship—"Collective bargaining is an adversary approach to decision making."[10] This can result in divisiveness within the library or the college, and educational or library policies may be negotiated, rather than determined through deliberations based on the recognized needs of the student within the educational process.
5. Standardization and innovation—opportunity and incentive for outstanding or innovative performance are lost in the standardized evaluation and promotion procedures, and in rigid work rules.

With this overview of the purported advantages and disadvantages of collective bargaining, the specific implications for academic libraries and librarians can now be analyzed. As suggested by John Weatherford in a recent issue of *Library Journal*, the involvement of librarians in faculty unions is so recent and still represents such relatively small numbers that it is difficult to define an established response.[11] Although the Association of College and Research Libraries (ACRL) statement on faculty status[12] is quite positive, the study conducted by Weatherford indicates that continuing analysis is needed, as well as a more concise definition of the terminology employed. It is apparent that a collective bargaining process for librarians, whether within a faculty union or not, will be using the ACRL statements as guidelines, and implications will inevitably relate to these concerns.

The nine rights and privileges outlined in the statement jointly sponsored by ACRL and the American Library Association have varying implications which fall primarily into two categories: (1) library management—from a library manager's point of view, the suggestion that libraries should adopt an academic form of governance has the most serious implications; and (2) library governance—"college and university libraries should adopt an academic form of governance. The librarians should form as a library faculty whose role and authority is similar to that of the faculties of a college, or the faculty of a school or a department."[13]

Writing in the June 1974 issue of *Library Journal*, Adeline Tallau and Benjamin Beede support this statement, suggesting that a "library director must think of himself or herself as an academic dean," who does not "issue orders but stands as a symbol of their collegial responsibility."[14] They suggest that with the collegial form of governance, library administrative organizations can cease to be bureaucratic, and library "faculty" can be involved in planning, decision-making, defining objectives, and problem-solving.

This view is contentious for two reasons. First, chief librarians or library directors, many of whom have the rank of dean, have a different accountability than does a dean. A library director is accountable to the university president for the operation of the library, so that it meets objectives usually set forth by the senate, with a budget approved by the vice-president, administration or the board of governors. Within that framework the library director balances a variety of complex functions and determines priorities for the allocation of diminishing resources covering many fields.

Colleges have one primary function: teaching. Research, usually funded separately and on an individual basis, is not the responsibility of the college dean. Within the teaching activity, each faculty member is independent as to methodology, timing, and even scheduling, to a certain extent. Any constraints placed on the teaching faculty are university-wide and are accepted university policy. The dean may be accountable for such coordination of teaching programs as is necessary, but he is not accountable for the performance of the teacher within the classroom.

Most, if not all, library directors are held accountable for the performance of all library activities. If a circulation clerk is rude to a faculty member, if there is a "mistake" in classification, or if a requested book takes six months to reach the library shelves, it is the library director who is accountable. The performance of professional librarians can be measured in a way that teaching cannot, and different operating systems can provide more effective service. Library directors can have more impact on a library than does a dean on a college, and more, or at least a different, accountability is involved.

As long as this form of accountability exists, the library director should have final decision-making authority in such areas as choice of department heads, establishment of short-term goals, and priorities for allocation of resources. Staff members voting for the head of the catalog department on a rotating basis would not necessarily result in the provision of effective access to the collections of a resource library.

The second reason for my reluctance to accept the collegial concept of library governance is that it is not the only alternative to bureaucratic administration. As stated above, a consultative or participatory library management system can achieve all the benefits of the collegial system, and yet still leave the library director with a role for which he or she can accept accountability.

At the University of Guelph Library, decision-making is done, within the framework of established objectives, at the department and division head meetings. Long-range planning considerations and university policy or budgetary limitations are provided by the four senior library staff members, and decisions are made in a democratic fashion (see Appendix). To communicate these decisions to all library staff, committee meeting minutes are distributed, and each department or division head is responsible for maintaining regularly scheduled meetings with his or her entire department. Professional and support staff can meet either separately or together, or in functional units. Department size may often be a determining factor in the structuring of such meetings.

Efficient operating and management information systems, with procedural manuals and standards of productivity and measurement for all library processes and services are also part of an effective library management system. Staff can then be allocated on an equitable basis related to established priorities and measured needs. Automated library sytems are most suitable for providing the kind of data necessary for such decisions; circulation, reserve, in-library use, reference, orientation, bibliographic, acquisition, cataloging and processing statistics should all be part of the library management system.

The librarians working in this type of library organization can assume a much greater degree of independence, since objectives, policies and procedures are all stated and understood. Working within an area of subject expertise, a librarian can do original cataloging, in-depth reference, or collection selection and evaluation, reporting officially in one division but working in several. As long as production or service schedules are met, librarians can be free to do research, participate in library or university committee work, or be involved in provincial or national library or academic affairs.

Librarian Benefits

For purposes of this paper I am categorizing the paragraphs in the ACRL statements relating to compensation, tenure, promotion, leaves and research funds as benefits which librarians are seeking. The statement on promotion is typical: "Promotion. Librarians should be promoted through ranks and steps on the basis of their academic proficiency and professional effectiveness. A peer review system similar to that used by other faculty is the primary basis of judgement in the promotion process for academic librarians. The librarians' promotion ladder should have the same titles, ranks, and steps as that of other faculty."[15]

The implications of this statement are many. Using the criteria for promotion which are contained in the ACRL "Model Statement of Criteria and Procedures for Appointment, Promotion in Academic Rank and Tenure for College and University Librarians," the following qualities would be judged in consideration for promotion: (1) professional and scholarly qualifications; (2) ability to perform at a high professional level; (3) contributions to the educational function of the university; (4) contributions to the advancement of the profession; and (5) activities related to inquiry and research.[16] Similar criteria are suggested for tenure, and peer evaluation is recommended. Rather than postulating the results of application of such standards, several questions can be posed: Who but the catalog department head or immediate supervisor can judge the performance of a senior professional cataloger? How many librarians are actively involved in research and publishing, or in professional or university activities? How many librarians have academic qualifications similar to the teaching faculty member?

If librarians are to be judged by faculty-directed criteria, they are going to have to adopt teaching faculty attitudes and commitments. They must also be prepared to accept unequal compensation, leave and tenure conditions, because the very nature of librarianship, as compared to teaching, does not provide identical opportunities or requirements. The statement of Paul Buck in describing the personnel program at Harvard in 1958 seems appropriate: "incorporation of Harvard's librarians into the 'officers of instruction' would be to impose upon them a personnel program that was not designed for librarians."[17]

Although not initiated by collective bargaining, in 1973 Harvard announced a new system for ranking and appointment of librarians. Librarians are to be assigned formal ranks with matching salary ranges; review and evaluation procedures have been established, and "there are up or out decisions to be made, because promotion or non-reappointment is the alternative at certain stages."[18] General librarians, for instance, can continue for a certain number of years in that classification, but after a stated interval they must be evaluated for promotion. If the evaluation is not successful the contract will not be renewed.

The new Harvard system appears desirable because all criteria for evaluation and the privileges established are directly related to the work and needs of librarians. A collective bargaining agreement in which standards designed for another profession are used to evaluate librarians for salary adjustments, promotion or tenure would not be as appealing.

Compensation is another of the important issues for librarians, and the ACRL model states that the "salary scale should be the same as that for other academic categories with equivalent education and experience."[1,9] Differing educational qualifications may be the justification for the discrepancy between the librarian and faculty scales displayed in the 1972-74 Wayne State University Contract (see Table 1).

An interesting and very different situation has developed in Ontario, and this may have a parallel in some American states. At the University of Guelph librarians belong to the faculty association which, although not designated as a bargaining unit, does negotiate with the administration for salaries. Librarians have always had comparable—if not exactly equivalent—salaries with the teaching faculty.

Within the past three years several Ontario universities have used a management consultant firm which has developed a system for evaluating all jobs within an institution and establishing a salary policy which is equitable for the campus. The University of Guelph hired this firm for such an evaluation, and all positions on campus except teaching or research faculty were evaluated. The faculty association protested the inclusion of the librarians within the project, but the protest was overruled.

The initial reaction of concern about inclusion of librarians was caused by the heavy weighting toward management criteria in the evaluation system which was to be used. Typical factors were number of people supervised, size of budget involved, and complexity of the decision-making in the job. It was felt that librarians had a stronger community of interest with the faculty, that their concerns were primarily educational and academic, and that any evaluation which compared librarians to accountants, engineers or the Computer Institute staff would not have favorable results for the librarians' compensation.

Without going into the details of a process that took almost two years to complete, the librarians achieved, as a result of the evaluation, classifications and salary grades that placed them well above equivalent faculty members. In some instances the salary increases for librarians which were needed to match the assigned grades were so high (up to 40 percent) that they could not be given in one year. Since this same result occurred on several other Ontario campuses, it can be suggested that a study of the academic

	Min.	Max.		Min.	Max.
Librarian I	$ 9,248	$12,049	Instructor	$ 8,400	$12,000
Librarian II	11,249	14,493	Assistant Professor	9,800	17,900
Librarian III	12,979	16,895	Associate Professor	12,500	22,800
Librarian IV	15,251	20,086	Professor	15,200	30,400

Table 1. Salary Schedules—Wayne State University, 1973-74

Source: Wayne State University. *Agreement Between Wayne State University and the Wayne State University Chapter of the American Association of University Professors, July 1, 1972 to June 30, 1974*, pp. 22, 24.

administrative salary and classification schedules in American universities might prove valuable.

It should also be noted that such an evaluation system is based on job content, not on personal ranking, and that this also conflicts with the established faculty procedures. The evaluation of job content is a premise basic to management theory, and is in direct opposition to the type of ranking recently accepted at Duke University Library: "Basic to the philosophy of the new structure is the idea that rank adheres to the individual rather than the position."[20]

There are, therefore, important issues which have to be resolved—issues which may have different solutions dependent on the view of the library administrator or the library staff. If collective bargaining is to be the accepted pattern for the establishment of personnel policies in the university libraries of the United States and Canada, those libraries not yet involved should consider the immediate development and implementation of policies which would be more acceptable in the present environment of academic libraries.

Since the recent study of university library directors determined that the second most common cause for their resignations was one of conflict between the director and the professional staff,[21] it might be of benefit if a task force representing several levels of the library staff studied the problem of the librarians' status and role in the academic community. Such an approach has been used at both Harvard[22] and the University of Toronto,[23] and certainly reduces the adversary condition referred to earlier.

Whatever the method of approach, several steps can be taken:

1. The ACRL standards for faculty status and the model statement of criteria and procedures for appointment and promotion should be re-evaluated as a basis for collective bargaining for academic librarians.

Each article should be defined in relation to the objectives of librarianship, with consideration for the differing needs of librarians and the particular circumstances on an individual campus.
2. Using this revised ACRL statement, a personnel policy for librarians, encompassing the management system, promotion, tenure, evaluation, compensation, leaves of absence and responsibility should be established within the library and approved by the university administration.
3. The library should also develop a classification schedule with detailed job descriptions, and define criteria for movement through the schedule which are realistically related to the library functions and librarian qualifications.
4. The need for study leaves as a vehicle for continuing education for librarians should be stressed in the personnel policy. This is separate from the issue of sabbaticals, which are rarely given for formal study in the teaching faculty context.
5. The library personnel office, or the task force suggested above, should work closely with the university personnel department so that the university administration is kept informed of the concerns of the librarians and of other directions being taken.
6. In universities or colleges where librarians are members of the faculty association, the association should also be made aware of policies being developed by the librarians.
7. If the faculty association, or some other group which includes librarians, is declared a bargaining unit, some representative of the library should sit on the committee which draws up the contract. Care should be taken to ensure the inclusion of a general statement of the educational and service objectives of the university.

STRIKES AND ACADEMIC LIBRARIES

Having presented this very brief overview of the implications of collective bargaining for academic libraries, I would like to conclude with a brief discussion of the problem presented by a strike on a university campus and the implications which this might have for the library. Since several such strikes have occurred in academic libraries in Canada, all involving unions of clerical or support staff only, I will limit this discussion to a strike of that nature.

Most strikes are based on economic factors, with the union seeking better working conditions, wages or fringe benefits. The union attempts to prevent the library from carrying out its normal functions, and brings pressure to bear by mobilizing support from members of the community not directly involved (e.g., the students).

It is usually a university decision whether services will be continued in all areas affected by the strike. Teaching and research activities usually continue fairly normally, with the library an area in which action has varied. Sir George Williams University in Montreal closed the library for five weeks during a strike (their second) in 1973. They also submitted to union demands. The University of Guelph, the University of Saskatchewan, and several others have elected to stay open, and in most instances have not acceded to union requests which were considered impossible to meet.

Contingency planning for a strike should begin as soon as there is any indication that negotiations are not proceeding smoothly. If the university does not have a statement of broad guidelines to be followed in the event of a strike, the library should prepare one. This should be expanded into a full manual if a strike occurs.

If an academic library is to remain open during a strike, depending entirely on professional and supervisory staff, priorities must be established concerning which services will be continued. It will undoubtedly be necessary to concentrate on services directly related to student use of the library: circulation and reserve systems, stack maintenance, reference service; such activities as cataloging, serial check-in and binding will be abandoned.

Steps such as reducing library hours and closing most of the washrooms can be of great assistance. During the strike at the University of Guelph in 1969 the most serious problem was the maintenance of the many washrooms in McLaughlin Library.

It must also be realized that no one can be asked to do such maintenance work if it is not normally his or her responsibility. At Guelph this was interpreted to mean that librarians shouldn't type catalog cards or paste book labels, but that book shelving and washroom cleaning were jobs necessary for our own welfare. A few librarians refused to participate in these activities and this attitude was accepted and understood.

Other actions which can or should be taken by a library about to be involved in a strike are: arrange for increased library security; post reduced hours and services; notify faculty of specific services which may be reduced (i.e., no new books on reserve, no interlibrary loan, no book requests processed, etc.); notify other libraries in your network of a strike possibility, and the discontinuation of interlibrary loan activities; arrange for library parcel delivery away from the campus (personal mail is usually taken care of by the university); and plan schedules and priorities for return to normal library operations after the strike.

A strike can have a very demoralizing and divisive effect on a library staff, since relationships between the unionized and the professional and supervisory staff can deteriorate. A meeting with the nonstriking staff prior to the return of the striking staff, in which advice on attitudes to be assumed can be given, is useful.

At the conclusion of the strike at the University of Guelph it was agreed by the librarians that no mention was to be made of the strike or its settlement, and work was continued, with former strikers and nonstrikers coping with a four-week backlog of unprocessed books and journals and with chaotic book stacks, as if this was the normal routine. All staff pitched in and helped with the backlogs with more enthusiasm than many of us had had for the washroom detail. We arranged a staff party (using library funds) and almost everyone came. Within a few weeks all bitterness was gone, and we could even joke together about the not quite normal activities that many of us—both strikers and those who had remained on duty—had performed during the strike.

The move toward collective bargaining for both support and professional staff in an academic library suggests the importance of improved management systems, with particular emphasis on consultative decision-making and the personnel function. It should be possible to design a library system in which librarians have the opportunity to perform independently within their area of academic expertise, and which encourages the development of procedures for evaluation and criteria for promotion more compatible with library goals and with librarianship. The unique position of the library—one which has managerial-oriented production goals as well as academic teaching and research objectives—must be recognized. Since a union contract can reduce the flexibility of a library and curtail the provision of effective library service, it is important that libraries participate in the development of the contract and be kept informed throughout any negotiation period.

Although the matrix of collective bargaining and academic libraries does not yet have exact or final definition, the outline is already apparent. By taking cognizance of the needs on which the collective bargaining movement focuses, academic libraries still have the opportunity to move toward improved management systems, anticipating some of the demands which a union might make and reducing the deleterious effects which can result.

The status of the library professional staff will probably be the most important issue. The resolution of this problem may well decide the direction and dimension of academic library service in the future.

APPENDIX

Following are some examples of library organization, classification and job descriptions.

Chief Librarian

Associate Librarian

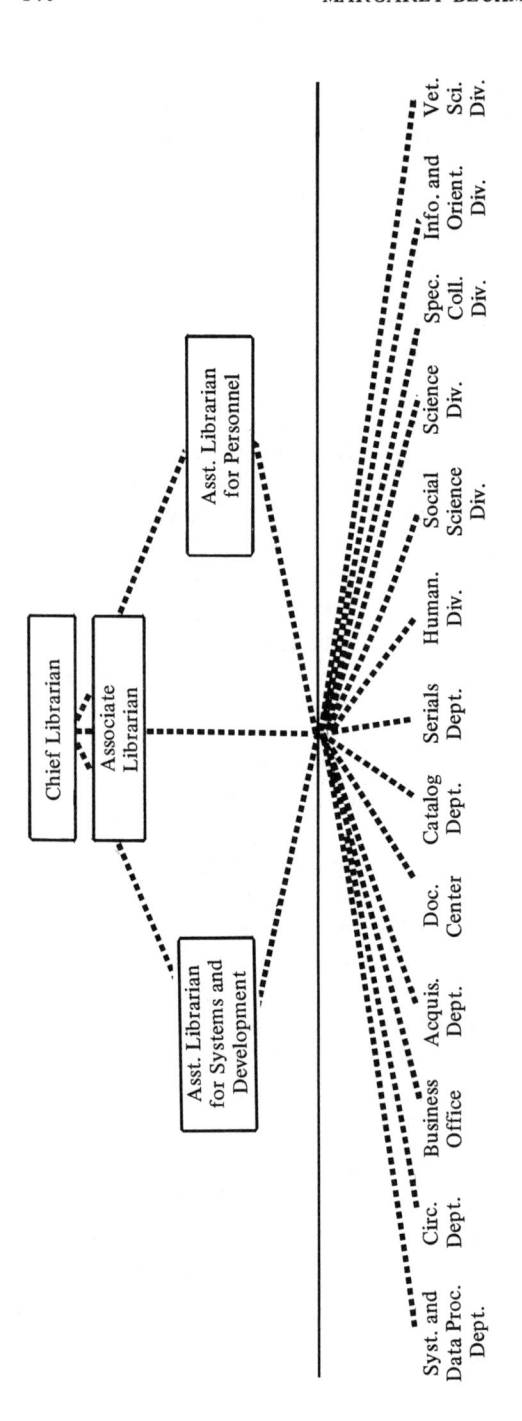

Asst. Librarian for Personnel

Asst. Librarian for Systems and Development

Syst. and Data Proc. Dept.
Circ. Dept.
Business Office
Acquis. Dept.
Doc. Center
Catalog Dept.
Serials Dept.
Human. Div.
Social Science Div.
Science Div.
Spec. Coll. Div.
Info. and Orient. Div.
Vet. Sci. Div.

COORDINATING COMMITTEES

Department/Division Heads
Allocations and Collections Development
Budget
Orientation
System Coordination
Serials
Documents
Rare Books, Regional and Agricultural History

Staff 159 (37 Professional)

Library Organization, January 1974

LIBRARY SUPPORT STAFF (SEPTEMBER 1973)

Grade	Job Category
1	Library Assistant 1
2	Library Assistant 2
3	Library Assistant 3 Senior Library Assistant Coordinator
4	Library Assistant 4 Senior Coordinator 1
5	Library Technical Assistant Senior Coordinator 2 Supervisor 1
6	Library Associate Senior Supervisor 1
7	Senior Library Associate Supervisor 2
8	Senior Supervisor 2

Grade 1

This is the entry level for library assistants in positions requiring simple clerical skills only.

Class Description
　　Under direct supervision, performs routine library tasks of limited complexity, following prescribed procedures and with a minimum requirement for independent judgment.

Qualifications for Eligibility
1. Secondary school graduation (grade 12) *or*
2. Relevant commercial or technical training or experience may be substituted, provided a minimum of grade 10 (two years of secondary school) completed, *or*
3. Equivalent basic qualifications accepted by the institution.

Typical jobs (Library Assistant 1)
　　Library assistant, file maintenance; library assistant, book processing; library assistant, photocopy; and library assistant, stack maintenance.

Grade 6

Staff in this classification apply library techniques and/or university education (bachelor's degree) at a general senior level of responsibility and complexity. This is the entry level for library associates.

Class Description
Under general supervision, is accountable for the performance and/or supervision of complex library tasks requiring extensive in-service training, university education and/or experience in library techniques. Consults supervisor on difficult problems or new policies only. Generally uses independent judgment and initiative in performing duties within assigned objectives.

Library associate uses subject and/or language proficiency at bachelor's degree level in performing, under the direction of a department or division head or other professional librarian, complex library tasks such as bibliographic searching, Library of Congress cataloging, and reference assistance to library users.

Senior supervisor 1 Under the general direction of the department head, supervises and trains library assistants and coordinators in grades up to 4. This job may be done by a supervisor 1 at grade 5 level, but, by virtue of training or experience, the senior supervisor 1 exercises a greater degree of independence and judgment than at grade 5 level.

Qualifications for Eligibility
1. Bachelor's degree
2. Diploma in library technology, representing two years of post-secondary training, plus at least one year of library experience; one year must be in the same library
3. Two years post-secondary education and two years of library experience, one year to be in the same library
4. Secondary school graduation (grade 12) and three years of library experience, of which at least one year must be in the same library *or*
5. Equivalent experience and education, provided at least one year of experience is in the same library.

Note: Not every one of these alternatives is acceptable for every position in the grade. Library associates' and senior supervisors' positions require different qualifications.

Typical jobs
Library associate: library associate, acquisitions; library associate, bibliographic search; library associate, L.C. cataloging; library associate, documents coding; library associate, humanities division (social science division, science division, information and orientation division, special collections division, O.V.C. branch).

Senior supervisor 1: senior supervisor, data input; senior supervisor, coding; senior supervisor, current subscriptions; senior supervisor back issues.

LIBRARY STAFF MANUAL, SEPTEMBER 1974

Classification: Librarian III

Title: Senior librarian; or, Assistant Department/Division Head
Recommended Minimum Qualifications
　　Master's degree in a subject field in addition to master's degree in library science plus demonstrated professional competence and expertise.
Summary of Responsibility
　　Independent performance of duties requiring extensive theoretical knowledge of librarianship, practical experience in application of this knowledge, extensive subject knowledge in a specific discipline or broad knowledge of the function and operation of a library in an academic institution; *and either* organizational and administrative skill to initiate, direct and expand the structure and operation of a discrete section of an academic library, *or* skill and experience to perform difficult assignments without established routines and guidelines; supervision of general professional staff and nonprofessional staff assisting in these assignments.
　　The assistant head of a department shares in the administration of the department, acts as deputy head when necessary, and may have entire responsibility for certain functions such as training and supervision.
Characteristic Duties
1. Undertakes extensive and difficult bibliographic tasks (including difficult original cataloging and classification)
2. Undertakes major responsibility to operate or coordinate bibliographic projects at institutional or wider levels within area of subject specialty
3. Applies bibliographic, library or information science techniques and theory to new or special fields of knowledge or forms of material
4. Initiates, recommends and conducts selection and acquisition of special materials
5. Undertakes and is responsible for resource service to library users at many levels
6. Offers instruction in library, bibliographic information or subject areas, either formally (classroom) or informally, to both library staff and library users
7. Participates in research activities of a bibliographic, information science or scholarly nature, usually resulting in publication.

Assistant Head of Department/Division
1. Is responsible for preparation of departmental procedure manuals, in-service training of professional and support staff, maintenance of standards of performance

2. Represents the department head on committees or deputizes for him when necessary; acts as department head in his absence.

Authority, Responsibility and Contacts

In a specialist position, a senior librarian is free from responsibility for function of a unit of staff (other than staff directly assisting his tasks of content, bibliographic detail, or clerical support), but may have responsibility for effective personal service to a distinct body of users, and for effective relationships with persons and groups affected by the objectives of his own tasks and duties. He receives instruction as to general policy and objectives, with independence of decision on methods. He frequently represents the library in functions and meetings in the area in which he is a specialist.

The assistant head works under the general supervision of the department head but has considerable freedom of action in the areas of responsibility which have been delegated to him. He must also be able to speak and act for the department head in his absence, on any matter concerning the department.

Experience and Advancement

Advancement to and within this grade is dependent solely on qualifications and experience, on difficulty of duties, and on the independent professional initiative required for effective performance. Five years of professional experience at Librarian II would normally be considered the minimum necessary for assignment to the Librarian III classification.

The senior librarian is responsible for maintaining personal professional development and competence including appropriate knowledge of library and information science, methodology, and of subject area.

Promotion to assistant department head is entirely dependent on the needs of the library system.

REFERENCES

1. Houser, L., ed. "Labor Relations Information Exchange," *IPLO Quarterly*, 16:37-38, July 1974.
2. "Collective Bargaining," *Spec Flyer*, 8:1, June 1974.
3. Gotwals, Joan I. "Review of Collective Bargaining Activities in Academic and Research Libraries," *ARL Management Supplement*, 1:3, June 1973.
4. Booz, Allen and Hamilton, Inc. *Organization and Staffing of the Libraries of Columbia University*. Westport, Conn., Redgrave Information Resources Corp., 1973.
5. Redmond, Donald A. *Annual Report on the Libraries for the Year Ended April 30, 1974*. Kingston, Ontario, Queen's University, 1974, unpaged.

6. Wayne State University. "Agreement Between Wayne State University and the Wayne State University Chapter of the American Association of University Professors, July 1, 1972-June 30, 1974," p. 3.

7. Weatherford, John. "Librarians in Faculty Unions," *Library Journal*, 99:2443, Oct. 1974.

8. Academic Collective Bargaining Information Service. *Some Suggested Advantages and Disadvantages of Collective Bargaining; A Short Review*. Washington, D.C., 1973.

9. *Ibid.*, p. 1.

10. *Ibid.*, p. 4.

11. Weatherford, *op. cit.*, p. 2444.

12. Herbison, Michael, *et al.* "Joint Statement on Faculty Status of College and University Librarians," *College and Research Libraries News*, 33:209-10, Sept. 1972.

13. *Ibid.*, p. 211.

14. Tallau, Adeline, and Beede, Benjamin R. "Faculty Status and Library Governance," *Library Journal*, 99:1522, June 1, 1974.

15. Herbison, *op. cit.*, p. 211.

16. Committee on Academic Status. "Model Statement of Criteria and Procedures for Appointment, Promotion in Academic Rank and Tenure for College and University Librarians," *College and Research Libraries News*, 34:193, Sept. 1973.

17. Buck, Paul H. "A New Personnel Program for Harvard Librarians," *Harvard Library Bulletin*, 12:292, March 1958.

18. Williams, Edwin E. "Harvard's Study Committee on Professional Library Personnel," *Harvard Library Bulletin*, 21:277, July 1973.

19. Herbison, *op. cit.*, p. 211.

20. Dyson, Allan J., ed. "Ranking Structure Instituted in Duke Libraries," *College and Research Libraries News*, 35:216, Oct. 1974.

21. McAnally, Arthur M., and Downs, Robert B. "The Changing Role of Directors of University Libraries," *College & Research Libraries*, 34:110, March 1973.

22. Williams, *op. cit.*, p. 277.

23. University of Toronto. "President's Working Group on the Library," *Report*, June 1974.

MARGARET A. CHAPLAN
Librarian
Institute of Labor and Industrial Relations
University of Illinois
Urbana-Champaign, Illinois

Collective Bargaining in Libraries: A Bibliography

This bibliography was compiled for those who wish to pursue further the topics discussed in the papers included in this volume. From a great amount of material on collective bargaining by public employees and about labor relations in libraries, I have selected those items I thought important contributions to an understanding of the subject. Because circumstances are changing rapidly, recent works are emphasized. Some items were included not because they are the latest or the best, but because they represent a subject or viewpoint that needs to be recognized. In order to take advantage of the whole of our collective bargaining experience, items relating to both the public and private sectors are included; the basic principles are the same, and so are some of the problems. In addition, there are references to some topics that were not covered in the Allerton Park Institute papers. The guiding question in both the selection of topics and of individual items was: What would someone with little prior knowledge of collective bargaining and the activities of labor unions need to know, or want to know, if faced with a bargaining situation?

ORGANIZING

Basic to an understanding of the subject of collective bargaining in libraries is some background in the nature of labor unions—their structure and administration, their programs and activities, and their relationship to other organized groups and to the communities in which they exist. Perhaps the best general introduction to labor and labor unions is the volume by Bok and Dunlop (2). The books by Barbash (1) and Estey (3) concentrate on the structure and administration of unions and their relationships with their members. How union members feel about their union is described in the Seidman, et al., (4) study. Specifically for the public sector, these same types of general studies of unions have been done by Spero and Capozzola (5), Stieber (6), and Wellington and Winter (7).

1. Barbash, Jack. *American Unions: Structure, Government, and Politics.* New York, Random House, 1967. 183p.
2. Bok, Derek C., and Dunlop, John T. *Labor and the American Community.* New York, Simon and Schuster, 1970. 542p.
3. Estey, Marten. *The Unions: Structure, Development, and Management.* New York, Harcourt, Brace and World, 1967. 125p.
4. Seidman, Joel, et al. *The Worker Views His Union.* Chicago, University of Chicago Press, 1958. 299p.
5. Spero, Sterling D., and Capozzola, John M. *The Urban Community and Its Unionized Bureaucracies.* New York, Dunellen, 1973. 361p.
6. Stieber, Jack. *Public Employee Unionism.* Washington, D.C., Brookings Institution, 1973. 256p.
7. Wellington, Harry H., and Winter, Ralph K. *The Unions and the Cities.* Washington, D.C., Brookings Institution, 1971. 226p.

The History of Organizing in Libraries

Union organizing in libraries is not a new phenomenon. The 1930s, which was a great period of labor union growth in general, also saw the formation of unions in libraries, with the first, according to McDonald (23), in 1934. Some of the same arguments used today in discussing the advantages and disadvantages of joining unions were brought up at that time also (see Falkoff (12) and Hale (18)). A summary of the organizing activity up to the end of the 1930s is included in Berelson's article (8), although he is more concerned with analyzing whether unionism and librarianship are compatible. Spicer (27) gives a short historical summary, and Clopine's thesis (10) provides, among other information, a history of library unions local by local, including where they were located, how long they were in existence, and when and why they disappeared. While some librarians were joining labor unions, others were forming staff associations as a response to the same kind of problems. The question of whether to form a union or a staff association is discussed by Phelps (25).

An upsurge of organizing activity in libraries has occurred since the formation of the University of California library local in 1965. This activity has been accompanied by a voluminous literature, much of which consists of case studies of organizing efforts at particular libraries. The more theoretical and analytical essays have been concerned with the status of organizing efforts, the reasons for an increase of interest in joining unions on the part of librarians, the pros and cons of joining unions, and assessments of whether the American Library Association or other professional organizations could function as substitutes for labor unions. Boaz (9), Cottam (11), Goldstein (14), Golodner (15), Guyton (17), Harrelson (19), Hopkins (20), Kirkpatrick (21), Letson (22), Nyren (24), and Suleiman and Suleiman (28) are representative examples of such essays. The situation in specific types of libraries is discussed by Trelles (29) and Tucker (30), and organizing activities among nonprofessional library employees are described by Flanagan (13) and Greenberg (16).

8. Berelson, Bernard. "Library Unionization," *Library Quarterly*, 9:477-510, Oct. 1939.
9. Boaz, Martha. "Labor Unions and Libraries," *California Librarian*, 32:104-08, April-July 1971.
10. Clopine, John J. "A History of Library Unions in the United States." Unpublished master's thesis, Catholic University, 1951.
11. Cottam, Keith M. "Unionization is not Inevitable," *Library Journal*, 93:4105-06, Nov. 1, 1968.
12. Falkoff, Barbara. "Should Librarians Unionize? Part II. The Librarian and the Closed Shop," *Library Journal*, 62:590-93, Aug. 1937.
13. Flanagan, Leo N. "A Sleeping Giant Awakens: The Unionization of Library Support Staffs," *Wilson Library Bulletin*, 48:491-99, Feb. 1974.
14. Goldstein, Melvin S. *Collective Bargaining in the Field of Librarianship*. Brooklyn, Pratt Institute, 1968. 167p.
15. Golodner, Jack. "The Librarian and the Union," *Wilson Library Bulletin*, 42:387-90, Dec. 1967.
16. Greenberg, Herman. *Unionization of White Collar Employees: A Case Study of the Free Library of Philadelphia*. Philadelphia, 1963. 92p.
17. Guyton, Theodore L. "Unionization of Public Librarians: A Theoretical Interpretation." Unpublished Ph.D. dissertation, University of California, Los Angeles, 1972. 332p.
18. Hale, Ruth. "Should Librarians Unionize? Part I: The Librarian and the Open Shop," *Library Journal*, 62:587-89, Aug. 1937.
19. Harrelson, Larry E. "Library Unions: Introduction and History," *Oklahoma Librarian*, 22:6-8, July 1972; Part 2: "Library Unions: Some Issues," *Oklahoma Librarian*, 22:11-13+, Oct. 1972.
20. Hopkins, Joseph S. "Unions in Libraries: A Review of the Recent Period of Renewed Union Activity in American Public and Academic Libraries," *Library Journal*, 94:3403-07, Oct. 1, 1969.
21. Kirkpatrick, Oliver. "Professional Librarian as Unionist." *In* E. J. Josey, ed. *What Black Librarians are Saying*. Metuchen, N. J., Scarecrow Press, 1972, pp. 192-201.

22. Letson, C. G. "Collective Bargaining Organizations in Public Libraries of Nassau County, New York." Unpublished research paper, Long Island University, 1971. 81p.
23. McDonald, Elizabeth. "First Librarians' Union," *Wilson Library Bulletin*, 10:675-76, June 1936.
24. Nyren, Karl E. "Libraries and Labor Unions," *Library Journal*, 92:2115-21, June 1, 1967.
25. Phelps, Orme W. "Organization of Employees with Special Reference to Library Personnel," *Library Quarterly*, 16:20-34, Jan. 1946.
26. Smith, Eldred. "Librarians and Unions: The Berkeley Experience," *Library Journal*, 93:717-20, Feb. 15, 1968.
27. Spicer, Erik J. *Trade Unions in Libraries (the Experience in the United States)* (Occasional Paper No. 23). Ottawa, Canadian Library Association, 1959. 14p.
28. Suleiman, Fuad K., and Suleiman, JoAnn D. "Collective Bargaining: Alternatives for Academic Librarians," *Protean*, 2:26-31, Summer 1972.
29. Trelles, Oscar M. "Law Libraries and Unions," *Law Library Journal*, 65:158-80, May 1972.
30. Tucker, William P. "Unionization for Special Librarians," *Special Libraries*, 30:41-45, Feb. 1939.

Why Workers Join Unions

Studies of why workers join unions fall generally into one of two categories: (1) studies of the motivations of employees, and (2) studies of the characteristics of union members, i.e., studies of the kinds of people who are likely to belong to unions. Theories of labor union growth attempt to account for membership expansion and contraction on a nationwide level. The article by Blum (34) is a survey of the literature on theories of union growth. In the first category, that of studies of motivation, Bakke (31), Seidman, *et al.* (47), and Viteles (49) are studies of workers in private industry; Christrup (36), Tyler (48), Imundo (40 and 41), and Biles (32) deal specifically with government employees; and Jones (42), Haro (39), and Bulger (35) analyze factors stimulating interest in unionization among librarians. A final group of motivational studies concerns psychological studies of attitudes toward joining unions, represented here by Messick (44), Dubin (37), and Nagi (45). Quantitative studies of the characteristics of union members, like those by Scoville (46) and by Blinder (33), assess the influence of certain socio-economic variables of the population on union membership. Kornhauser's article (43) is a non-quantitative analysis of the same type. Preliminary results from a study of union and management actions in organizing campaigns and how they affect a worker's vote for or against the union in an NLRB-supervised representation election are reported in Getman, *et al.* (38).

31. Bakke, E. Wight. "Why Workers Join Unions," *Personnel*, 22:37-46, July 1945.
32. Biles, George E. "Allegiances of Unionized Public Employees toward Employer and Union," *Public Personnel Management* 3:165-69, March-April 1974.
33. Blinder, Alan S. "Who Joins Unions" (Working Paper No. 36). Princeton, N. J., Industrial Relations Section, Princeton University, February 1972. 25p.
34. Blum, Albert A. "Why Unions Grow," *Labor History*, 9:39-72, Winter 1968.
35. Bulger, William T. "Librarians and Collective Bargaining," *Michigan Librarian*, 38:10-12, Spring 1972.
36. Christrup, Helen J. "Why do Government Employees Join Unions?" *Personnel Administration*, 29:49-54, Sept.-Oct. 1966.
37. Dubin, Robert. "Attachment to Work and Union Militancy," *Industrial Relations*, 12:51-64, Feb. 1973.
38. Getman, Julius G., *et al.* "The National Labor Relations Board Voting Study: A Preliminary Report," *Journal of Legal Studies*, 1:233-58, June 1972.
39. Haro, Robert P. "Collective Action and Professional Negotiation: Factors and Trends in Academic Libraries," *ALA Bulletin*, 63:993-96, July-Aug. 1969.
40. Imundo, Louis V., Jr. "Attitudes of Non-Union White Collar Federal Government Employees toward Unions," *Public Personnel Management*, 3:87-92, Jan.-Feb. 1974.
41. ———. "Why Federal Government Employees Join Unions: A Study of AFGE Local 916," *Public Personnel Management*, 2:23-28, Jan.-Feb. 1973.
42. Jones, Margaret P. "Staff Organizations Roundtable Survey: Opinions on Collective Bargaining," *ALA Bulletin*, 63:803-09, June 1969.
43. Kornhauser, Ruth. "Some Social Determinants and Consequences of Union Membership," *Labor History*, 2:30-61, Winter 1961.
44. Messick, David M. "To Join or not to Join: An Approach to the Unionization Decision," *Organizational Behavior and Human Performance*, 10:145-56, Aug. 1973.
45. Nagi, Mostafa H. "Social Psychological Correlates of Membership in Teachers' Organizations," *Teachers College Record*, 74:369-78, Feb. 1973.
46. Scoville, James G. *"Influences on Unionization in the U.S. in 1966,"* *Industrial Relations*, 10:354-61, Oct. 1971.
47. Seidman, Joel, *et al.* "Why Workers Join Unions," *Annals*, 274:75-84, March 1951.
48. Tyler, Gus. "Why They Organize," *Public Administration Review*, 32:97-101, March-April 1972.

49. Viteles, Morris S. "Attitudes toward the Union." *In* Morris S. Viteles. *Motivation and Morale in Industry.* New York, W. W. Norton and Company, 1953, pp. 333-58.

Discussions and Histories of the Various Unions Trying to Organize Librarians

A variety of unions have organized or are attempting to organize librarians in all kinds of libraries. There are the traditional labor unions, such as the American Federation of State, County, and Municipal Employees (AFSCME) and the American Federation of Teachers (AFT); there are professional organizations that have taken on collective bargaining functions, such as the National Education Association (NEA) and the American Association of University Professors (AAUP); and, finally, there are independent employee unions and associations. Most of the librarians covered by collective bargaining agreements are represented by one of the above organizations. The items listed in this section present histories of these organizations and discussions of their goals and programs. Billings and Greenya (52) and Kramer (57) write about AFSCME. Braun (53) and the Commission on Educational Reconstruction (55) present opposing viewpoints on the AFT's activities, and Stinnett (64) chronicles the struggle between the AFT and the NEA for the support of teachers. Strauss (65) and Belasco (51) discuss the AAUP, and Schlachter (61 and 62) analyzes the potential of the American Library Association for representing employee interests. The official positions of the AFT, NEA and AAUP on collective bargaining in colleges and universities are found in items 50, 56, 60, and 63. The nature and functions of the independent unions and associations are discussed by Krislov (58) and Marshall (59), while Chaison and Rock (54) analyze the success rates of such local independent unions in organizing campaigns in private industry.

50. "AFT Statement of Position; Academic Freedom and the Rights of Faculty." *In* Clarence R. Hughes, *et al.,* eds. *Collective Negotiations in Higher Education, a Reader.* Carlinville, Ill., Blackburn College Press, 1973, pp. 218-21.
51. Belasco, James A. "The American Association of University Professors: A Private Dispute Settlement Agency," *Industrial and Labor Relations Review,* 18:535-53, July 1965.
52. Billings, Richard N., and Greenya, John. *Power to the Public Worker.* Washington, D.C., R. B. Luce, 1974. 224p.
53. Braun, Robert J. *Teachers and Power: The Story of the American Federation of Teachers.* New York, Simon and Schuster, 1972. 287p.

54. Chaison, Gary N., and Rock, William K. "Competition between Local Independent and National Unions," *Labor Law Journal*, 25:293-97, May 1974.
55. Commission on Educational Reconstruction. *Organizing the Teaching Profession; The Story of the American Federation of Teachers*. Glencoe, Ill., Free Press, 1955. 320p.
56. "Faculty Participation in Strikes," *AAUP Bulletin*, 54:155-59, Summer 1968.
57. Kramer, Leo. *Labor's Paradox—the American Federation of State, County, and Municipal Employees, AFL-CIO*. New York, Wiley, 1962. 174p.
58. Krislov, Joseph. "The Independent Public Employee Association: Characteristics and Functions," *Industrial and Labor Relations Review*, 15: 510-20, July 1962.
59. Marshall, James F. "Public-Employee Associations—Roles and Programs," *Public Personnel Management*, 3:415-24, Sept.-Oct. 1974.
60. "NEA Statement of Position; Professional Negotiation and Grievance Procedures." In Clarence R. Hughes, *et al.*, eds. *Collective Negotiations in Higher Education...*, *op. cit.*, pp. 222-23.
61. Schlachter, Gail A. "Professional Librarians' Attitudes toward Professional and Employee Associations as Revealed by Academic Librarians in Seven Midwestern States." Unpublished Ph.D. dissertation, University of Minnesota, 1971.
62. _____. "Quasi Unions and Organizational Hegemony within the Library Field," *Library Quarterly*, 43:185-98, July 1973.
63. "Statement on Collective Bargaining," *AAUP Bulletin*, 59:167, Summer 1973.
64. Stinnett, Timothy M. *Turmoil in Teaching: A History of the Organizational Struggle for America's Teachers*. New York, Macmillan, 1968. 406p.
65. Strauss, George. "The AAUP as a Professional Occupational Association," *Industrial Relations*, 5:128-40, Oct. 1965.

THE LEGAL FRAMEWORK

Collective bargaining in libraries comes under the jurisdiction of a variety of state and federal legislation, as well as court decisions and federal and state agency rulings. A general background to U.S. labor law can be found in Wellington (69). The other three works listed deal specifically with legal aspects of collective bargaining by public employees: those by Hanslowe (66) and Sullivan (68) are treatises, while Smith's (67) is a casebook.

66. Hanslowe, Kurt L. *The Emerging Law of Labor Relations in Public Employment* (ILR Paperback No. 4). Ithaca, New York State School of Industrial and Labor Relations, Cornell University, 1967. 117p.
67. Smith, Russell A., et al. *Labor Relations Law in the Public Sector: Cases and Materials.* Indianapolis, Bobbs Merrill, 1973. 1222p.
68. Sullivan, Daniel P. *Public Employee Labor Law.* Cincinnati, W. H. Anderson Company, 1969. 312p.
69. Wellington, Harry H. *Labor and the Legal Process.* New Haven, Yale University Press, 1968. 409p.

Permissive Legislation

Libraries in the private sector, and in private colleges and universities, are subject to federal labor legislation, i.e., to the National Labor Relations Act (Wagner Act), as amended by the Labor Management Relations Act (Taft-Hartley Act) and the Labor-Management Reporting and Disclosure Act (Landrum-Griffin Act). An explanation of the provisions of these acts can be found in item 74. The sections of the law relating to organizing campaigns are discussed by Schlossberg (70), and Silverberg (71) explains the procedure for taking a case before the NLRB. In several sessions of Congress, bills have been introduced that would provide for federal regulation of collective bargaining by public employees. The provisions and prospects for passage of one of the latest of these (H.R. 8677) are discussed by Stone (72) as well as how passage of this bill would affect organizing in libraries. Until such a bill is passed, however, public employees are covered by various state laws and state court decisions. A comparative outline of the basic provisions of state public employee bargaining laws can be found in item 73.

70. Schlossberg, Stephen I. *Organizing and the Law.* Rev. ed. Washington, D.C., Bureau of National Affairs, 1971. 304p.
71. Silverberg, Louis G. *How to Take a Case before the National Labor Relations Board.* 3d ed., rev. by Kenneth C. McGuiness. Washington, D.C., Bureau of National Affairs, 1967. 442p.
72. Stone, Dennis. "The Prospect of Unionism," *American Libraries*, 5:364-66, July-Aug. 1974.
73. U.S. Department of Labor. Division of Public Employee Labor Relations. *Summary of State Policy Regulations for Public Sector Labor Relations: Statutes, Attorney Generals' Opinions and Selected Court Decisions.* Washington, D.C., U.S.G.P.O., 1973. 37p.
74. U.S. National Labor Relations Board. Office of the General Counsel. *A Layman's Guide to Basic Law under the National Labor Relations Act.* Washington, D.C., U.S.G.P.O., 1971. 59p.

Strikes

The issues here are: Should public employees have the right to strike and, if so, should employees in essential services, however "essential" may be defined, also be allowed to strike? If strikes are not permitted, what other dispute settlement procedures should be adopted? What should be the policy of the unions regarding strikes by public employees? Burton and Krider (78) and Wellington and Winter (81) present the basic arguments for and against strikes. Aboud and Aboud (75) review the literature and add a bibliography on these issues, the provisions of the laws regarding strikes, and alternatives to the strike. Barrett and Lobel (76) review the legislative provisions regarding public employee strikes and court decisions interpreting them. Dispute settlement procedures other than the strike are analyzed by Bernstein (77) and Gilroy and Sinicropi (79).

75. Aboud, Antone, and Aboud, Grace Sterrett. *The Right to Strike in Public Employment* (Key Issues Series, no. 15). Ithaca, New York State School of Industrial and Labor Relations, Cornell University, 1974. 40p.
76. Barrett, Jerome T., and Lobel, Ira B. "Public Sector Strikes—Legislative and Court Treatment," *Monthly Labor Review*, 97:19-22, Sept. 1974.
77. Bernstein, Merton C. "Alternatives to the Strike in Public Labor Relations," *Harvard Law Review*, 85:459-75, Dec. 1971.
78. Burton, John F., and Krider, Charles. "The Role and Consequences of Strikes by Public Employees," *Yale Law Journal*, 79:418-40, Jan. 1970.
79. Gilroy, Thomas P., and Sinicropi, Anthony V. *Dispute Settlement in the Public Sector: The State-of-the-Art*. Report submitted to the Division of Public Employee Labor Relations, U.S. Department of Labor. Washington, D.C., U.S.G.P.O., 1972. 141p.
80. Muir, J. Douglas. "The Strike as a Professional Sanction: The Changing Attitude of the National Education Association," *Labor Law Journal*, 19:615-27, Oct. 1968.
81. Wellington, Harry H., and Winter, Ralph K., Jr. "The Limits of Collective Bargaining in Public Employment," *Yale Law Journal*, 78:1107-27, June 1969.

COLLECTIVE BARGAINING

A widely used text for courses in collective bargaining is Chamberlain and Kuhn (87). Text-like books for public employee bargaining are item 83, Lowenberg and Moskow (95), Moskow, *et al.* (97), and Walsh (101). In addition to basic texts, a large number of studies on specific subjects have been done, of which only a representative sample can be mentioned here. The significance of the differences between the public and private sectors is assessed by Lewin (93). Alexander (82), Burton (86), and Weber (102) analyze bargaining structure and its effect on the bargaining relationship as well as organizational changes it may bring about. The problems of financial limitations and other constraints and of the treatment of managerial and confidential employees are discussed by Rehmus (98) and Bers (85), respectively. Political activity by public employee organizations and their influence on the political process is reported by Love and Sulzner (96). Several researchers have attempted to measure whether or not collective bargaining actually increases salaries, and Lipsky and Drotning (94), as well as presenting their own model, review the results of previous studies of the question. General problems of bargaining in libraries, concerns about procedures, and attitudes of various sectors of the profession are summarized in the *ALA Bulletin* (88), Gardiner (91), Vignone (99 and 100), and Wyatt (103). Factors to keep in mind when deciding whether the ALA should assume a bargaining role are pointed out by Auld (84). Librarians in colleges and universities have, for the most part, joined with faculty members for collective bargaining, and the situation in higher education is described in Ladd and Lipset (92), Duryea (89), and Tice (90).

82. Alexander, Kenneth O. "Union Structure and Bargaining Structure," *Labor Law Journal*, 24: 164-72, March 1973.
83. American Assembly. *Public Workers and Public Unions.* Sam Zagoria, ed. Englewood Cliffs, N.J., Prentice-Hall, 1972. 182p.
84. Auld, Lawrence W. S. "ALA and Collective Bargaining," *ALA Bulletin*, 63:96-97, Jan. 1969.
85. Bers, Melvin K. *The Status of Managerial, Supervisory, and Confidential Employees in Government Employment Relations.* Albany, New York State Public Employment Relations Board, 1970. 190p.
86. Burton, John F., Jr. "Local Government Bargaining and Management Structure," *Industrial Relations*, 11:123-39, May 1972.
87. Chamberlain, Neil W., and Kuhn, James W. *Collective Bargaining.* 2d ed. New York, McGraw-Hill, 1965. 451p.
88. "Collective Bargaining: Questions and Answers," *ALA Bulletin*, 62:1385-90, Dec. 1968.
89. Duryea, Edwin D., et al. *Faculty Unions and Collective Bargaining.* San Francisco, Jossey-Bass, 1973. 236p.
90. *Faculty Power: Collective Bargaining on Campus.* Terence N. Tice, ed. Ann Arbor, Institute of Continuing Legal Education, 1972. 368p.
91. Gardiner, George L. "Collective Bargaining: Some Questions Asked," *ALA Bulletin*, 62:973-76, Sept. 1968.

92. Ladd, Everett C., and Lipset, Seymour M. *Professors, Unions and Higher Education.* Berkeley, Carnegie Commission on Higher Education, 1973. 124p.
93. Lewin, D. "Public Employment Relations: Confronting the Issues," *Industrial Relations*, 12:309-21, Oct. 1973.
94. Lipsky, David B., and Drotning, John E. "The Influence of Collective Bargaining on Teachers' Salaries in New York State," *Industrial and Labor Relations Review*, 27:18-35, Oct. 1973.
95. Loewenberg, J. Joseph, and Moskow, Michael. *Collective Bargaining in Government: Readings and Cases.* Englewood Cliffs, N.J., Prentice-Hall, 1972. 362p.
96. Love, Thomas M., and Sulzner, George T. "Political Implications of Public Employee Bargaining," *Industrial Relations*, 11:18-33, Feb. 1972.
97. Moskow, Michael H., et al. *Collective Bargaining in Public Employment.* New York, Random House, 1970. 336p.
98. Rehmus, Charles M. "Constraints on Local Governments in Public Employee Bargaining," *Michigan Law Review*, 67:919-30, March 1969.
99. Vignone, Joseph A. "An Inquiry into the Opinions and Attitudes of Public Librarians, Library Directors and Library Board Members Concerning Collective Bargaining Procedures for Public Library Employees in Pennsylvania." Unpublished Ph.D. dissertation, University of Pittsburgh, 1970. 204p.
100. _____. *Collective Bargaining Procedures for Public Library Employees: An Inquiry into the Opinions and Attitudes of Public Librarians, Directors and Board Members.* Metuchen, N.J., Scarecrow Press, 1971. 179p.
101. Walsh, Robert E., ed. *Sorry...No Government Today; Unions vs. City Hall.* Boston, Beacon Press, 1969. 325p.
102. Weber, Arnold R. "The Structure of Collective Bargaining: Introduction." In Arnold R. Weber, ed. *The Structure of Collective Bargaining.* New York, Free Press of Glencoe, 1961, pp. xv-xxxii.
103. Wyatt, James. "A Study of Attitudes toward Library Union Organization and Collective Bargaining Held by Academic Librarians, Library Directors, and Deans in Colleges and Universities of Eight Southern States." Unpublished Ph.D. dissertation, Florida State University, 1973.

Unit Determination

The composition of the bargaining unit has important implications for both organizing and collective bargaining, and the criteria for inclusion or exclusion of various classes of employees are often disputed. Related to this is the question, discussed by Sullivan (108), of whether the criteria used for private sector unit determinations are applicable to public employee unit determinations. A thorough review of practices, problems, and policy questions is presented in Gilroy and Russo (104). Rock (107) deals with the particular problem of proliferation of units and what this means for orderly collective bargaining. McHugh (106) and Kahn (105) discuss the special problems of unit determination in colleges and universities, and Kahn particularly examines the NLRB's policy on inclusion of non-teaching academic staff in units with teaching faculty.

104. Gilroy, Thomas P., and Russo, Anthony C. *Bargaining Unit Issues: Problems, Criteria, Tactics* (Public Employee Relations Library, no. 43). Chicago, International Personnel Management Association, 1973. 62p.
105. Kahn, Kenneth. "The NLRB and Higher Education: The Failure of Policymaking through Adjudication," *UCLA Law Review*, 21:63-180, Oct. 1973.
106. McHugh, William F. "Collective Bargaining with Professionals in Higher Education: Problems in Unit Determination," *Wisconsin Law Review*, 1:55-90, 1971.
107. Rock, Eli. "The Appropriate Unit Question in the Public Service: The Problem of Proliferation," *Michigan Law Review*, 67:1001-16, March 1969.
108. Sullivan, Daniel P. "Appropriate Unit Determinations in Public Employee Collective Bargaining," *Mercer Law Review*, 19:402-17, Summer 1968.

How to Negotiate

Negotiating a collective bargaining contract is a three-stage process. The first stage is preparation—formulating demands, counterproposals, and strategy. Negotiation manuals, such as that prepared by the AFT (109), are intended to help local unions become informed on various issues and to suggest possible clauses for the contract. Management, too, has its reference tools; Morse (121) and the National Industrial Conference Board (123) give general guidelines, and Overton and Wortman (122) describe methods for preparation of proposals. The book by Ryder, *et al.* (124), is a survey of company practices when preparing for bargaining, with a detailed discussion of the various steps in the process.

An important question in public employee negotiations is: With whom should the union negotiate? In many instances fiscal control and managerial control are vested in two different bodies, and deciding who should conduct the negotiations has important consequences, as Derber (112) points out.

Practical guides for the conduct of negotiations, the second stage, can be found, for the public sector, in Hastings (114), Heisel and Hallihan (115), and

Warner and Hennessy (125). For colleges and universities, Howe (116) offers guidelines and Coe (111) a description of actual practices. Lewis' article (119) presents management's view of the negotiation of a contract at the Brooklyn Public Library, and Lubin and Brandwein (120) present the union view of the same negotiations. Levin (117) describes various kinds of fringe benefits, along with their advantages and disadvantages, and points out things to keep in mind when negotiating benefits. How to calculate the cost of specific contract provisions and the pitfalls that may be encountered when doing so are analyzed by Granof (113) and Levine (118).

The final stage of negotiation is to embody the proposals agreed upon in a contract, described by Clark (110).

109. American Federation of Teachers. Department of Collective Bargaining Services. *Negotiations Manual.* John Oliver, comp. Washington, D.C., AFT, 1972. Looseleaf.
110. Clark, R. Theodore, Jr. *Drafting the Public Sector Labor Agreement* (Public Employee Relations Library, no. 13). Chicago, Public Personnel Association, 1969. 35p.
111. Coe, Alan C. "A Study of the Procedures used in Collective Bargaining with Faculty Unions in Public Universities," *Journal of the College and University Personnel Association,* 24:1-22, March 1973; 24:1-44, May 1973; 24:1-25, Sept. 1973.
112. Derber, Milton. "Who Negotiates for the Public Employer?" *In* Keith Ocheltree, ed. *Perspective in Public Employee Negotiation* (Public Employee Relations Library, special issue). Chicago, Public Personnel Association, 1969, pp. 52-58.
113. Granof, Michael H. *How to Cost Your Labor Contract.* Washington, D.C., Bureau of National Affairs, 1973. 147p.
114. Hastings, Robert H. "How to Bargain in the Public Service," *Good Government,* 87:8-14, Winter 1970.
115. Heisel, W. D., and Hallihan, J. D. *Questions and Answers on Public Employee Negotiation.* Chicago, Public Personnel Association, 1967. 214p.
116. Howe, Ray A. "The Bloody Business of Bargaining," *College and University Business,* 48:63-67, March 1970.
117. Levin, Noel A. *Negotiating Fringe Benefits* (AMA Management Briefing). New York, AMACOM, 1973. 39p.
118. Levine, Gilbert. "Assessing the Cost and Benefits of Collective Bargaining: The Potential Use of Costing," *Relations Industrielles,* 28:817-25, Oct. 1973.
119. Lewis, Robert. "A New Dimension in Library Administration– Negotiating a Union Contract," *ALA Bulletin,* 63:455-64, April 1969.

120. Lubin, Martin, and Brandwein, Larry. "Negotiating a Collective Bargaining Agreement—the Union Perspective," *ALA Bulletin*, 63:973-79, July-Aug. 1969.
121. Morse, Bruce. *How to Negotiate the Labor Agreement; An Outline Summary of Tested Bargaining Practice Expanded from Earlier Editions.* Detroit, Trends Publishing Co., 1971. 83p.
122. Overton, Craig, and Wortman, Max S., Jr. "Proposals and Counterproposals in Public Sector Collective Bargaining," *Journal of Collective Negotiations in the Public Sector*, 2:125-34, Spring 1973.
123. *Preparing for Collective Bargaining.* Part I—Studies in Personnel Policy, no. 172. Part II—Studies in Personnel Policy, no. 182. New York, National Industrial Conference Board, 1959, 1961.
124. Ryder, Meyer S., et al. *Management Preparation for Collective Bargaining.* Homewood, Ill., Dow Jones-Irwin, 1966. 151p.
125. Warner, Kenneth O., and Hennessy, Mary L. *Public Management at the Bargaining Table.* Chicago, Public Personnel Association, 1967. 490p.

Scope of Bargaining

The scope of bargaining refers to what items can be subjects for bargaining, or, to put it in Wildman's terms (131), "What's negotiable?" A subset of that question is: What should be negotiable and what have the law and the courts said must be negotiated? Two general surveys of the concepts and problems connected with the scope of bargaining are those by Gerhart (127) and Prasow (130). For the public employer, scope is especially a problem because of its possible conflict with sovereignty. Helburn (128) discusses the principles involved and what appropriate public policy might be. Historically the scope of bargaining has tended to widen and, particularly with governmental and professional employees, to include non-labor policies of management as well as its labor policies (126). This does not mean, however, that economic issues have declined in importance, as Johnson's study (129) reveals.

126. "Collective Bargaining and the Professional Employee," *Columbia Law Review*, 69:277-98, Feb. 1969.
127. Gerhart, Paul F. "The Scope of Bargaining in Local Government Labor Negotiations." In *Proceedings of the 1969 Annual Spring Meeting, Industrial Relations Research Association.* Madison, Industrial Relations Research Association, 1969, pp. 545-52.
128. Helburn, I. B. "The Scope of Bargaining in Public Sector Negotiations: Sovereignty Reviewed," *Journal of Collective Negotiations in the Public Sector*, 3:147-66, Spring 1974.

129. Johnson, Paul V. *Wages and Hours as Significant Issues in Collective Bargaining* (Paper No. 309). Lafayette, Ind., Herman C. Krannert Graduate School of Industrial Administration, Purdue University, 1971. 28p.
130. Prasow, Paul, et al. *Scope of Bargaining in the Public Sector—Concepts and Problems.* Washington, D.C., Division of Public Employee Labor Relations, U.S. Department of Labor, 1972. 156p.
131. Wildman, Wesley A. "What's Negotiable?" *American School Board Journal*, 155:7-10, Nov. 1967.

Administering the Contract, Including Grievances and Arbitration

Frequently, if management has never been a party to a collective bargaining relationship before, the day-to-day operation under the contract brings about administrative changes (132, 137, and 143). Mechanisms and procedures have to be instituted by both parties to carry out the terms agreed upon (136, 138, 139, and 140) and to promote a smooth working relationship. Some (141) would argue that a union can be a help in administration. Should there be any dispute about the interpretation or application of the contract terms, a grievance procedure can usually be resorted to. In general, the grievance procedures prevailing in the private sector have been adopted into the public sector (133). The details of the procedures may vary considerably (144), but the mechanisms are all intended to insure due process (145). The final step in many grievance procedures is arbitration, and the books by Elkouri and Elkouri (134), Fleming (135), and Prasow and Peters (142) offer thorough discussions of the nature and operation of arbitration as well as analyses of arbitration awards.

132. Association of Research Libraries. Office of University Library Management Studies. *Review of Collective Bargaining Activities in Academic and Research Libraries* (ARL Management Supplement, vol. 1, no. 3). Washington, D.C., Association of Research Libraries, 1973. 4p.
133. Begin, James P. "The Private Grievance Model in the Public Sector," *Industrial Relations*, 10:21-35, Feb. 1971.
134. Elkouri, Frank, and Elkouri, Edna. *How Arbitration Works.* 3d ed. Washington, D.C., Bureau of National Affairs, 1973. 819p.
135. Fleming, R. W. *The Labor Arbitration Process.* Urbana, University of Illinois Press, 1965. 233p.
136. Geller, William S. "Working with the Library Union, an Administrator's Experience," *California Librarian*, 3:50-62, Jan. 1972.
137. Gibson, Frank E. "Effects of the Activities of the Unions in the Minneapolis Public Library on Library Functions and Administrative

Processes and upon Union Members." Unpublished master's thesis, University of Minnesota, 1952.
138. Heisel, W. Donald. *Day-to-Day Union-Management Relationships* (Public Employee Relations Library, no. 31). Chicago, Public Personnel Association, 1971. 34p.
139. Krause, Robert D., et al. *Making the Collective Bargaining Agreement Work* (Public Employee Relations Library, no. 14). Chicago, Public Personnel Association, 1969. 29p.
140. Marceau, LeRoy, ed. *Dealing with a Union.* New York, American Management Association, 1969. 256p.
141. Mleynek, Darryl. "Unions—What's in it for Administrators?" *Wilson Library Bulletin,* 43:752-55, April 1969.
142. Prasow, Paul, and Peters, Edward. *Arbitration and Collective Bargaining: Conflict Resolution in Labor Relations.* New York, McGraw-Hill, 1970. 426p.
143. Stanley, David T. *Managing Local Government under Union Pressure.* Washington, D.C., Brookings Institution, 1972. 177p.
144. Ullman, Joseph C., and Begin, James P. "The Structure and Scope of Appeals Procedures for Public Employees," *Industrial and Labor Relations Review,* 23:323-34, April 1970.
145. Volkersz, Evert. "The Grievance: First Step in Improved Library Government," *ALA Bulletin,* 63:1566-69, Dec. 1969.

RELATED ISSUES

This section is not meant to present an exhaustive list, but rather an indication of some of the more important issues that can affect, or be affected by, collective bargaining.

Professionalism vs. Unionism

The literature on this subject falls into two groups: (1) analyses of how professionalism influences employee behavior and attitudes toward unions (147, 149, 150, and 152), and (2) arguments about whether librarians are professionals (146 and 148). Mleynek (151) suggests librarians use collective bargaining to achieve professional goals.

146. Bundy, Mary Lee, and Wasserman, Paul. "Professionalism Reconsidered," *College & Research Libraries,* 29:5-26, Jan. 1968.
147. Etzioni, Amitai, ed. *The Semi-Professions and their Organization: Teachers, Nurses, Social Workers.* New York, Free Press, 1969. 328p.

148. Flanagan, Leo N. "Professionalism Dismissed?" *College & Research Libraries*, 34:209-14, May 1973.
149. Kleingartner, Archie. *Professionalism and Salaried Worker Organization.* Madison, Industrial Relations Research Institute, University of Wisconsin, 1967. 113p.
150. Lipset, Seymour M. "White Collar Workers and Professionals—their Attitudes and Behavior towards Unions." *In* William A. Faunce, ed. *Readings in Industrial Sociology.* New York, Appleton-Century-Crofts, 1967, pp. 525-48.
151. Mleynek, Darryl. "Professional Unions," *California Librarian*, 31:110-18, April 1970.
152. Myers, Donald A. *Teacher Power: Professionalization and Collective Bargaining.* Lexington, Mass., Lexington Books, 1973. 199p.

Merit Systems

Subjects of bargaining, such as hiring, promotions, transfers, training, grievance procedures, job classification, wages and benefits are often regulated by civil service systems for public employees. There may be conflicts where they overlap. A general review of the problem can be found in item 160. The rest of the references that are listed offer assessments of whether the two systems are compatible and, if not, how they can be reconciled, except for Lelchook (155), who looks at the nature of civil service employee associations and how they are responding to collective bargaining.

153. Feigenbaum, Charles. "Civil Service and Collective Bargaining: Conflict or Compatibility," *Public Personnel Management*, 3:244-52, May-June 1974.
154. Helburn, I. B., and Bennett, N. D. "Public Employee Bargaining and the Merit Principle," *Labor Law Journal*, 23:618-29, Oct. 1972.
155. Lelchook, Jerry. *State Civil Service Employee Associations; An LMSA Staff Study.* Washington, D.C., U.S.G.P.O., 1974. 89p.
156. Nesbitt, Murray B. "The Civil Service Merit System and Collective Bargaining." Unpublished Ph.D. dissertation, New York University, 1962. 305p.
157. Shils, Edward B. "Collective Bargaining Can Strengthen the Merit System," *Public Employee*, 32:11, Oct. 1967.
158. Stanley, David T. "What are Unions Doing to Merit Systems?" *Public Personnel Review*, 31:108-13, April 1970.
159. _____. "What's Happening to the Civil Service?" *Good Government*, 91:16-19, Summer 1974.
160. U.S. Labor-Management Services Administration. Office of Labor-Management Policy Development. *Collective Bargaining in Public Em-*

ployment and the Merit System. Prepared by Jerry Lelchook and Herbert J. Lahne. Washington, D.C., U.S.G.P.O., 1972. 114p.

Women in Unions

Women have a long history of activity in labor unions, and some have been nationally known leaders of the labor movement. As more and more women join the labor force, their concerns will have to be incorporated into union policies and programs. Union policies on "women's issues" are historically examined by Cook (162). Figures on the status of women union members can be found in Dewey (163), and Bergquist (161) offers statistical data to support the thesis that the increase in female union membership has not been accompanied by a proportional increase in the number of union leadership positions held by women.

In order to make the influence of women in the labor movement stronger, in the spring of 1974 a convention of union women was held, out of which grew the Coalition of Labor Union Women. The convention and the founding of the coalition are described in 164, 165, and 166.

161. Bergquist, Virginia A. "Women's Participation in Labor Organizations," *Monthly Labor Review*, 97:3-9, Oct. 1974.
162. Cook, Alice H. "Women and American Trade Unions," *Annals*, 375: 124-32, Jan. 1968.
163. Dewey, Lucretia M. "Women in Labor Unions," *Monthly Labor Review*, 94:42-48, Feb. 1971.
164. Sexton, Patricia Cayo. "Workers (Female) Arise!" *Dissent*, 21:380-95, Summer 1974.
165. Weiner, Lois. "Women Trade Unionists Organize," *New Politics*, 11:31-35, Winter 1974.
166. "Women Push for Union Power," *Business Week*, 2324:102, March 30, 1974.

Sex Discrimination

The status of women in the labor force is described in the *Monthly Labor Review* (178), while Kreps (172) concentrates on the labor market for women. A quantitative analysis of the extent of sex discrimination is presented in Tsuchigane and Dodge (177). The case study by Malkiel and Malkiel (173) suggests that the real source of economic discrimination lies in exclusion from higher paying jobs rather than in salary differentials for men and women in the same job.

Data on the status of women in libraries is presented by Blankenship (167), Schiller (175), and Carpenter and Shearer (168), who update their previous study of pay differentials (*Library Journal*, Nov. 15, 1972). The particular situation in law libraries and in archives is discussed by Hughes (171) and Deutrich (170), respectively.

Several types of remedial action have been suggested. Schiller (174) suggests what the ALA might do to draw attention to the unequal status of women librarians. De Fichy (169) advocates affirmative action committees and suggests steps they might take. Smith (176) relates a case study in which collective bargaining was used to remedy sex discrimination.

167. Blankenship, W. C. "Head Librarians: How Many Men? How Many Women?" *College & Research Libraries*, 28:41-48, Jan. 1967.
168. Carpenter, Raymond L., and Shearer, Kenneth D. "Sex and Salary Update," *Library Journal*, 99:101-07, Jan. 15, 1974.
169. De Fichy, Wendy. "Affirmative Action: Equal Opportunity for Women in Library Management," *College & Research Libraries*, 34:195-201, May 1973.
170. Deutrich, Mabel E. "Women in Archives: Ms. versus Mr. Archivist," *American Archivist*, 36:171-81, April 1973.
171. Hughes, Marija. "Sex-Based Discrimination in Law Libraries," *Law Library Journal*, 64:13-21, Feb. 1971.
172. Kreps, Juanita. *Sex in the Marketplace: American Women at Work*. Baltimore, Johns Hopkins Press, 1971. 117p.
173. Malkiel, Burton G., and Malkiel, Judith A. "Male-Female Pay Differentials in Professional Employment," *American Economic Review*, 63:693-705, Sept. 1973.
174. Schiller, Anita R. "The Disadvantaged Majority: Women Employed in Libraries," *American Libraries* 1:345-49, April 1970.
175. _____. "The Widening Sex Gap," *Library Journal*, 94:1098-1100, March 15, 1969.
176. Smith, Georgina M. "Faculty Women at the Bargaining Table," *AAUP Bulletin*, 59:402-06, Winter 1973.
177. Tsuchigane, Robert and Dodge, Norton. *Economic Discrimination against Women in the United States: Measures and Changes*. Lexington, Mass., Lexington Books, 1974. 152p.
178. "Women in the Workplace: A Special Section," *Monthly Labor Review*, 97:3-58, May 1974.

Glossary of Collective Bargaining Terms

Agency Shop A provision in a collective agreement which requires that all employees in the negotiating unit who do not join the exclusive representative pay a fixed amount monthly, usually the equivalent of organization dues, as a condition of employment. Under some arrangements, the payments are allocated to the organization's welfare fund or to a recognized charity. An agency shop may operate in conjunction with a modified union shop. (See *Union Shop*.)

Agreement See *Collective Bargaining*. A written agreement between an employer (or an association of employers) and an employee organization (or organizations), usually for a definite term, defining conditions of employment, rights of employees and the employee organization, and procedures to be followed in settling disputes or handling issues that arise during the life of the agreement.

American Arbitration Association (AAA) A private nonprofit organization established to aid professional arbitrators in their work through legal and technical services, and to promote arbitration as a method of settling commercial and labor disputes. The AAA provides lists of qualified arbitrators to employee organizations and employers on request.

American Federation of Labor-Congress of Industrial Organizations (AFL-CIO) A federation of approximately 130 autonomous national/international unions created by the merger of the American Federation of Labor (AFL) and the Congress of Industrial Organizations (CIO) in December 1955. More than 80 percent of union members in the United States are members of unions affiliated with the AFL-CIO. The initials AFL-CIO after the name of a union indicate that the union is an affiliate.

Annual Improvement Factor Wage increases granted automatically each contract year, which are based upon increased employee productivity.

Arbitration (Voluntary, Compulsory, Advisory) Method of settling employment disputes through recourse to an impartial third party, whose decision is usually final and binding. Arbitration is voluntary when both parties agree to submit disputed issues to arbitration and compulsory if required by law. A court order to carry through a voluntary arbitration agreement is not generally considered as compulsory arbitration. Advisory arbitration is arbitration without a final and binding award.

Arbitrator (Impartial Chairman) An impartial third party to whom disputing parties submit their differences for decision (award). An ad hoc

---

Prepared by the Labor Relations Training Center, Bureau of Training, U.S. Civil Service Commission.

arbitrator is one selected to act in a specific case or a limited group of cases. A permanent arbitrator is one selected to serve for the life of the agreement or for a stipulated term, hearing all disputes that arise during this period.

Authorization Card A statement signed by an employee authorizing an organization to act as his representative in dealings with the employer, or authorizing the employer to deduct organization dues from his pay (check-off). (See *Card Check*.)

Bargaining Rights Legally recognized rights to represent employees in negotiations with employers.

Bargaining Unit Group of employees recognized by the employer or group of employers, or designated by an authorized agency as appropriate for representation by an organization for purposes of collective negotiations.

Boycott Effort by an employee organization, usually in collaboration with other organizations, to discourage the purchase, handling or use of products of an employer with whom the organization is in dispute. When such action is extended to another employer doing business with the employer involved in the dispute, it is termed a secondary boycott.

Bumping (Rolling) Practice that allows a senior employee (in seniority ranking or length of service) to displace a junior employee in another job or department during a layoff or reduction in force. (See *Seniority*.)

Business Agent (Union Representative) Generally a full-time paid employee or official of a local union whose duties include day-to-day dealing with employers and workers, adjustment of grievances, enforcement of agreements, and similar activities. (See *International Representative*.)

Business Unionism ("Bread-and-Butter" Unionism) Union emphasis on higher wages and better working conditions through collective bargaining rather than political action or radical reform of scoiety. The term has been widely used to characterize the objectives of the trade union movement in the United States.

Call-in Pay (Callback Pay) Amount of pay guaranteed to a worker recalled to work after completing his regular work shift. Call-in pay is often used as a synonym for reporting pay. (See *Reporting Pay*.)

Card Check Procedure whereby signed authorization cards are checked against a list of employees in a prospective negotiating unit to determine if the organization has majority status. *The employer may recognize the organization on the basis of this check without a formal election.* Card checks are often conducted by an outside party, e.g., a respected member of the community. (See *Authorization Card*.)

Certification Formal designation by a government agency of the organization selected by the majority of the employees in a supervised election to act as an exclusive representative for all employees in the bargaining unit.

Check-off (Payroll Deduction of Dues) Practice whereby the employer, by agreement with the employee organization (upon written authorization from each employee where required by law or agreement), regularly withholds organizational dues from employees' salary payments and transfers these funds to the organization. The check-off is a common practice and is not dependent upon the existence of a formal organizational security clause. The check-off arrangement may also provide for deductions of initiation fees and assessments. (See *Union Secutity*.)

Closed Shop A form of organizational security provided in an agreement which binds the employer to hire and retain only organization members in good standing. The closed shop is prohibited by the Labor-Management Relations Act of 1947 which applies, however, only to employers and employees in industries affecting interstate commerce.

Collective Bargaining A process whereby employees as a group and their employers make offers and counter-offers in good faith on the conditions of their employment relationship for the purpose of reaching a mutually acceptable agreement, and the execution of a written document incorporating any such agreement if requested by either party. Also, a process whereby representatives of the employees and their employer jointly determine the conditions of employment.

Company Union An employee organization that is organized, financed or dominated by the employer and is thus suspected of being an agent of the employer rather than of the employees. Company unions are prohibited under the Labor-Management Relations Act of 1947. The term also survives as a derogatory charge leveled against an employee organization accused of being ineffectual.

Compulsory Arbitration (See *Arbitration*.)

Conciliation (See *Mediation*.)

Consultation An obligation on the part of employers to consult the employee organization on particular issues before taking action on them. In general, the process of consultation lies between notification to the employee organization, which may amount simply to providing information, and negotiation, which implies agreement on the part of the organization before the action can be taken.

Continuous Negotiating Committees (Interim Committees) Committees established by employers and employee organizations in a collective negotiating relationship to keep an agreement under constant review, and to discuss possible changes in it long in advance of its expiration date. The continuous committee may provide for third-party participation.

Contract Bar A denial of a request for a representation election, forced on the existence of a collective agreement. Such an election will not be conducted by the National Labor Relations Board if there is in effect a written agreement which is binding upon the parties, has not been in effect for more than a "reasonable" time, and its terms are consistent with the National Labor Relations Act. "Contract bars" in state governments are established by state laws and state agencies.

Cooling-off Period A period of time which must elapse before a strike or lockout can begin or be resumed by agreement or by law. The term derives from the hope that the tensions of unsuccessful negotiation will subside in time so that a work stoppage can be averted.

Craft Union A labor organization which limits membership to workers having a particular craft or skill or working at closely related trades. In practice, many so-called craft unions also enroll members outside the craft field, and some come to resemble industrial unions in all major respects. The traditional distinction between craft and industrial unions has been substantially blurred. (See *Industrial Union*.)

Craft Unit A bargaining unit composed solely of workers having a recognized skill, e.g., electricians, machinists, or plumbers.

Credited Service Years of employment counted for retirement, severance pay, seniority. (See *Seniority*.)

Crisis Bargaining Collective bargaining taking place under the shadow of an imminent strike deadline, as distinguished from extended negotiations in which both parties enjoy ample time to present and discuss their positions. (See *Continuous Negotiating Committees*.)

Decertification Withdrawal by a government agency of an organization's official recognition as exclusive negotiating representative.

Dispute Any disagreement between employers and the employee organization which requires resolution, e.g., inability to agree on contract terms or unsettled grievances.

Downgrading (Demotion) Reassignment of workers to tasks or jobs requiring lower skills and with lower rates of pay.

Dual Unionism A charge (usually a punishable offense) leveled at a union member or officer who seeks or accepts membership or position in a rival union, or otherwise attempts to undermine a union by helping its rival.

Dues Deduction (See *Check-off*.)

Election (See *Representation Election*.)

Escalator Clause Provision in an agreement stipulating that wages are to be automatically increased or reduced periodically according to a schedule related to changes in the cost of living, as measured by a designated index or, occasionally, to another standard, e.g., an average earnings figure. Term may also apply to any tie between an employee benefit and the cost of living, as in a pension plan.

Escape Clause General term signifying release from an obligation. One example is found in maintenance-of-membership arrangements which give union members an "escape period" during which they may resign from membership in the union without forfeiting their jobs.

Exclusive Bargaining Rights The right and obligation of an employee organization designated as majority representative to negotiate collectively for all employees, including nonmembers, in the negotiating unit.

Fact-finding Board A group of individuals appointed to investigate, assemble and report the facts in an employment dispute, sometimes with authority to make recommendations for settlement.

"Favored Nations" Clause An agreement provision indicating that one party to the agreement (employer or union) shall have the opportunity to share in more favorable terms negotiated by the other party with another employer or union.

Federal Mediation and Conciliation Service (FMCS) An independent federal agency which provides mediators to assist the parties involved in negotiations, or in a labor dispute, in reaching a settlement; provides lists of suitable arbitrators on request, and engages in various types of "preventive mediation." Mediation services are also provided by several state agencies.

Free Riders A derogatory term applied to persons who share in the benefits resulting from the activities of an employee organization but who are not members of, and pay no dues to, the organization.

Fringe Benefits Generally, supplements to wages or salaries received by employees at a cost to employers. The term encompasses a host of practices (paid vacations, pensions, health and insurance plans, etc.) that usually add to something more than a "fringe," and is sometimes applied to a practice that may constitute a dubious "benefit" to workers. No agreement prevails as to the list of practices that should be called fringe benefits. Other terms often substituted for fringe benefits include "wage extras," "hidden payroll," "nonwage labor costs," and "supplementary wage practices." The Bureau of Labor Statistics uses the phrase "selected supplementary compensation or remuneration practices," which is then defined for survey purposes.

Grievance Any complaint or expressed dissatisfaction by an employee in connection with his job, pay, or other aspects of his employment. Whether such complaint or expressed dissatisfaction is formally recognized and handled as a "grievance" depends on the scope of the grievance procedure.

Grievance Procedure Typically a formal plan, specified in a collective agreement, which provides for the adjustment of grievances through discussions at progressively higher levels of authority in management and the employee organization, usually culminating in arbitration if necessary. Formal plans may also be found in companies and public agencies in which there is no organization to represent employees.

Impartial Chairman (Umpire) An arbitrator employed jointly by an employee organization and an employer, usually on a long-term basis, to serve as the impartial party on a tripartite arbitration board and to decide all disputes or specific kinds of disputes arising during the life of the contract. The functions of an impartial chairman often expand with experience and the growing confidence of the parties, and he alone may constitute the arbitration board in practice.

Industrial Union (Vertical Union) A union that represents all or most of the production, maintenance, and related workers, both skilled and unskilled, in an industry or company. Industrial unions may also include office, sales and technical employees of the same companies. (See *Craft Union*.)

Injunction (Labor Injunction) Court order restraining one or more persons, corporations or unions from performing some act which the court believes would result in irreparable injury to property or other rights.

International Representative (National Representative, Field Representative) Generally, a full-time employee of a national or international union whose duties include assisting in the formation of local unions, dealing with affiliated local unions on union business, assisting in negotiations and grievance settlements, settling disputes within and between locals, etc. (See *Business Agent*.)

International Union A union claiming jurisdiction both within and outside the United States (usually in Canada). Sometimes the term is loosely applied to all national unions, i.e., "international" and "national" are used interchangeably.

Job Posting Listing of available jobs, usually on a bulletin board, so that employees may bid for promotion or transfer.

Joint Bargaining Process in which two or more unions join forces in negotiating an agreement with a single employer.

Jurisdictional Dispute Conflict between two or more employee organizations over the organization of a particular establishment or whether a certain type of work should be performed by members of one organization or another. A jurisdictional strike is a work stoppage resulting from a jurisdictional dispute.

Labor Grades One of a series of rate steps (single rate or a range of rates) in the wage structure of an establishment. Labor grades are typically the outcome of some form of job evaluation, or of wage-rate negotiations, by which different occupations are grouped, so that occupations of approximately equal "value" or "worth" fall into the same grade and, thus, command the same rate of pay.

Labor-Management Relations Act of 1947 (Taft-Hartley Act) Federal law, amending the National Labor Relations Act (Wagner Act), 1935, which, among other changes, defined and made illegal a number of unfair labor practices by unions. It preserved the guarantee of the right of workers to organize and bargain collectively with their employers, or to refrain from such activities, and retained the definition of unfair labor practices as applied to employers. The act does not apply to employees in a business or industry where a labor dispute would not affect interstate commerce. Other major exclusions are: employees subject to the Railway Labor Act, agricultural workers, government employees, nonprofit hospital workers, domestic servants, and supervisors. Amended by Labor-Management Reporting and Disclosure Act of 1959. (See *National Labor Relations Act; National Labor Relations Board; Unfair Labor Practice.*)

Labor-Management Reporting and Disclosure Act of 1959 (Landrum-Griffin Act) A federal law designated "to eliminate or prevent improper practices on the part of labor organizations, employers," etc. Its seven titles include a bill of rights to protect members in their relations with unions, regulations of trusteeships, standards for elections, and fiduciary responsibility of union officers. The Labor-Management Relations Act of 1947 was amended in certain respects by this act.

Maintenance of Membership Clause A clause in a collective agreement providing that employees who are members of the employee organization at the time the agreement is negotiated, or who voluntarily join the organization subsequently, must maintain their membership for the duration of the agreement, or possibly a shorter period, as a condition of continued employment. (See *Union Security.*)

Management Prerogatives Rights reserved to management, which may be expressly noted as such in a collective agreement. Management prerogatives usually include the right to schedule work, to maintain order and efficiency, to hire, etc.

Master Agreement A single or uniform collective agreement covering a number of installations of a single employer or the members of an employers' association. (See *Multi-employer Bargaining.*)

Mediation (Conciliation) An attempt by a third party to help in negotiations or in the settlement of an employment dispute through suggestion, advice, or other ways of stimulating agreement, short of dictating its provisions (a characteristic of arbitration). Most of the mediation in the United States is undertaken through federal and state mediation agencies. A mediator is a person who undertakes mediation of a dispute. Conciliation is synonymous with mediation.

Merit Increase An increase in employee compensation given on the basis of individual efficiency and performance.

Moonlighting The simultaneous holding of more than one paid employment by an employee, e.g., a full-time job and a supplementary job with another employer, or self-employment.

Multi-employer Bargaining Collective bargaining between a union or unions and a group of employers, usually represented by an employer association, resulting in a uniform or master agreement.

National Labor Relations Act of 1935 (Wagner Act) Basic federal act guaranteeing employees the right to organize and bargain collectively through representatives of their own choosing. The act also defined "unfair labor practices" as regards employers. It was amended by the Labor-Management Relations Act of 1947 and the Labor-Management Reporting and Disclosure Act of 1959.

National Labor Relations Board (NLRB) Agency created by the National Labor Relations Act (1935) and continued through subsequent amendments. The functions of the NLRB are to define appropriate bargaining units, to hold elections to determine whether a majority of workers workers want to be represented by a specific union or no union, to certify unions to represent employees, to interpret and apply the act's provisions prohibiting certain employer and union unfair practices, and otherwise to administer the provisons of the act. (See *Labor Management Relations Act of 1947.*)

National Union Ordinarily, a union composed of a number of affiliated local unions. In its union directory, the Bureau of Labor Statistics defines a national union as one with agreements with different employers in more than one state, or an affiliate of the AFL-CIO, or a national organization of government employees. (See *International Union*.)

No-strike and No-lockout Clause Provision in a collective agreement in which the employee organization agrees not to strike and the employer agrees not to lockout for the duration of the contract. These pledges may be hedged by certain qualifications, e.g., the organization may strike if the employer violates the agreement.

Open-end Agreement Collective bargaining agreement with no definite termination date, usually subject to reopening for negotiations or to termination at any time upon proper notice by either party.

Open Shop A policy of not recognizing or dealing with a labor union, or a place of employment where union membership is not a condition of employment. (See *Union Security*.)

Package Settlement The total money value (usually quoted in cents per hour) of a change in wages or salaries and supplementary benefits negotiated by an employee organization in a contract renewal or reopening.

Past Practice Clause Existing practices in the town, sanctioned by use and acceptance, that are not specifically included in the collective bargaining agreement, except, perhaps, by reference to their continuance.

Pattern Bargaining The practice whereby employers and employee organizations reach collective agreements similar to those reached by the leading employers and employee organizations in the field.

Payroll Deductions Amounts withheld from employees' earnings by the employer for social security, federal income taxes, and other governmental levies; may also include organization dues, group insurance premiums, and other authorized assignments. (See *Check-off*.)

Picketing Patrolling, usually near the place of employment, by members of the employee organization to publicize the existence of a dispute, persuade employees and the public to support a strike, etc. Organizational picketing is carried on by an employee organization for the purpose of persuading employees to join the organization or authorize it to represent them. Recognitional picketing is carried on to compel the employer to recognize the organization as the exclusive negotiating agent for his employees. Informational picketing is directed toward advising the public that an employer does not employ members of, or have an agreement with, an employee organization.

Preventive Mediation Procedures designed to anticipate and to study potential problems of employment relations. These procedures may involve early entry into employment disputes before a strike threatens.

Probationary Employee A worker in a probationary period. Where informal probation is the practice, a worker who has not yet attained the status of regular employee may be called a temporary employee.

Probationary Period Usually a stipulated period of time (e.g., 30 days) during which a newly hired employee is on trial prior to establishing seniority or otherwise becoming a regular employee. Sometimes used in relation to discipline, e.g., a period during which a regular employee, guilty of misbehavior, is on trial.

Raiding (No-raiding Agreement) Term applied to an organization's attempt to enroll members belonging to another organization or employees already covered by a collective agreement negotiated by another organization, with the intent to usurp the latter's bargaining relationship. A no-raiding agreement is a written pledge signed by two or more employee organizations to abstain from raiding and is applicable only to signatory organizations.

Ratification Formal approval of a newly negotiated agreement by vote of the organization members affected.

Real Wages Purchasing power of money wages, or the amount of goods and services that can be acquired with money wages. An index of real wages takes into account changes over time in earnings levels and in price levels as measured by an appropriate index, e.g., the Consumer Price Index.

Recognition Employer acceptance of an organization as authorized to negotiate, usually for all members of a negotiating unit.

Reopening Clause Clause in a collective agreement stating the time or the circumstances under which negotiations can be requested, prior to the expiration of the contract. Reopenings are usually restricted to salaries and other specified economic issues, not to the agreement as a whole.

Reporting Pay Minimum pay guaranteed to a worker who is scheduled to work, reports for work, and finds no work available, or less work than can be done in the guaranteed period (usually 3 or 4 hours). Sometimes identified as call-in pay. (See *Call-in Pay*.)

Representation Election (Election) Election conducted to determine whether the employees in an appropriate unit desire an organization to act as their exclusive representative. (See *Bargaining Unit*.)

Right-to-Work Law Legislation which prohibits any contractual requirement that an employee join an organization in order to get or keep a job.

Runoff Election A second election conducted after the first produces no winner according to the rules. If more than two options were present in the first election, the runoff may be limited to the two options receiving the most votes in the first election. (See *Representation Election*.)

Seniority Term used to designate an employee's status relative to other employees, as in determining order of promotion, layoff, vacation, etc. *Straight seniority*—seniority acquired solely through length of service. *Qualified seniority*—other factors such as ability considered with length of service. *Department or unit seniority*—seniority applicable in a particular department or agency of the town, rather than in the entire establishment. *Seniority list*—individual workers ranked in order of seniority. (See *Superseniority*.)

Shop Steward (Union Steward, Building Representative) A local union's representative in a plant or department elected by union members (or sometimes appointed by the union) to carry out union duties, adjust grievances, collect dues, and solicit new members. Shop stewards are usually fellow employees, and perform duties similar to those of building representatives in public schools.

Standard Agreement (Form Agreement) Collective bargaining agreement prepared by a national or international union for use by, or guidance of, its local unions, designed to produce standardization of practices within the union's bargaining relationships.

Strike Temporary stoppage of work by a group of employees (not necessarily members of a union) to express a grievance, enforce a demand for changes in the conditions of employment, obtain recognition, or resolve a dispute with management. *Wildcat or outlaw strike*—a strike not sanctioned by a union and one which violates a collective agreement.

Quickie strike—a spontaneous or unannounced strike. *Slowdown*—a deliberate reduction of output without an actual strike in order to force concessions from an employer. *Sympathy strike*—strike of employees not directly involved in a dispute, but who wish to demonstrate employee solidarity or bring additional pressure upon employer involved. *Sitdown strike*—strike during which employees remain in the workplace, but refuse to work or to allow others to do so. *General strike*—strike involving all organized employees in a community or country (rare in the United States). *Walkout*—same as strike.

Strike Vote Vote conducted among members of an employee organization to determine whether a strike should be called.

Superseniority A position on the seniority list ahead of what the employee would acquire solely on the basis of length of service or other general seniority factors. Usually such favored treatment is reserved for union stewards, or other workers entitled to special consideration in connection with layoff and recall to work.

Sweetheart Agreement A collective agreement exceptionally favorable to a particular employer, in comparison with other contracts, implying less favorable conditions of employment than could be obtained under a legitimate collective bargaining relationship.

Taft-Hartley Act (See *Labor-Management Relations Act of 1947*.)

Unfair Labor Practice Action by either an employer or employee organization which violates certain provisions of national or state employment relations acts, such as a refusal to bargain in good faith. *Unfair labor practices strike*—a strike caused, at least in part, by an employer's unfair labor practice.

Union Security Protection of a union's status by a provision in the collective agreement establishing a closed shop, union shop, agency shop, or maintenance-of-membership arrangement. In the absence of such provisions, employees in the bargaining unit are free to join or support the union at will, and, thus, in union reasoning, are susceptible to pressures to refrain from supporting the union or to the inducement of a "free ride."

Union Shop Provision in a collective agreement which requires all employees to become members of the union within a specified time after hiring (typically 30 days), or after a new provision is negotiated, and to remain members of the union as a condition of continued employment. *Modified union shop*—variations on the union shop. Certain employees may be exempted, e.g., those already employed at the time the provision was negotiated and who had not yet joined the union.

Wagner Act (See *National Labor Relations Act of 1935*.)

Welfare Plan (Employee-Benefit Plan) Health and insurance plans and other types of employee-benefit plans. The Welfare and Pension Plans Disclosure Act (1958) specifically defines welfare plans for purposes of compliance, but the term is often used loosely in employee relations.

Whipsawing The tactic of negotiating with one employer at a time, using each negotiated gain as a lever against the next employer.

Work Stoppage A temporary halt to work, initiated by workers or employer, in the form of a strike or lockout. This term was adopted by the Bureau of Labor Statistics to replace "strikes and lockouts." In aggregate figures, "work stoppages" usually means "strikes and lockouts, if any"; as applied to a single stoppage, it usually means strike or lockout unless it is clear that it can only be one. The difficulties in terminology arise largely from the inability of the Bureau of Labor Statistics (and, often, the parties) to distinguish between strikes and lockouts since the initiating party is not always evident.

Zipper Clause An agreement provision specifically barring any attempt to reopen negotiations during the term of the agreement. (See *Reopening Clause*.)

INDEX

Academic libraries, advantages of unionization, 130-131; collective bargaining in, 122-123; disadvantages of unionization, 131; future of unionization, 139; unionization of, 130; unionization of in Canada, 123.

Academic library directors, role of, 132-133.

Academic library governance, collegial concept, 132-133.

Administration of a collective bargaining agreement, 78-79.

American Federation of State, County and Municipal Employees, bargaining in the public sector, 23-29; history of, 24.

American Library Association, ix, 132; history of union position, 9-10; membership of, 9; position on library unionism, 9-11.

Arbitration, defined, 89-90; evaluation of, 96-98; its effect on libraries, 120; future of, 105; types of, 98-101.

Association of College and Research Libraries, 131-132; statements on library benefits, 134-135.

Association of Research Libraries, 122-123.

Brooklyn Public Library, 119.

Canadian Association of College and University Libraries, 129.

Collective bargaining, defined, 77; negotiating process, 77-78; process, future of, 105; in the private sector, negotiation simulation, 109-113; for professional employees, history of, 1-3; representatives of parties, 55-66; techniques of, 78-83, 87-90, 93-105.

Collective bargaining in the public sector, x, 23-29, 84-86; effect of budget cuts, 26-27; effect of civil service laws and regulations, 68-70; grievances, 82; history of, 24-25, 30; legislation, 25-26, 31-40; professional negotiations, 60-61; scope of negotiations, 60-72; unit of determination, 33-36.

Columbia University libraries, 124.

Continuous bargaining, 90; evaluation of, 103.

INDEX

Duty to bargain, 47; definition of, 54-55; obligations of employer and union, 47-48.

Factfinding, defined, 88-89; evaluation of, 95-96; present status of, 105.
Final-offer arbitration, evaluation of, 98-99.

Grievance procedures, 79-82; use and application of, 82-83.
Grievances, reason for, 79; use in the public sector, 82.

Harvard University, library personnel policies, 134-135.

Job classification, 124.

Labor-management contract negotiations, simulation of, 107-116.
Librarians, numbers unionized, 4-6; professional status of, 6-8; response to unionization, ix-x, 117.
Libraries, effect of budget cuts, 128.
Library service, effects of unionization on, 125-126.

Management system in libraries, 123-124.
Med-arb, evaluation of, 99-101.
Mediation, defined, 87-88; evaluation of, 93-94.

National Labor Relations Act, 1, 43-52; definition of professional employee, 45; jurisdiction of, 43; jurisdiction over librarians, 46; in relation to libraries, 44-45.
National Labor Relations Board, 43-52; cases involving librarians, 50-51; designation of supervisor, 50; determination of unit by, 49-50; jurisdiction of, 44; processing of cases by, 48-50; professional employees and supervisory status, designation by, 50; professional status, determination of, 46; supervision of union elections by, 48.

Negotiation process, 77. *See also*: Collective bargaining.
New York, regulation of public libraries, 119.
Nonstoppage strikes, defined, 90; evaluation of, 103.

Personnel offices in libraries, 124.
Professional library associations, number of, 8.
Professionalism, 6-8; effect on collective bargaining, 27-29; in relation to collective bargaining, ix. *See also*: Collective bargaining.
Professionals, goals of, 16-19.
Public Employees Relations Board, 117.
Public library unions, coping with special legislation, 119; evolution of, 117; negotiations of, 119-120; operating in the public sector, 118-119; resolving grievances, 120-121; variety of, 118. *See also*: Collective bargaining in the public sector.

Queens Borough Public Library, 119.

Referendum, definition of, 90.

Staff association, definition of, 117; position on collective bargaining, 15; purpose of, 15, 117-118.
Strikes, definition of, 90; evaluation of, 101-103; history of in the public sector, 31; legality of in the public sector, 31, 36-37; present attitude toward, 104-105; in the public sector, 31, 36-37, 101-103.

Taft-Hartley Amendments (1947), effect on professional employees, 2.

Unfair labor practices, 46.
Unionism in the public sector, of federal and postal employees, 92-93; legislative protection for, 3; of municipal employees, 92; in the 1970s, 3; of police and firefighters, 91; of teachers, 91-92. *See also*: Public library unions.

Unionization of libraries, cost of, 121; future of, 19-20, 29; legal status of, 30, 39-40.
Unions, representing librarians, x, 12-16.
Unions and professional associations, convergence of, 12.
United States Department of Labor, negotiation simulation, 107-116.

University of Guelph, staff association, 135.
University of Guelph Library, 126, 129, 130, 133; effects of strike on, 138-139.

Wayne State University, 135.